Last
Letters
from the
Shoah

DEVORA
PUBLISHING
JERUSALEM ◆ NEW YORK

Yad Vashem
Jerusalem

Editorial comment
The letters in this volume were collected from various sources. Most of them were translated from different languages; some of them were published in Hebrew in memoirs and a few were written originally in Hebrew. We have tried to remain faithful to the writing style of the letters, correcting only what was necessary for linguistic purposes.

LAST LETTERS FROM THE SHOAH

Published by DEVORA PUBLISHING COMPANY and YAD VASHEM

Copyright © 2004 English Language Edition by Devora Publishing Company
Translator: Batsheva Pomerantz
Editor: Zwi Bacharach
Editor of the English version: Toby Weissman

Cover and Book Design: David Yaphe

Translated from *Eleh Devarei HaAchronim* with permission from Yad Vashem, Jerusalem, Israel. Website: www.yadvashem.org

Library of Congress Cataloging-in-Publication Data
Editor Dr. Walter/Zwi Bachrach
p.cm.
ISBN 1-930143-94-X (hc: alk.paper)
1. Shoah/The Holocaust. 2. Last Letters/Last Words of Victims of the Holocaust. 3. The Holocaust reflected through personal experience. 4. Testimony. 5. Sense of doom, despair and hope. 6. Concern for children. 7. Revenge, faith, acceptance, resistance, personal dilemmas, suicide. 8. Resistance/The Underground. 9. Coded Language found in the letters. I. Title

Library of Congress Control Number: 2004112423

ISBN: 1-930143-94-X

Email: publisher@devorapublishing.com
Web Site: www.devorapublishing.com

Printed in Israel

TABLE OF CONTENTS

ABOUT THE LETTERS

This book enriches the wealth of existing basic resources on the Holocaust, constituting an essential tool for research, for direction in education and for the reader seeking to glimpse at the depths of the period's years of darkness.

This volume, the first of a projected series, is the result of the collation of letters over many years; these letters have been categorized and elucidated with commentary before going to print. The compilation includes the last letters written by Jews and sent off from the countries engulfed by the Holocaust to beyond the walls enclosing them, as well as to their friends and acquaintances within the boundaries of Nazi rule. Part of the letters made their way to public archives; others were kept in private collections published in books of the destroyed communities or in personal or family memoirs.

The last letters can be seen as a branch of documentation left by the murdered victims themselves. Here, we become acquainted with their names and the conditions under which they wrote, and we even sense the fear as it tightens around them. The personal and familial letters in this collection are of unique significance, differing from other types of documentation, such as official documents, testimonies and memories of the survivors, and even from diaries written during the period itself. The letters gathered here were written by a relatively large and varied group of people, with origins in distant and distinct countries and communities; they tell of a multi-faceted reality influenced not only by the temperament and nature of the individual, but also by the accumulated collective experience and the prevalent attitude in a range of places. The letters relate what has happened and what looms in the near future, with their writers thirsting to know what was going on beyond their blockaded area. Their words are loaded with distress and the yearning for rescue. Details given about each family member and close ones show the unity and the feeling of oneness of Jewish families during this unprecedented time of distress and trial. Their faith, the devotion to their people, their shudder some farewell words and the powerful cry of the rebels and insurgents are all evident in their words.

Most of the letters presented here were sent over a period of several years, and via the mail, thus passing through the channel of the German censorship. For this reason, only hints of the distressing news and the anticipated critical situations emerge from the letters, or else they are related in coded terms. The letters include details about the events and the vain attempts to flee the trap, as well as information and a warning about the killing surrounding them. A clear impression emerges: Even those Jews who were aware of the killing in their midst, did not internalize the fact that the murder decree was general and included every Jew wherever he may be; the writers assumed that the worst would affect only their area or its vicinity, and therefore it was necessary to try to find refuge in another city or district.

Indeed, each letter was intended for a specific addressee, and conveyed personal details about the writer and his family, but those who peruse these letters today — people distant from them and their period — have a feeling that the letters were actually intended personally for them, as a sign and remembrance for the future.

Israel Gutman

5

INTRODUCTION

Then for the first time we became aware that human language lacks words to express this searing humiliation, the demolition of the image of a man. In a moment, with almost prophetic intuition, the reality was revealed to us: we had reached the bottom. It is not possible to sink lower than this; no human condition could be more miserable. Nothing belongs to us any more; they have taken away our clothes, our shoes, even our hair; if we speak, they will not listen to us, and if they listen, they will not understand. Soon they will even take away our names: and if we want to keep them, we will have to muster all of our strength to do so, to manage somehow to salvage something of ourselves of what we once were.

I know that my words cannot be easily understood, and this is as it should be. But try to consider what value, what meaning is continued in even the smallest of our daily habits, in the many possessions which even the *poorest beggar owns: a handkerchief, an old letter, the photo of a cherished person. These things are part of our being almost like limbs of our body; we cannot imagine that we can be deprived of them, for we immediately find others to replace the old ones; they are ours because they evoke our thoughts and our memories.*

Now imagine a man deprived at once of everyone he loves, and of his house, his habits, his clothes, in short, of everything he possesses: he will be a hollow shell, reduced to suffering and helplessness, bereft of dignity, no longer able to discern between good and bad. He has been robbed of his personality as well, becoming a downtrodden creature whose life and death can be lightly decided with no sense of human affinity, in the most fortunate of cases, on the basis of a pure judgment of utility. It is in this way that one can understand the double sense of the term "extermination camp" and it is now clear what we seek to express with the phrase: "to lie on the bottom". [1]

These words of Primo Levi are the starting point of this collection. They reflect a somber description of the loss of the human image within the reality of the extermination camp. But his words reflect the character of the humiliated Jew, as the murderers had wished to see him, "to lie on the bottom", in his language. From his experience, Primo Levi unfolds before us the method and means employed by the Nazis to make the Jew miserable and helpless. The description of the humiliated Jew in the death camp is shocking in its authenticity.

These last letters are the subjective testimony of the victims about the situations that the writers had undergone, as they themselves perceived them — and not as they were depicted by the enemy. A letter is naturally personal, and the unique voice of its writer is the guide for writing about the events: "A letter is a living soul, a faithful echo of the voice of the speaker". The "faithful echo" is sounded in these last letters with an outcry, with anger, with pleading, with love, with a call for revenge and many other emotional experiences, as these people faced their death. They did not write for the purpose of historical coverage, but out of personal pain, concern and grief. The letters constitute testimony from an unconventional viewpoint of the events of the Holocaust, the personal experience of the victim and his vision. This is their distinctiveness; the message is direct, devoid of any commentary from an outside observer.

It must be stressed that among the writers are those who wrote their last letter at the moment they were taken away from their homes and put on the transport, at a time when they sensed this would be their last road. These letters were usually written at an earlier period, during 1938–1942 in Western Europe and Central Europe. Some people knew precisely the appointed time of their execution and therefore they sent us their last words; others wrote their letters with the assumption that perhaps they would not return. These emotional states, of certainty and doubt have prevailed throughout the entire period of the Holocaust, over the years and in various places.

The writers can be divided into three groups:

a. Writers from Western Europe and Central Europe, usually from large cities, in the period prior to the implementation of the mass murders;

b. Writers from the ghettos and concentration camps, transit camps and death camps;

c. Writers from the underground in various places, and those belonging to ideological groups, such as Zionists, members of the Bund, Socialists and Communists.

This division emphasizes the geographical difference of Western Europe and Eastern Europe, as well as the division into periods of time.

Obviously, the question arises as to how we obtained these letters; the method depended of course on the circumstances. For instance, Jews from Central Europe and Western Europe who received deportation orders at home during the first years of the war — and even prior to the war — managed to send letters to their relatives by mail. Even if these letters underwent censorship, their relatives and friends received them, and finally they reached different archives. In quite a few cases, victims already aboard the railroad cars on their last road, managed to throw letters and postcards through the openings hoping that the person finding them would give them over to their destination — and this indeed happened.

There were Jews who knew that they would be executed within a few hours, and they handed over their last letter to a guard or jailer of good will, or to a friend in trouble — hoping that he would survive and give it over to their families or dear ones. Thus, in perilous ways, the last messages written in the different countries of the Holocaust, were preserved. The numeric comparison between the countries is significant; for example, out of 800 letters, 230 came from Poland as compared to some 60 from France. This reflects the centrality of Poland in the terrible events of 1941–1944. There is a difference too between the letters of the 1940s and the anticipatory "fear" that characterized the letters coming from Germany in 1933–1938. These are known facts in historical research, and the last letters add a personal touch.

The considerable diversity of personal testimonies — from the ghetto, the different types of camps and the undergrounds — raises the problem of which subject matter to focus on. It would have been possible to present the letters as adding a personal touch to the existing historical research, as a further corroboration and confirmation of the research findings. This could have been an important contribution, but in our opinion, it would have been secondary. This is because the content of the letters and their personal tone do not allow us to see them only as secondary revelations; the words written in them teach a primary issue. Perceptually, their content unifies an awareness of their inner world with an exposure of their personal experience. We are exposed here to a complex chapter of private and individual testimony existing in its own right. These are not revela-

10

tions about the destiny of a community, a group or some collective, but rather the personal expression of the individual on his way to the grave.

The uniqueness of the last letters is evident in two aspects: The first one is the genuine, honest and direct exposure of emotions, and mainly the sense of coping with impending death. Certainly phrases like the "murder of six million people" or "mass murder with gas" also provoke a dreadful feeling beyond human comprehension, of the inconceivable. Yet, when the sentiments while confronting the most terrible of all events emerge as a personal voice, identifiable by name — the testimony sounds more concrete, more convincing and more reliable. The phrase "six million" comes out of its conceptual obscurity and takes form, and the reader identifies with the solitary victim.

The other aspect is in the actual commemoration. Many times the writers expressed the wish that their name should be remembered for future generations; and even when it was not an explicit request, the personal letter becomes like a *"Yizkor"* [memorial prayer], widely accepted in Jewish tradition: a prayer in which the deceased is mentioned by name. For the person reciting the prayer, identification with the deceased person becomes more intimate and meaningful.

The Nazis murdered the Jews because they were Jews, and the following question is called for, surfacing from the subject matter of the letters: Did the victims stress their Jewish awareness in their last words; did they stress their bitter fate as Jews during their last experiences and emotions? It can be assumed that during moments of crisis, during those extremely critical moments, the condemned saw before them neither the Nazi ideology and scheming, nor their Jewish pride, for this was not the time for conceptual musings of any kind. The voice of the Jewish person confronting his end resonates from the letters, the exceptions being the letters of the underground people and of various ideological groups. They sacrificed themselves for the sake of collective Jewish ideals like Zionist, religious, socialistic-Jewish and national Jewish ideals. They saw their march to death as the fulfillment of a mission for the sake of the Jewish people, but as was noted, this group of writers stands on its own and is not the rule.

As was stated, most of the Jews going to their end found relief for their emotions as Jews demanding justice, expressing concern for others, making final requests with a sense of maintaining their human dignity. This principle of maintaining a human image is seen through a range of experiences and feelings expressed in the last letters — whether in the wills and last requests, whether in the sense of doom, the concern for the descendants, dilemmas and faith. Maintaining a human image was a contradiction and complete nega- tion of the Nazis' intentions and plans — to display the Jew as a non- human, as a sub-human. Thus the vital message passes through these words like a scarlet thread. Until his last breath the Jew maintained the human image.

The personal response, the experience and wishes of those going to their death are apparent in a range of revelations. These revela- tions have mostly corresponded with the similar human responses to various situations. This is how similar expressions, even identical ones, were found in the last letters. For example, the requests to set a memorial day ("yahrzeit") for the writer of the letter, usually the request mentioned the last deportation date or the minutes preced- ing the execution.

This collection includes therefore the following themes: testi- mony, a sense of doom, hope, wills and last requests, concern for children, revenge, dilemmas, acceptance, faith and resistance, sui- cide, underground and coded language. In general, one can say that it is difficult to divide the themes precisely, since many motifs are repeated, recurring again and again in the different themes. We will try to shed light on the conceptual continuity inherent in the inner connection of each and every theme.

Many felt the need to leave testimony about what had happened to them. This need grew out of the intention to document history for future generations, because the writers felt that the horrors they had experienced were unprecedented in the history of man. The horrors must be perpetuated by providing testimony from a primary source. The testimonies were written during the event or nearby, and therefore frequently led to pessimistic exposures of the soul, such as an impending sense of doom and despair emerging from the personal experience.

Along with despair, hope still prevailed, because it is a component of the structure of man's soul and spirit: there is no life without hope. So long as man still lives, even during the Holocaust, hope accompanies him, whether consciously or not, because this is the guarantee for maintaining a human image. By its nature, hope looks forward to the future, to a better, more promising future. The will and last requests express the yearning for better days in the future. The writers asked for a better future for their children, their parents, and for their dear ones, for all those for whom the hope that they would survive helped keep the writers alive.

A delicate and sensitive theme among the final requests was the concern for children. Love of children is an ingrained, unconditional emotion. It is impossible to produce, purchase or control it. A primeval love and the wish for continuity is expressed in the concern for children, more than with other beloved people and relatives. When these primeval love relationships are hurt, the pain cries out to Heaven, and from this cry the demand for revenge is born. It has been stated already: "Revenge is a confession of pain"[3]. But the demand for revenge raised a dilemma: whether to forgive or to take revenge. The wish to forgive the dreadful deeds of the enemies is not found in the letters, but other dilemmas do arise. For example, should one person be rescued on the account of another; should one save a life and thus endanger lives of benefactors and supporters; should one flee and abandon his parents. These dilemmas and others which the writers had to determine, and the decisions themselves, are evident in the letters. In the crucial decisions the wish of the victim is expressed, motivated more than once by the need for acceptance — or the absence of acceptance — of his difficult situation.

The crucial decision between the various options was a direct result of the personality and ethical upbringing of the writer of the letter, and was related to his Jewish faith. A Jew is not commanded about faith, but his consciousness is what pushes him to fulfill the command of an inner voice. The internal religious-ethical command is what caused him to behave as he did. According to the letters, if he accepted his grim situation, he usually would place his burden on the will of the Creator. If he refused to accept the decree, the letters would express anger, distrust and heresy.

The absence of acceptance leads naturally to the theme of the test of resistance, which is stressed in many letters. Two types of resistance are revealed in the letters: personal resistance of the individual, and resistance nourished by an awareness of mission. The latter characterized the underground fighters, partisans and other ideological groups, to whom a separate chapter is devoted.

The test of personal resistance was expressed in different ways, all sharing the fact that the resistance was shown as a spiritual opposition. Two motifs stand out in many letters: The resistance stemming from an awareness of a person's dignity which went hand-in-hand with optimistic feelings, an optimism rooted in the hope that perhaps they would withstand the hardships and survive. In contrast to this optimism, the occurrence of suicide or the volition to commit suicide, also latent with an element of opposition, was apparent: These people, whose considerations are revealed in the letters, were not willing to allow the enemy to abuse them — and they thwarted their scheming with the act of suicide. The small amount of suicide letters indicates the very low rate of those who willingly ended their lives on their own; for the most part, suicide as a response was not evident in the consciousness of the victims.

Quite a few letters were written in coded language. This is another original way of waging war against the enemies: The writers relayed their positions and wishes in code words, in coded names so managing to deceive the enemy and circumvent the decrees. They described their situation and requests, and the person who read the letter received a genuine picture of what was happening.

As was stated, it is very difficult to divide precisely between the themes, because the emotional and excited person, pained and hurting, dazed by what was happening to him, was not able to put his soul in order. We, generations after the victim died, try to enter his experiences, while making some sort of "artificial order" in his inner world, in order to better understand and sense what is going on inside him. Yet, when dividing between the themes there are often certain areas of overlap. Paragraphs of the letter presented here as an introduction clearly illustrate the aforementioned merge of the many themes, showing the diverse mosaic of emotions and expressions of the Holocaust victim during his last test.

Dr. Elchanan Alex, who was appointed as head of the Council of the Elders in the Kovna Ghetto, is the writer of the letter.[4] It is unique in that it invites the reader to be a partner in the emotions of the man who was at the helm of the ghetto. An intimate revelation of the character of such a leader is rare, and there is no equivalent to this in the entire corpus of letters presented here. The sense of doom resonates from the first paragraphs, like "We found out that in the next few days our fate will be decided" or "We are awaiting our fate in a very short time". The man writes to his children, and when reading his words, we grasp the depths of his pain and anxiety. He gives shocking testimony about the fate of the Lithuanian Jews, about "the last slaughter, the largest one, cost us ten thousand victims at once. It was on October 28, 1941". His aspiration, perhaps a glimmer of hope, is hidden behind his longing that he might yet see his children and hug them. He requests from his son and daughter in a will and last request, to be loyal to their people, to try to settle in the Land of Israel, to go together throughout their lives, and to remember what the nation of Amalek has done to the Jewish people. The concern for his children cries out from this will, and from the description of him sitting together with his wife, during long, dark nights, dreaming about their children's lives and future. We feel here the worry of all parents in that vale of tears. The writer demands revenge by pointing an accusing finger at the Lithuanians who cooperated with the Nazis. As a sacred will for future generations, he commands them to show no regard for the murderers throughout their lives. The dilemma shows up between the lines, when people — "many scarcely dressed and hungry" — turn to him in his role as head of the ghetto. His strength is insufficient, and he feels naked and bare with no words to offer. Faith has not abandoned him, and he explains to his children that the power of faith is great and it can "transfer and move mountains from their place". We, the readers, comply with Dr. Alex's plea to his children: "Understand what I wished for you and wanted to tell you at this time".

It can be stated that this anthology is unique in its originality, a sampling of the authentic personal voice of the Holocaust victim revealing the turmoil of his soul on the verge of his end without falsifications. The memory of the Jew as a person, as a human being, with his stormy soul, emerges and is reflected in this anthology. It is difficult to imagine a more vivid commemoration. This is the first volume that we present to the public. We hope that those who possess last letters will submit them to Yad Vashem to be included in future volumes.

◆ ◆ ◆

The letters in this book were gathered from the Yad Vashem Archives in Jerusalem, the archives of Bet Lohamei HaGetaot, the Massua Archives in Tel-Yitzchak, the Central Zionist Archives in Jerusalem, the Religious Kibbutz Archives in Kibbutz Yavne, the Moreshet Archives in Givat Chaviva, the Kibbutz Chafetz-Chaim Archives, the Kibbutz Chulda Archives, The Kibbutz Ein Gev Archives, the archives in Safed, the archives in the Nir Galim community, the Leo Beck Institute Archives in Jerusalem, the YIVO Archives in the United States, private sources, memorial books of communities, and the "Encyclopedia of the Exiles" series. My sincere thanks and appreciation go to the staff at these archives, who provided me with gracious help.

Many prominent people have stood by my side while compiling the letters and writing the book. First of all, Prof. Israel Gutman, who initiated the anthology of letters in his position as director of the International Institute for Holocaust Research. Prof. Gutman, the former chief scientist of Yad Vashem and its academic advisor today, has granted me the great privilege to publish this anthology and thus immortalize the victims' memory. The trust given to me by Prof. Gutman and his thoughtful suggestions have given me the strength to complete this heavy task. Prof. Yehuda Bauer, the former director of the Institute and an academic consultant today, has assisted my work with his useful suggestions. Mrs. Malka Tor, the director of the Testimony Division in the Yad Vashem Archives, has done the initial work of summarizing the corpus of letters in a thorough and comprehensive way; her work forms the basis for in-depth examination and analysis of the text. The devoted staff of the International Institute for Holocaust Research of Yad Vashem, directed by Ms. Dr. Tikva Fattal-Cana'ani and her secretary Carmela Meron, spared no effort to support me whenever necessary. I feel obliged to express sincere and special thanks to Ms. Lilach Stadler, who went beyond the call of duty to help me classify the letters and bring them to print. Without her kind support I would not have been able to complete this work. Thanks to Chedva Malchior Cohen for her devoted work. Prof. David Bankier, director of the International Institute for Holocaust Research, Prof. Dan Michman, the chief historian of Yad Vashem and Dr. Bella Gutterman, director of Yad Vashem Publications have reviewed the completed work, enriching it with comments and clever suggestions.

Mr. Shmuel Ahuvia of Rishon Lezion volunteered to translate the letters from the Polish language.

Many people, whom I cannot mention here by name, have given me the last letters of their dear ones from their private bequests. Dr. Eliezer Even, who volunteered with great devotion, has collected the letters in the different archives, and translated them according to the different themes. His praiseworthy work in Israel and Hungary was the cornerstone for publishing the last letters from the Holocaust. Mention must also be made of Dr. Yael Peled who greatly assisted with the collection of the letters.

Many thanks and gratitude to all of these people, and may this book be their reward.

Zwi Bacharach

THE HOLOCAUST
REFLECTED THROUGH
PERSONAL EXPERIENCE

We learn the history of the Holocaust from the comprehensive research literature published in the world, documenting the Jews' experience during the period of terror, usually from the perspective of Jews as a collective group. This perspective deals with Jews as a group of people, the fate of communities, the destinies of villages and towns, or the chronology *testimony* of the ghettoes and camps. The following letters are not verified testimony, elucidated and analyzed by a researcher, but rather the personal, experiential testimony of an eyewitness from the location of the atrocity. The combination of testimonies presented here constitutes the history of the Holocaust from a personal perspective. It is not a researcher's commentary, distant in time and locale, but rather an expression of the immediate and direct experience emerging from the shock of the moment, the personal astonishment and pain, all of which afford the description its authenticity. There is no concern here as there is with contemporary testimony about the possibility vague, clouded memory, sometimes rendering this type of testimony problematic.

Today, tens of years after the Holocaust, we stand as observers and commentators of the testimonies. We determine what is testimony. But in those times, during the inferno, was the writer of the letter aware of the fact that his words would ever serve as historical testimony? What motivated him to document? Most of the letters provide no answer to these questions, but there were writers who were aware of the importance of their writings, for example: "In my opinion, the material that I have collected in my anthology is of historical importance. For this reason I made sure that it would not get lost. I gave it to an archive in a secure place, in order to protect it for future generations"[5].

Emmanuel Ringelblum wrote in September 1942 about the activities of the "Oneg Shabbat", the underground documentation center in the Warsaw Ghetto. Historical awareness is clearly emphasized in his words:

> *Friday, September 26, 1942 is a great day for the O.Sh. [Oneg Shabbat]. This morning London Radio broadcast to the Jews of Poland. We know about everything, the radio transmitted about Slonim, Vilna, Lemburg [Lvov], and Chelmno and more. Thus the O.Sh. has fulfilled its great historical mission, by alarming the world, by telling about our fate [...], I do not know who will remain alive from among us, who will be privileged to edit the material we have accumulated. But one thing is clear to us all: Our toil, our efforts, our sacrifice and the constant living in fear, these have not all been in vain.*[6]

Researcher Ruta Sakowska has published a collection of letters from the archive of Ringelblum: They are all directed to relatives in the Warsaw Ghetto. The letters were written from other ghettoes, before deportation or during deportation; some messages were thrown as notes from railroad cars en route to the death camps. The main recurrent tone in all of the letters is one of despair and the sense of doom. Some of them express an acceptance of fate, of the will of the Creator, and even hope. As mentioned, the main arena for the terrible events was Poland and so it is also the source of this collection.

The individual testimonies give the events of the Holocaust a genuine historical dimension. We do not simply present new testimonies to enrich the research; the facts are known and have been greatly researched. Our interest focuses on the personal, inner-experiential attitude of the person giving testimony in his letter, in other words what the writer felt when relating his testimony. For example, the fact that the victims were deported in cattle cars is known, but the personal description enhances the understanding of what really happened inside the car, and we possess notes that were thrown by Jews from the cars.[7] Mrs. Blanca Levi, on her last road, describes the living conditions of being imprisoned in a railroad car for eight days, in the deportation journey to Bergen Belsen. In the morning, at about 8:00–9:00 the prisoners were let out to relieve themselves, but they were forced to do this near the railroad car. Once a day they received a slice of bread with a morsel of canned food. For a sip of water "the heart nearly passes out […] Already at 5:00 in the afternoon it gets dark and a person curls up over his bag. Until 7:00 the next morning he cannot even budge". She is distressed over how "a decent person gets completely lost in all the muck here".[8]

"A decent person gets completely lost" — these words are reminiscent of Primo Levi's definition "to lie on the bottom". Those that managed to survive in the railroad car, arriving at their destination, were sent to odd types of labor. Some had to write a letter immediately before their annihilation;[9] others were forced to work for the Nazis and killed after completing the task. One of them, Lodek was led "with the entire division, by way of Pilichovsky Street — to the sands, instead of to his sleeping board … the smell of burnt bodies and bones remained in the air until the next day". Also the writer of the letter expects death: "I have nothing and I will leave nothing after me… There will be just a slight smell of fire"[10]. Tzipporah from Malet probably also, senses her end; 20 years went by until the Lithuanian woman to whom Tzipporah had given her letter, handed it over, and we do not know the reason for this. Tzipporah relates in the last letter that already on the eve of the New Moon (*Rosh Chodesh*) of the month of Av, they were separated, undressed and awaiting death by shooting. Tzipporah gives the date of her yahrzeit.[11]

Many writers gave personal testimony with the precise number of those deported or murdered in their area of residence, according to countries. We will bring here some personal examples that are likely to form a diverse base for chapters in the history of the Holocaust.

Daniel wrote from Lublin in March 1942 that in a deportation going on for two weeks already, 14,000 Jews were deported from the city. Nobody knew when the deportation would end, hospitals closed down and "terrible things are happening in Lublin".[12] A letter from Athens in 1943, relates that in June 1942, "8,500 Jews of Saloniki were sent to hard labor".[13] In 1943 all the Jews of Saloniki were forced to wear the yellow Star of David, leave their homes and assemble in the ghetto. The writer testifies about the deportations in cattle cars, with some 3,000 people in each one, sent off to an unknown destination. According to his testimony, 53,000 Jews were deported, so that "no Jew remains in Saloniki and the cities of Macedonia". Those that fled the deportation decree, some 3,000 people, reached Athens. One can learn from his letter that 350 Jews of Saloniki, who were Spanish subjects, traveled to Spain via Germany. Another letter states that "great mourning befell the city of Athens, too. Now that the Germans took over authority from the Italians, they called in the Chief Rabbi half-an-hour ago and told him that here, too, they would do all that was done to the Jews in Saloniki [...] If you are able to save us, hurry and do not slumber".[14]

Many letters arrived from Poland and generally from Eastern Europe. A letter appears in the Byten Ledger[15] from 1942 in which Zlotka Wishniatzky describes the events in the town of Byten. She tells of "mass slaughters". 350 people survived, 850 were killed in "a dreadful death". Her daughter Yuta also write a few lines to her father in which comes forth the cry of a ten-year-old girl who wants to live and is terrified of death. Human intelligence cannot fathom this combination, a young girl confronting death.[16]

"We remained in the camp a total of 70 Jews out of 15,000 from the entire Snokai Region". The reader can sense that the writers themselves could not grasp what was happening: "I don't want to give details, since no human being can describe it", writes Asher son of Yitschak Schwartz, who snuck out from the Zaslaw camp,[17] adding: "I'm forced to say that this was some nightmarish dream, but to my regret it is entirely true", as if he is trying to convince himself that this is what really is happening to him.[18]

In the set of letters that we gathered in this book, the personal perspective of the victims is expressed together with their comments and commentaries. These letters introduce us, the readers, to the inner world of the writers. A woman from Tarnopol[19] tells in her letter about the murder of some 5,000 people, including her husband, and we feel her sense of loss. As she continues, she describes all the details of the executions in the different actions: before the open grave they must undress, kneel and stand in line, in a row, awaiting the shooting, so that "the place will be used to capacity".[20] That which we already know becomes more and more incomprehensible because of the personal traumas. The wickedness of the murderers is depicted even more intensely by their cynicism in charging the Judenrat 30,000 zloty to cover the cost of the bullets.

At times the testimonies are dry and straight to the point, but they are astounding because of the writer's personal involvement and the added personal remarks. As a writer tells about the Jews of Slovakia: "Here remains only a small part […] Despite this, our situation is better than that of the majority who were transferred to Poland". In a letter to the World Center of the Mizrachi movement, the writer notes that 60,000 Jews, who are 80 percent of the entire Slovakian Jewish population, were deported to Poland and later "most of them' like the Jews of Poland, fell there sanctifying the name of God among Israel".[21] Thus the reports and testimonies pile up, about the fate of the Jews of Czechoslovakia, about the town of

Moletai in Lithuania,[22] where a father and son write about the tragic death of a Jewess who was shot. When you read the sentence "and tomorrow they are going to shoot us", you cannot but shudder and imagine yourself in their place. According to their words, all Jews in the town were shot during seven days, in the month of Elul 1941, and they themselves, so they testify, were caught and imprisoned in jail: "We are counting the minutes until they come to take us and execute us. In a few minutes".[23]

Shmuel Minzberg describes in July 1944 the situation in the Shavli Ghetto:[24] "In the ghetto, 2,000 Jews await the order to go. Our destiny is unknown. The mood is terrible".[25] In 1942 those imprisoned in Poland knew, as is evident in a letter from Lublin, what happened to the Jews of Chelmno and Belzice, and the despair is pouring out. In Shloamek's postcard it says: "I already have no strength to cry",[26] and we feel the sense of indifference affecting many of the victims. The eyes of the sufferers are dry, even while crying, an experience that offers release for the person undergoing tragedy. This was a common phenomenon during the entire period of the Holocaust.

Many of the victims had hoped for a new life in the Land of Israel, and life and the Homeland became like one: The meaning of "to meet with the Homeland" is to live. In a letter from Bedzin[27] from July 1943, the fate of the Jews of Lithuania, in Warta and in General-government is told. Testimony is given here about the murder of Jews with gas in Chelmno, and about execution by shooting in Ponary[28]. In General-government only three places remained that were forced labor camps: Trawniki, Poniatowa and Prokocim. The writers have no chance to "to meet with the Homeland [the Land of Israel]".[29]

Melech Goldenberg describes the destruction of the town of Beresteczko. In addition to the Nazis' atrocities, the testimony stresses the cooperation of the Ukrainians with the Germans: the writer calls them "the grandsons of Patelyura and Taras Bolva" who were known for the pogroms they led against the Jews. The S.S. and the Gestapo, with the assistance of the Ukrainians, assembled together on one occasion some 300 Jews, men aged 14 to 65, and murdered them brutally.[30]

The shock is greatest when reading about the despair of infants and children. Here is ten-year-old Yuta as she faced death and wrote to her father: "I am parting from you before my death. We want to live very much, but what's to be done — they don't allow it. I am so terrified of death, because little children are thrown into the grave when still alive. I am parting from you forever. I kiss you strongly, strongly".[31] Hannah from the Warsaw Ghetto writes to her brother-in-law, shortly before being sent to the Treblinka camp. She notes that the ghetto is gradually being terminated and that its days are numbered. Her brother-in-law, Pesach Bezradki, had received on the same day another letter from his friend, Mottl Bornstein. This letter is testimony to the situation in the ghetto and the decision to rebel against the "Nazi beast". According to the writer, a fighting organization was founded, which included many printing workers. At their head was Lazar Sklar. The writer gives advice to do the same also in Miechow. From Bornstein's testimony one can learn about the head of the Judenrat in Warsaw, Adam Czerniakov. The attitude of the Jews towards him was split: some supported his way of leadership, and some negated this as well as his personage. Bornstein tells how he, together with two other friends, threatened Czerniakov with arms, forcing him to refuse the Nazis' deportation orders. Without relating to the veracity of this story, his testimony is important since it confirms the double-valued attitude towards Czerniakov: "Regarding Czerniakov's death [he committed suicide], specific elements wanted to make him into a national hero, but we know that Czerniakov and heroism are a contradiction in terms. Yes, he was a hero compared to Jews who went like sheep to the slaughter, but he served the Germans faithfully".[32]

In the following collection of letters, testimonies are compiled from across Europe and also from the words of the writers of the Underground. As was stated, details and descriptions that are historical testimony from a primary source about what happened are embedded in these outpourings of their stormy and pained souls. But the purpose of this anthology is to expose their inner world, the personal experience and the personal impressions in the last words of the victims. For this reason, we did not present the words of testimony in chronological order, or in a systematic division of geographical regions. Even though geographical distinctions — such as Athens compared to Cracow — portray various historical circumstances and different surroundings, it does not bear in any way on the expressions and inner feelings of the individual. There is no difference between the suffering and feelings of the individual in this camp or another camp — the voice of the individual as a Holocaust victim is conveyed by the letters.

The historical importance of the personal testimonies written in real time is exceptional. This is because today's researcher who gathers and verifies testimonies, usually orally, is hampered by the question of reliability and historical truth of testimony given 60 years after the events happened, due to the possibility of faded and weak memory, obscuring the past and other reasons. The testimonies in these last letters were given at that time or shortly thereafter and therefore they have great authenticity. This is the history of the Holocaust by those who experienced it on their own flesh, a description of the horrors as they were engraved on the souls of the writers.

The sense of impending doom, despair or hope is singled-out as the expression of the individual stormy soul more than any other theme in this collection. The individual destiny of the writer is the focus of the letter, and we as readers are partners in his emotions and experiences. Every person

a sense of doom, despair and hope

is a world unto himself, and thus the responses and feelings reflected in the letters are different and unique. Each individual has his own image of the Holocaust. Grief and indifference, acceptance and amazement, a mosaic of varying degrees of emotions and turmoil, are interwoven in these images.

Presumably despair was felt by all those persecuted during the Holocaust, although the manner of coping with it differed. Some were overtaken with despair, while others found a way to overcome their despair. The letters reveal that the force of life was more powerful than surrender to fate, and countering despair was hope, even when they realized that it was a delusion. It seems from the letters that despair was a temporary mental state, transient, while hope breathed some spirit of life for the victims. It is stated in the Talmud: "As long as a person is alive, he has hope; when he is dead, his hope is gone" (Yerushalmi, Tractate Brachot, 89, a). Despair stemmed from what actually happens concerning the person: the deportation order, the shortage, the suffering, hunger, humiliation, the conditions of arrest and imprisonment — all of these brought the victim to feel despair. Hope is rather a consciousness that is imprinted in man's soul, an inherent spiritual force. When reading the words of the writers, it becomes ever so clear that with all the malicious plans of the Nazis, this vital force of man was not taken into account: the murderers did not understand the power of survival of their victims. Therefore, hope was not just a response to the sense of doom and despair, but also the cause for the wonderous resistance against the enemy.

Sense of Doom

The theme that unifies the following letters is the impending sense of doom. Despair and fear are thrust upon a person mainly when confronting death face to face, when there is a sense of finality with no escape.

In this situation the words are mostly written out of stormy emotions. They are an outpouring of the soul, with a pervading intimate tone. More than in any other letters, the personal sentiment is prominent. Grief and suffering transform the written words into a humane document, into a testimony of the individual for generations. At times, a realistic perspective pervades the letters, like a personal assessment of the situation, and the reader is touched by the clarity of thought with which the emotional words are stated.

Parents who sense the end convey advice and last ambitions for their children. Julius Joseph of Magdeburg[33] wrote such a letter in June 1942 to his son Arno. The son was in the United States and the letter was given to him by a priest. The father assumes that this is the last letter he will ever write, because "deportation to Poland awaits us, that's where we'll find our graves", and he delivers a last piece of educational advice to his son: "Stay decent in deed and in spirit! Stay away from all filth, whatever its color is! [...] Don't get involved with politics. I am today of the opinion that Jews who are involved in politics are the grave-diggers of their people". The father encloses in the letter a curl that he had cut from the mother's hair in 1919.[34] An interesting fact is that a Jew who still lives in Germany in 1942 feels that Poland is the last stop. The father's warning to his son not to get involved in politics attests to the passive condition of the Jew in the Diaspora, excluded from political action. Perhaps the father intended to say that the Jew's political involvement, while tolerated, could endanger his position.

In contrast to the certainty felt by Julius Joseph about his end, doubt emerges from the parting letter of Fredric and his wife to their children, written in Vienna in September 1941: "if we don't reach a situation when we can see you again", but "may it be that God will allow us to see each other soon".[35] The possibility of final separation exists, but is not yet certain. Some face imminent death: "We are fasting for two days and are going to be slaughtered. The date of our death (*yahrzeit*) will be the 28/9 of August [sic]", writes Tzipporah from Malet, whom we have already mentioned. The feature of remembrance is repeated here. In accordance with the custom in Jewish tradition, Tzipporah centers not on her certain death, but on remembrance, the *yahrzeit*, lest she be forgotten in future generations. By setting the *yahrzeit*, the claim for continuity is anchored, with the memory of the dead in the awareness of those who live.[36]

Adolph Michaelovitch wrote to his family from a military prison on February 21, 1942. He was sentenced to death and notes in his words that these are his final moments, "if there is anyone who interprets my death as a heroic act — I tell you this: We have no need for heroes [...] Listen, these are the last words of one who is about to die!". He requests from his family to take care of his parents, to sell his possessions and to send them the proceeds. If children are born to his family, he requests to name the firstborn Dan or Francesca. The doomed person does not view his death as heroism; he calls for the perpetuation of the family chain by giving names to the progeny. Humanism stands out in all its might, with all its spiritual strength, at a time when barbarism subjugates the victim's body.[37] A father named Nechemia leaves his son Emmanuel flowery letter written on the festival of Shavuot 1944 in the Williampola camp in Kovna. "We await rescue by a miracle", wrote the father, and with the impending sense of doom he decides "to leave at least some information for those remaining after us, so you will know what happened to us from a primary source". Nechemia sensed the importance of his last letter as a primary source, which is the prominent significance of the entire body of last letters.[38]

A woman named Frieda who was part of a group of some 600 Jews executed in March 1943 in the city of Borislaw,[39] wrote to her husband Avraham and to her son Meir. A Jewish policeman kept her note. She requests that her children, whom she terms "orphans", should be taken care of, because "I am going to eternal rest".[40] Salla wrote to her sister that "I know that it is hard for you to recognize the fact that you have already lost us, but what can we do!".[41] Sometimes the letters expose a psychological truth, like the question about the easiest way to die — as an individual or as part of a community. For example Mina Hibshman was so certain of her imminent death that she took a dramatic step, understandable only to those subject to the same pressures she had: knowing that she had no chance of carrying on with life, and since she was lonely and isolated from the community — she gave herself in to the Gestapo. "Dying alone is much harder", she wrote, and was sorry that "I didn't go to die with everyone". And you wonder: Was the motive for her action fear of death, or actually its acceptance?[42]

Ida Goldisch wrote her last letter in 1941 to her sister Clara Schwartz, before her deportation in the transport from Kishinev.[43] Ida's son froze to death and Ida herself died three days later. In her letter she expresses her pleadings: Like others, she worries in her final moments for her mother and asks her sister Clara to take care of her. The strong will for life on the one hand and the concern for the mother on the other, are additional testimony to the great humanism of those condemned, a humanism that the greatest forces of evil could not suppress.[44]

Chaim, a son of Jewish farmers, was caught in Ratzia and led to the camp in Pustkow, Galicia where he was put to death. The 14-year-old boy inserted his last letter in the camp's barbed wire. He writes: "The day before yesterday two boys escaped, so they lined us up in a row, and every fifth one in the line was shot to death. I was not the fifth but I know that I will not leave here alive. I part from you, dear Mother, dear Father, dear brothers, and I cry…". When a 14-year-old boy senses and realizes that he will not come out of the inferno alive and all he can do is cry, this is not an acceptance of death. All the horrors of the Holocaust, all the upheavals of the world order, shout out to us from the weeping of Chaim.[45] The same sense of doom, the same pain and objection of a young person emerges from the letter of 17-year-old Pinchas'l from Budapest to his brother Mordechai: "At the age of 17, I am forced to confront certain death […] I think that I've also felt that I would die young". Like an actual adult he manages to explain his emotions: "Plans, ambitions and hopes are before my eyes. I yearn for the unknown. I would like to know, to live, to see, to do, to love… but now it is all over".[46] Five days after writing this letter he was taken to Csomad near Budapest. There, in the forest, he was ordered together with others to dig a pit. He was shot into his grave, dug with his very own hands.

We learn from the letters that the older a person is, the more capable he is of grasping the secrets of the soul. But here, too, one is awed at the emotional capability, the inner strength, shown by an anonymous Jewess from Tarnopol. She identifies her husband's corpse at the cemetery and in the turbulence of pain and sorrow over the loss of her husband, with death looming over her, she asks: "Is it possible to describe the overflowing extent of sorrow and pain? […] In the course of time we became so used to it all, that we were like dummies. We didn't react at all when we lost those who were closest. No one cried. We ceased to be human beings. We were like stones without feeling. There was no news that made an impression on us any more. We went silently, even to die. The people in the square where we assembled were reserved and silent". This description of the mental state of apathy and dulled senses, from a first person account, is relevant to many of the victims, and it deepens our understanding today about the victims' souls.[47] This authentic psychological description provides the convincing response to the frequently asked question: Why didn't those condemned to death resist? In order to resist, physical ability and inner strength are necessary, and not apathy and dulled senses. True, not all were apathetic and quite a few people in the camps and ghettoes were aware of their situation; but here the victims saw death facing them.

There were those who described their fate, wrote and then were silent. For example, a mother named Regga from Rimanow,[48] who wrote to her sister: "My last wish: Take care of my children and Mother. We were punished in a cruel way and suffer harshly, but we don't know for what. Goodbye. It's impossible to say: see you again".[49]

Today, many years after the Holocaust, we know quite a lot about the physical suffering, the hunger and the abuse of those imprisoned in the vale of death. In contrast, it remains difficult until today to document the emotional anguish they experienced, and these letters open a window to their suffering and pained souls: "Since we already expect and sense the impending footsteps of death […] Don't think that we are full of despair, we must and we force ourselves to make peace with our fate […] Hunger wasn't the main cause of our suffering, our slow dying has tortured us many times more […] We are parting from you forever".[50] These words of Faige Krauss from the Sambor Ghetto in Galicia describe a slow death, a condition of decline, of ongoing and debilitating suffering stemming from the sense of doom.

The letters present a variety of responses to the situation. There is no identical, uniform response; there is no structured order of what transpires in the soul. In contrast to the desperate and apathetic, there were those who bore with pride their bitter destiny. Fanya Brovkov of Druya writes:[51] "I don't know exactly the day that I and my relatives will be killed, only because we're Jews", but on the day of her death she declares that everyone is marching proudly towards death: "I am proud that I am a Jewess. I am dying for my people". These words were written on the day she was executed, at four a.m.[52] The letters therefore express not only an awareness of their situation, but also display the pride felt prior to the hour of execution, and perhaps they rose to such an inexplicable degree because they knew their precise hour of death?

In the letter of Genia of Zolkiew[53] to her brother Mundak, she reveals the disappointment about there being no way out of her situation: "It must certainly be difficult for you to imagine that we couldn't find any solution whatsoever, but to our sorrow, we didn't find a way! Only friends, non-Jews, could help, and as you know, everyone abandoned us in troubled times, and everyone remains indifferent. Indeed, if God has abandoned us, what can we say and speak of friends, who would endanger themselves when helping". Nevertheless she was left with emotional distress without finding peace. "All this causes us to be insane", writes Genia, and she interprets her impending death that will "redeem us from these moral tortures".[54]

Dvorah Dohl writes from the Mukhavka camp to her brother, a short time before she was murdered. The tone of her words is altruistic: "I am going to die aware that you, my dear brothers, were saved from my bitter fate, and it is very possible that all of the agonies that I suffered here, I suffered on your behalf, as well".[55]

In most of the letters the absence of anger and crying out is noticeable. The responses of those going to their death and their feelings differed from each other showing how each person reacts according to his nature, education and outlook. But the extent of the humanism and magnitude of the spirit displayed by the victims prior to their tragic end unifies all the letters.

Despair

The difference between expressions of a sense of doom and despair is evident: A sense of doom does not leave room for hope, while despair is mostly associated with the possibility of finding a way out, or expressing hope that the writers will see their precious ones again. When people contemplated about the distant future, they would be overcome with despair, while a sense of doom shook the spirit, and cried out during the event itself or near by. We are discussing here a compilation of letters combining despair and hope. Two letters in this compilation were written at relatively early times, in 1939 and 1940, while the rest of the letters were written later from the ghettos and camps in Poland. The fear in the early letters differs from the latter ones: The parents writing from Berlin are desperate because they sense that their destiny is sealed because they did not get visas for the Land of Israel, yet despite the despair they have not abandoned hope that perhaps they will see the Land. When the parents parted from the daughter, the mother took comfort in what is written [in the Scriptures]: "For it shall endure and your hope will not be cut off". (Proverbs 23, 18).[56] In a letter from Hungary from 1940, Polish refugees arriving in Budapest complain about the indifference of the local Jews to them. The Poles saw themselves "nearing the edge of the abyss, the edge of the abyss that swallows us […] Despair began creeping in our hearts". Between the lines a glimmer of hope peeks through: "And now that we received news about the new quota of certificates that the Agency obtained for Polish refugees, we awakened again and shook off our despair".[57] The writers of the letter sensed the despair despite the fact that they did not have any actual experience of the atrocities in the camps, but they held on to the hope that they would be rescued because of the change in policy regarding the certificates.

But when despair originates from the awareness that there is no point in expecting rescue by man, faith in divine Providence serves as a source of hope. Sophia Pelheimer notes when she relates to Theresienstadt[58] that "we are all desperate", but "perhaps there will yet be a miracle from Heaven, I'm always optimistic".[59] And another writer hopes in his despair that "May God the Blessed One say 'enough' already to the Angel of Death and that we should merit salvation, if not..."[60] Two letters are sent from Vienna to Mr. Netzel; it is impossible to decipher the writer's first name. She writes that her brother has been hospitalized for 14 months already "but we still hope that he will recuperate". And she is desperate, crying from morning until night. At the opening of her letter she expresses the wish that God protect them "from a cruel destiny and keep us together, or lead us together — this is all that I hope for and for this I live".[61] Somewhere off in Poland an anonymous person describes the Jewish brigades murdered after they had worked for the Wehrmacht. He writes that for him it is obvious that now his turn has come; it is a matter of a few days, and "I am ready for my last road [...] on the way to eternity". But this writer also doesn't conceal the hope for rescue, "Perhaps destiny will have us meet again and we will survive this disaster".[62]

Some of the people felt desperate because their hope was based on the response to their request for extending help. In the letter of a father and his daughter Gutta, written in 1943 in Warsaw, it is related that 40,000 Jews were still alive in Warsaw in the month of Shevat, but after Passover only some tens of Jews remained in hiding, and they too, "are in great danger, the danger of death". A complaint is lodged in this letter to the addressees, who are not doing enough to rescue them: "If only you would be obligated to break the heifer's neck over us, too. And you should not have to say: But we are guilty. The daughter thinks that there is still an opportunity to help, and she ends with the call: "Send certificates for exchange: Gutta".[63] Despair and the loss of hope emanate from the postcard of Yisrael Gold from Bedzin to the Schwartzbaum family. He thinks that they will not see each other again, but Lasker can save him.[64] Roz'a Kaplan relies on the fact that the murder is not kept secret any longer: "I would shout with all my might, but where can I run? After all there is such terrible frost here and the children will certainly freeze to death. When the frost eases up — it will perhaps be too late. Meanwhile I have no other choice, but to sit and wait. Maybe this disease will stop because the whole matter is becoming so public".[65]

In their despair, some people viewed their imminent death as a punishment. A mother confesses before her daughters that she had committed "severe crimes" towards them and "I myself bear my sins". But she does not want to die — she still wants to live. We do not know what she meant when mentioning "her sins", but the victim felt the need to find a cause and explanation for her approaching death. It exposes the reader to the emotional turmoil, the inner dilemmas and the despair befalling these hapless people.[66]

In a postcard from Vienna to Elsa Gross, David Berger writes that he is ready for everything. He was actually supposed to meet her, but "the worst of it all is the lack of knowledge of when I will return and see you". The postcard is his farewell from her, and the suppressed and desperate tone is understood from the sentence: "If something happens, I would want there to be a person who would remember that someone named D. Berger had once lived".[67] A father from Hungary writes in June 1944 a last letter to his son; he is about to be deported to an unknown destination. The letter expresses his profound despair: "I'm on the verge of despair. I already gave up on life, and I'm full of pain and sorrow [...] Why do we have to suffer from such despicable discrimination?"[68]

Shlemak, who fled Chelmno but was killed in Belzice,[69] told about a 15-year-old boy in Chelmno, Monik Halber, who would lean on him and sob: "Oh Shlomo, if only I would be dead instead of my mother and sister". Meir Pitrovski, his neighbor in the layer of straw, would weep: "I left behind at home my beloved wife and children, and who knows whether I will live to see them again. What will become of them?"[70] Shlemak wrote in desperation, probably in March 1942, his last testimony addressed to Mr. Wasser: "I received regards from my cousin in Lublin. They write that people went to the afterworld in the same way as in Chelmno. Imagine my despair. I have no more strength to cry. This is probably my last letter and I am about to go the same way and in the same manner as my parents [...] There is a House of Eternity [cemetery] in Belzice. It is the same as in Chelmno [...] He is cold [the murderer] in the same way as in Chelmno, and now we are in line. The cemetery is in Belzice. He already froze the towns mentioned in the letter".[71]

From the disclosures of despair, it is possible to learn that during the first stages of the Holocaust, the Jews did indeed grasp what was about to happen, but because they were not yet completely torn away from surrounding frameworks and humane conditions, the letters still expressed hope — alongside the despair. In contrast to this, those facing imminent death and far removed from any humane framework, viewed such hope as a delusion.

Some of the letters present total despair, while others show the recurring motif of a sense of confidence in the continuity of future generations. The yearning for life was stronger than the fear and dread of death; paradoxical as it seems, this was expressed as optimistic despair.

Hope

The psychologist Erich Fromm has correctly determined that hope is the guarantee for life: "When hope has gone, life has ended, actually or potentially".[72] The sense of doom, despair and suffering propels one to struggle for life, and the awareness of life does not allow "life to end actually". Expressions of hope do appear in the letters fueled by some inner force, motivated by optimism or by a goal that the writers had sought to achieve.

Hope can grow out of a strong sense of confidence, like that expressed in the letter by an anonymous writer who threw it from a train going from Westerbork headed to an unknown destination. In his letter he declares to his addressees that they can be sure and confident that he will certainly come back; he feels strong and can definitely withstand the future.[73] Differing circumstances determined the degree of hope: When the writers were surrounded by relatively normal conditions, they felt greater hope for a better future. For example Ruth Hadassah from Bonn writes a letter in July 1942. According to her it is the last one before deportation. She still hopes to start a new life in the Land of Israel and that the war will not go on for long, however "It's lucky that the three of us are still young and that we're not deterred from any work. Additionally, we will manage in any situation in life […] For thousands of years, Jews are used to bearing a difficult fate and withstanding it. And nobody will see our generation show fear".[74]

In May 1940, parents, a grandfather and grandmother, sent a letter to their sons Yitzchak and Yehuda Koren who were living in the Land of Israel. The letter was written in Gorlice[75] and expressed the hope that "with God's help we can also emigrate to the Land, and the entire family will be together again". The entire family was killed, as testified by the son, Yitzchak Koren.[76] The last letter of Bertha Cohen Goldschmidt in April 1943, was written in the Dutch city of Doorn and was addressed to her children and grandchildren. Bertha was 73 and realized that in two days she would be sent to the concentration camp. She hoped to reach the Land of Israel and come back again to Doorn, and if not — she hoped that her children would get there in order to thank those who were kind to her.[77]

Today's reader asks himself how long hope can nourish the soul. After all, as time went on, the scope of the Jews' persecution, as it became more and more brutal and atrocious, was increasingly apparent. Perhaps with this worsening situation, hope was slowly being crushed. We indeed find this process in some individuals, as expressed in the letters of Dr. Nohl to his son. The letters were written between June 1941 and November 1942. Dr. Nohl, a teacher and intellectual, lived in Vienna and later on in the Czech city of Hradec Kralove. He writes to his son letters full of despair where he blames himself for not using the opportunity to immigrate illegally to the Land. The distress is initially expressed in phrases like: "In my mind, I'm beginning to suspect that we will not see each other again". In 1942 the tone is more gloomy: "Nobody knows how long it will take and we must get more and more used to the idea that we will not stay alive". In June he writes: "It is slowly, slowly becoming apparent that we won't see each other again". He describes how the cities and communities in Prague and Vienna and their surroundings are becoming empty of Jews who are being sent to Poland, to Mauthausen[78] and to Theresienstadt. Despite the gloom, hope is interwoven throughout: In January, on his son's 21st birthday, the father makes a wish that he would still have a beautiful life, and writes an encouraging sentence: "I hope that you have a beautiful life ahead of you; perhaps I may live to be part of it". In June 1942 he ends optimistically: "I will still write before the parting". He claims that he is ready to bear every shortage, "in hope of seeing you again, while having a clear conscience". In his last letter, in November 1942, he again declares his hope: "I hope to endure", but "It is hard for me to picture now the happiness of a meeting".

We can learn many issues from Dr. Nohl's letters, such as his faith in the Jewish people, the importance of Zionism, the significance of family and more. But for our purpose it is important to note that in the early stages, when living conditions were relatively tolerable, a sense of hope was actually expressed — but it was stated with a realistic vision of the future. The reader cannot let go of the feeling that hope was slowly being crushed, and the optimistic tone was probably intended primarily to encourage his son, more than to convince himself.[79]

Some writers explained that their strength to endure hardships was due to past life experiences. It seems that the writers searched for every possible reason to grab hold of, convincing themselves that they have the strength to bear the suffering. Leopold, for example, sought the origin of his strength in the period of World War I. He writes that the following week they would be sent to Poland, mentions Ilsa and determines that the both of them are strong and courageous, going upright to their destiny. Leopold reminds the addressee, Victor, that during World War I the two of them became strong and gained experience, and with the help of God he hopes they would see each other soon.[80]

Other writers find the source of their strength and hope in love. In November 1941 Regina Kandet, a native of Belgrade, hands over her last letter to a Christian women, who gave it over to Regina's relatives in Israel. The letter is addressed to Max, Regina's husband: "I suffered a lot, but survived because I believed in the kind Lord and because my great love to you, Mutz'ek, gave me strength […] I've never loved a person in the whole world as much as I've loved you. Therefore you also must be strong and patient, one day an end will come to this, too […] I'm writing this just in case I'm not saved. But I have a feeling that we will return and see each other again".[81]

Whatever the motives of hope may have been, it served as a support for the Holocaust victims. Perhaps it can be determined, that if not for hope, the will to live flowing from the love between a husband and wife, the love for children, the love of man, and the love of the Land of Israel — murderous barbarism would have triumphed. Hope is the guarantee for the preservation of the human image, since it nourishes the strength to endure suffering. It seems that the revelations of hope expressed in the letters contradict philosopher Friedrich Nietsche's pessimistic statement that 'hope is actually the worst of evils, because it prolongs man's tortures'.[82] Reading about the voices of the sufferers during the Holocaust, the reader gains the impression, that hope strengthened them like a remedy, like faith in continuity, and not as a prolonging of the tortures.

The last requests portray a wide array of issues and emotions of those sensing their imminent end. Significant, fundamental and conceptual issues are revealed alongside mundane and trivial matters. Concern for others occupied the writers of the wills and requests

wills and last requests

even when they were at their lowest ebb and most difficult moments. The personal disclosures, put down on paper at the peak of an emotional crisis, enable us to glimpse into the inner world of the condemned, providing a rare documentation of personal and experiential history. In this chapter, a humane perspective of the children's concern for their parents is greatly expressed. Concern for the other person, close or distant, for the next generation, resonates like a cry and plea to maintain the continuity of life, the cry of one about to die. Exhortations for a life of good and worthy deeds emerge from the last requests, as our Sages have said: "Better is the day of the death of a great person than the day of his birth, because on the day of his birth man does not know his deeds, but when he is dead his deeds become known to the public" (Midrash Shmot Rabba). The source refers not only to a "great person", but also to a regular person.

The concept of continuity surfaces many times in the words of the writers; after all, this concept is inherent to the act of writing a will. The need to perpetuate the memory of the deceased in the cognizance of those remaining alive is a part of the essence of a will. Usually material instructions for the next of kin are presented in wills, but they also include ethical commands. An example of this is the will from the Shavli Ghetto, signed by Shmuel Minzberg. He presents the future generations with the names of four people ordered to prepare for evacuation from the ghetto. Minzberg instructs future generations, with the ethical duty, to remember the victims.[83]

In the will of a father called Moshe, his children were ordered to divide the property. He requests that the division be honest and to "live in peace and harmony". He expresses sorrow for missing the opportunity to emigrate because of a lack of agreement between him and his brother about the division of common property.[84]

At times, we find a combination of the material and the ethical in the wills. Shalom Eliyahu the son of Leah reveals in his will where he hid and buried money and jewelry: "If you get this letter, look in the places mentioned here", he writes, and adds, requesting from his children "to go about this in an honest and kind way, with fear of God your Lord, and follow His ways, and observe His laws and commandments that are written in the sacred book of Torah, and in this merit you shall be privileged for the complete redemption speedily in our times, Amen".[85] An idealistic tone comes across in the will of Frieda Niselevitch which was found in the area where the Shavli Ghetto had stood in July 1944. She requests that her Jewish brothers, who remain "after the inquisition", should be "loyal sons to our holy homeland, the Land of Israel". She left some photographs of the people most precious to her, hoping that "somebody will find them while digging, and will search in the ground".[86]

The wills also constitute a source of historical testimony. In April 1943, the names of 12 people who worked for the Gestapo is presented. A wish is expressed in the will to let the entire world should know that all Jews deported from Lodz were murdered in a brutal manner. The following command is added: "If you are saved — you must take revenge".[87]

Unique is the will of artist Gella Sakstein; she sought to impart her emotions not in words, but in her personal language — art. The painting speaks to us and awakens our sentiments as if the artist has spoken from the soul, as it says in the Talmud: "God Blessed be He formed a shape within a shape, placing in it the spirit of the soul".[88] Gella spoke from her soul when she commemorated her small daughter Margalit in her works of art, and therefore the paintings that survived embody a double significance which is very meaningful.[89] Amid the cases of the Ringelblum Archives, nearly 300 paintings, aquarelles, drawings and sketches were found. A will was also found in which she expresses her concern for the fate of her works of art.

Gusta Berger-Erlich writes from prison in Montelupich in Krakow.

Probably considered at first to be a non-Jewish Pole, she finally admitted under mental stress that she is indeed a Jewess; presumably this admission brought about her execution on August 4, 1942. In the prison cell, while awaiting her end, what are her thoughts, what occupies her? Neither reflections of reckoning nor thoughts about her life; even during these fateful hours, her thoughts are with her daughters Vladz'ia and Agussia. And she gives them advice, suggestions that could have been given by any mother in normal times, under normal conditions. These words are of human, motherly concern, pushing aside her bitter personal fate. We learn from the letter that the husband of the daughter, the writer's son-in-law, has already been sent to the camps, and Gusta raises the possibility that he will not return. She counsels her daughter to be independent, to learn a profession and to remarry. And if indeed she sets up home a second time — she should keep her sister Agussia at home only until the age of 16, because "you mustn't have at home a younger woman"![90] A mother's love transforms this will into a touching document with its subject matter taken from life —the kind of advice given by every mother. The issues may seem trivial when compared to the mother's fate, but emotional greatness is truly evident with this triviality.

Some sought their last request from within a deep connection to Jewish tradition and its special customs. A father and son from the Nutlevich family, from Moletai in Lithuania, write that in 1941 all Jews of that town were murdered during seven days in the month of Elul. The father and son have managed to escape but were caught, and realized that they will be executed. Thus says the father: "Be well. These are my last words [...] Today is 21.12.1941 and it will be our day of remembrance".[91] Asher son of Yitzchak wrote to his sister that he wants to inform her about the tragedy of the family and the memorial days. In a letter from January 1943 he relates that he snuck out of the Zaslow camp in order to give over this letter to a gentile, and he relays the memorial dates of his father, mother and Losha: a day after Yom Kippur 1942. Rachel was shot on October 25, 1942, and Hinda, Shaul and Melech were taken from the camp on January

15, 1943.[92] In November 1943, before her deportation to Auschwitz, Germana Ravena writes from the Carmine Monastery where she was hidden until caught by the Nazis: "Make sure that there will be some memorial plaque for Mother and me at the cemetery in Ferrera, near the graves of our family".[93] Most of these letters stress the anniversary, the "yahrzeit" and the matter of remembrance and the memorial — important cornerstones in Jewish tradition for the religious and secular person alike.[94]

Anchored in Jewish tradition, the fundamental concept of continuity, the need to perpetuate the memory of the deceased in the cognizance of the living, comes up again: "All that is done before the burial is done in honor of the deceased […] while nearly everything that is done after the burial is done for the benefit of the mourners".[95]

Jewish tradition deals with commemorating the deceased — in this case the Holocaust victims — within the hearts of the relatives, and it seems that this custom stood before the writers of the requests.

One acute issue apparent in the last requests is the concern for the welfare of the parents. Hours before they were killed, the condemned left their last requests to the survivors, to sell their possessions and transfer payment to the parents, to make sure the parents are happy, never to forget them and to constantly protect them.[96] In an inhumane situation, the preserving of the human image is illustrated here.

There were special requests, expressing somewhat unusual matters. For example, in August 1942, Elsa Klauber of Vienna writes to her daughter Anne-Marie, that she should forget the German language; if she gives birth to children — they should not know this language.[97] Another unusual request was written in October 1941 in the letter of Regina von Sin of Hamburg to her daughter Ilsa: When she mourns for her parents — she is not to wear black. This is the father's explicit last request because "we are all mortals".[98] In August 1942 Esther and David Lam write from Westerbork[99] to the parents of the wife and her two brothers; their request has an unusual suggestion — to forget them, this is their most reasonable suggestion, and if they ever get to see each other after the war, they will again "be reminded of us".[100]

But concern appears in the last requests not only for those closest like parents and children, but also for non-Jews. Among them were kind and merciful people, who extended help and support to the Jewish victims, and the writers seek to return their kindness. Moshe Akar, in his letter from June 1943 reveals to his son that Henia and Yozek Lokschwitz had hid him; he promised them 20 morgen[101] of land as payment. But Akar is aware of the possibility that the authorities might not permit the sale of land, and in that case, "you must pay Yozek and Henia a handsome and generous payment, for what they have done for me". If he should die, he requests another request: "bury me in the Land".[102]

In an anonymous letter written in Bonn in June 1942 by parents about to be deported to the unknown, they request to thank and repay the kidness of the non-Jews who cared for them. They mention their names: The woman's name is Hella (Marichen) Bente and a family called Ordingen: "you cannot thank them enough"[103] In July 1943, a mother notifies in a letter addressed to her sister and brother-in-law that her daughter Shaindeleh is in the faithful hands of the Tourkin couple in the area of Dabrowa,[104] and she requests to pay the Tourkin family for their deeds, and for taking care of her daughter.[105] Before this she relates that her mother had passed away "naturally, thank God" in 1942, 6th of Tammuz according to the Hebrew date, so her sister can observe the yahrzeit.

In the preceding letters we have seen the blunting of the senses and the indifference, and even inhumanity among the victims. Indeed, these emotional states affected many, but not the entire public. The letters that are brought in this chapter affirm the sensitivity, consideration and humanism, and as was stated, we cannot generalize. Each person is a world unto himself, and the feelings and responses are complex, related to the circumstances and the writer's

44

personality. These personal messages show that during distress, during the atrocious entanglement and barbaric surroundings, individuals acted both with emotional fortitude as well as with human weakness. Fortitude and weakness are character traits imprinted in man, and at times one prevails the other. The picture rendered in the letters is mixed; at times the hero appears weak and at times the contrary.

C hildren are the most precious asset of parents. In a family with normal relationships, parents' concern for their children continues even after they have left home and stand on their own two feet. It seems that a universal-humanistic aspect is expressed here, and not necessarily a unique Jewish aspect. Love of children and concern for them are the lot of each *concern for* and every parent, Jewish or non-Jewish, without *children* distinction of origin, religion or nationality.

In the tragic moments, in the last minutes of the life of a father or mother, the letters express concern over petty and mundane issues, seemingly insignificant for the children, but the magnitude of parental humanity is apparent. One of the purposes set by the Nazi enemies was to dehumanize the Jew prior to his murder. The letters focusing on the concern for children are a sweeping testimony to the failure of this scheme. During the worst time of trial and tribulation, when he faced certain death, the human aspect of the condemned Jew was revealed; otherwise how is it possible to understand the concern of the father and mother for petty human matters, concerning the most marginal matters?

Pierre's father writes that he is about to die the following day and asks for his forgiveness that "not everything with us and between us was as it should have been". He leaves him his possessions — a watch, gold, money and books — in different places, and directs him: "Be courageous, be honest, be a Jew".[106] When the shadow of death hovered over Aaron Liwecant in the train to Auschwitz in 1943, he is disturbed by the idea that his children, Bertha and Simon, would probably neglect their health, and he warns them not to drink cold water when they sweat...[107] Another father writes to his daughters in May 1944, before he was sent to Auschwitz, that he is enclosing food coupons for which they could get 2.4 kilograms of bread in the Weitz bakery. This deed is also proof of concern for the everyday matters,[108] and these letters are unique in their detailed description of issues that in normal life may receive our attention, but certainly do not top our list of concerns. Perhaps the two fathers are implying that above all, it is necessary to take care of one's body and health for a tranquil soul.

In a postcard written from Rimanov, a woman requests from her sister, Hilda, to take care of her children and her mother. Another sister tells that she and her husband have permission to remain, while their small son was given an order to join the transport. The sister writes that they, the parents, have decided not to abandon their son, and therefore they are determined to go "together to death".[109] But there were those who decided to abandon their child in an attempt to save him. It is hard to describe in words what went on in the soul of the mother who threw off her child on her way to death. A note (the addressee is unknown) was found on a child, signed "the distressed mother, H.P".. The note said: "Save the child, may God repay you, don't hand over the child to the murderers! Everything will be paid for, he has two pieces of property in Lukow, everything will be paid for. Have mercy on the miserable child! This is the request of a mother unable to do otherwise".[110] Various and even opposing responses of the parents arise from the letters. Parents who decided to go with the child until his bitter end, and parents who threw their child off the transport so he would have a chance to live. This is a dreadful dilemma, hard for us to imagine, but the two responses are as one, an expression of the supreme love of parents. Both are understandable and we cannot question which is preferable.

Concern born of despair and anxiety over the future cry out from the writings on the wall of the "Hasag" factory in Czestochowa.[111]

Jews who were no longer found fit for work were marked as condemned for transport on July 20, 1943. "How will my children live? What will become of them?" signed Ch.S. in a last cry.[112] Max Kawer, a native of Poland, who was transferred to the Cherche-Midi camp and executed on May 14, 1942, wrote beforehand to his wife assigning her to educate the children and requesting her to be brave. He also requests from the children to be good to their mother[113] — a widespread request of every parent wherever they may be. Also, the mother Gabbi Epstein who was transported to Auschwitz via Drancy in September 1942 petitions her daughter in her last request: to be kind and honest, stand upright and never lose courage — and not to forget her parents.[114]

During the last hour, in September 1941, when no hope remained, Bluma Stirnberg, a mother who saw her father murdered, writes that her turn and her son's turn will come the following day. Every means is appropriate in her eyes to rescue her son: "I wanted to convert to Christianity (many would like to do this)", the priests asked permission for this, but they have no hope that permission will be granted. Therefore, writes Bluma, "I must part from life".[115] Concern is expressed here for children's lives at any cost. This is a humanistic message left for the future generations by parents on the verge of their death.

Menachem Meir and Friedrich Reimes, who during the Holocaust were Heinz and Manfred Meyer, published the letters they had received from their parents Carl and Matilda (Are the Trees Blossoming by You?, Yad Vashem Publications, Jerusalem 5761), whose dominant theme is the concern of the parents for their sons. The letters clearly express their concern for the children, concern for small matters and for the most significant of matters that occupy parents also in normal times. We have brought here a few of the letters: the older brother should take care of the younger one and supervise his studies; they should listen to their teachers, they should be good children,[116] they should not fight over things they receive. There is even an interest in the blossom of the trees; do they get enough food?[117] A tone of encouragement is apparent from the lines: Longstanding suffering will end well".[118] There is concern for everyday matters: "Who actually mends your socks? Do you have wool for mending? "[119] The mother is happy that the boys gained weight;[120] the sons should not worry about their parents — it is enough for the parents to worry about their sons.[121] The parents are interested in whether the two brothers will have the opportunity to emigrate to the United States.[122] In the last letter,[123] written before their deportation to the unknown, a note of sadness mingled with slight hope is disclosed. Perhaps they, the parents, will yet reach America.

It is actually the concern over petty matters, from socks to toothpaste, that shows that the fear of the worst of all has not caused them to forget the most important of all — life; and the concern for petty and trivial matters are indeed the elixir of life that parents grant their children.

T he letters presented until this point cover various themes and were directed to the other person. The writers have expressed their concerns for relatives, friends and their precious ones, especially children. They did not emphasize their interests or desires. But the letters also include issues of personal impulses, personal wishes and inner dilemmas. This is evident in themes like revenge, dilemmas, acceptance, faith and suicide.

revenge, dilemmas, acceptance, faith, resistance and suicide

The demand for revenge raises complex questions for today's reader, because in Jewish tradition and general human culture, the act of revenge is considered flawed and is viewed in a negative light. Should we therefore condemn the call of Holocaust victims for revenge? Our answer is negative, and in our opinion the indignant demands for revenge of those going to their deaths cannot be judged for two reasons: The first is that the acts and atrocities that the Nazis carried out towards them were so dreadful and so brutal that it is impossible to include them in the regular behavioral standards of human society. Thus the reaction to call for revenge is not a usual one and cannot be judged on the scale of today's prevailing standards. The second reason is that pain, both physical and emotional, is inherent in each act of revenge; the greater and more burdensome the harm to the victim, so the pain increases. When the pain is beyond human comprehension, who would dare judge those that demand revenge? As with many issues concerning the Holocaust, it is preferable to remain with the questions and avoid the answers.

Most of the calls for revenge were of course directed against the Germans and the Nazis who the victims perceived as one group united in their malice. This was not the case however, with regard to the Polish people. Indeed it is known that extensive anti-Semitism existed in Poland, and so, in the opinion of the Jews. quite a few Poles deserved revenge.

The dilemma confronting the Jew hidden in the house of a gentile about whether to endanger the life of his benefactor was not the only one. Within the Jewish family, there were crucial decisions of children towards their parents and parents towards their children; during the Holocaust people were faced with the necessity to determine who would live and who would die. Should parents be abandoned in order to protect a brother or sister, should a terminally ill person be forsaken, how should food be distributed — these were just some of the dilemmas. The Jew stood alone in those difficult hours, alone with the difficult crucial decision — and found the answer on his own. We cannot judge these decisions today. Our task is merely to document them in order to learn as much as possible about the inner world of the writers.

A significant dilemma of the Jewish victim concerned his belief in the Creator. The letters portray a picture of devotion to faith, which was maintained in most cases. It was anchored in the acceptance of fate, even if this faith was based on a supreme force according to the individual's understanding, and not as dictated by the commandments of tradition (mitzvoth). Faith stresses the element of withstanding the test, a form of resistance without employing force. The last letters mostly express a multifaceted personal resistance, thus adding an impressive perspective to the chronicles of resistance. In the letters of Jewish resistance fighters, motifs appear of revenge and a sense of mission usually linked to the fate of the general community. The personal expressions present the experiences of the underground fighters themselves but they naturally include expressions of national pride and sentiments. A special chapter is dedicated to the letters of the underground.

It seems that the phenomenon of suicide can also be viewed as an expression of resistance. Broaching death of their own volition, was done with clear awareness. Fear, weakness or bravery are human characteristics which functioned within the consciousness of the victims, urging them to end their lives. This deed paradoxically reflects human traits and the human spirit during the moments of the sense of doom.

Revenge

Fury, despair and helplessness found their expression in the call for revenge. In most letters, the call for revenge originated with the writer's experiencing the atrocities of the Nazis and their allies, and the reader senses the deep pain accompanying the cry for revenge. Sometimes this is an appeal for personal revenge, and sometimes the call is directed to the entire Jewish nation. Mostly the demand is to take revenge against the Nazis, but sometimes revenge is demanded from the Polish people who rejoiced at the Jews' misfortune and even assisted this. Father and son, Moshe and Binyamin Wald, in their letter from June 1943, call for revenge in a national tone: "in order to take revenge for the nation's fate against the Germans and also against most of the Poles". In the son's words the national-Zionist tone comes across even stronger: "because Eretz Yisrael was our hope until the last minute, and at the last minute, we saw how our ways were bad".[124] The father of Yehoshua Szeremi from the city of

Uzqorod/Ungvar in Hungary wrote in April 1944: "Don't forget that England and America — two democracies — are the ones responsible for the lives of five or six million of our Jewish brothers. When everything calms down — demand a report from England". It is difficult to understand the reference to England;[125] perhaps this demand stems, as written in another letter, from the rage at the British and their allies who, according to the writer, could have prevented the slaughter.

Descriptions of the atrocities serving as a motive for demanding revenge constitute historical testimony. The letter of the 17 prisoners in the Chelmno death camp from April 2, 1943 belong to this type of testimony. They were forced to carry out the chores of tailors and shoemakers for the Germans, but they wrote that they had only 11 hours left to live.[126]

Eliezer Unger relates shocking testimony in his letter from Pressburg[127] in June 1943. He is forced to watch the murder of many Jews, and he testifies that: "I myself heard hundreds of times from the martyrs whom I saw — I was forced to do this — as their souls departed in holiness and purity and their last words were: Our brothers, remember, take revenge, avenge our blood".[128]

In the city of Kovel[129] in Volhynia where 10,000 had once lived only one woman survived. The Jews who had not yet been murdered were pressed together into the synagogue in September 1942 and shot in groups. We shudder as we read the letters written in the blood of two women, Gina Atlas and Esther Shroll, on the walls of the synagogue. The combination of blood with the synagogue symbolizes, more than anything else, the persecution of Jews throughout the ages until the Nazi atrocity; the blood awakens associations of revenge: Esther seeks to avenge the blood of the murdered; Gina writes to her husband Reuven that her son Imus had cried bitterly because he did not want to die, "Go to war and take revenge for the soul of your wife and your one and only son".[130] In the chapter on testimony we brought the letter of Zlotka Wishniatzky from the town of Byten, ending with the cry "to take revenge against our murderers" — the only thing possible to do for her and her daughter.[131] A note preserved from Chelmno relates that all of the Jews deported from Lodz' were murdered in an awful and dreadful manner; first they were abused and finally burnt. Twelve Jews signed the note calling their last call: "you must take revenge".[132] In most of the letters, revenge becomes the final cry. Sometimes terrible sadness emerges, like in the one of a 19-year-old girl who pleads "and don't forget this one condemned to die when she was nineteen years old".[133] The other letters are characterized by fury when demanding revenge, as in the letter of Asher the son of Yitzchak from Linesk. He testifies that in the entire Snokai region, a total of 70 Jews remain out of 15,000, and his cry for revenge is strong and harsh: The blood of the Jews must be avenged, children should be educated in the spirit of arms and hatred towards the German nation, and one must murder "everyone you come across (from the German nation), people, women and small children, because that's what they did to us... Revenge! Revenge! Revenge!"[134]

Those joining the partisans or the Red Army had one purpose before them, and this was revenge. Peretz Levine fell as a soldier in the Red Army in February 1945, and in his letter from January 1945 he writes: "I feel good now — I'm participating in the destruction of the enemy".[135] Yitzchak Aron, from the town of Miur, managed to escape on June 2, 1942 from a crowd of Jews prior to their being sent to the killing pit. He hid for three months in "crates, in wheat, in the stable, in the forest and in the great mud", and during that time he recorded his memories in a notebook. He hopes that "if I cannot look forward to some comfort of revenge against the Hitlerian murderers and the local police while I am alive, at least my own torn notebook [...] written in blood and amid the most difficult moments of my life [...] somehow to help take revenge against the German murderers for our parents, brothers, sisters, children, for our blood spilled over no wrongdoing on our part".[136]

It is strange that the research studies do not deal much with revenge; because after all, the indescribable suffering justifies a collective bitter cry for revenge. Elie Wiesel wrote: "Were hatred a solution, the survivors, when they came out of the camps, would have had to burn down the whole world".[137] The words of Wiesel are appropriate for this issue. Two types of revenge are discernible in the last letters: One type is revenge that focuses completely on the murderer, with a demand to punish him, sort of like "an eye for an eye" in the literal sense of this saying. An example of this approach is the cry of Asher son of Yitzchak Schwartz brought above to murder Germans, "because that's what they did to us".[138] This type of revenge is apparent in the last letters of the prisoners in Chelmno mentioned above. The second type, far more prominent in these letters, stresses the centrality of the victim rather than the murderer, because the element of "remembrance" is inherent in revenge: Revenge is required to remember the beloved person who died. An illustrative example of this desperate cry for revenge was mentioned above, "don't forget this one condemned to die".[139]

The testimonies in the letters reflect on the behavior of the Polish people from two different aspects: Some wrote positively, while others harshly criticized the behavior of the Poles. In the letter of Moshe and Binyamin Wald from June 1943, written from a hiding place near Piotrkow, a heavy charge is presented. It is mentioned that most of the Poles do not help the Jews and are even joyous at the bitter fate of the Jews. "The [Polish] public is very bitter, and is happy with the fate of our people", and for this the writers demand to take revenge against them.[140] There is known research that verifies the existence of hostility and anti-Semitism among the Polish population.

But among the hostile Poles there were exceptions who helped the Jews during the period of the Holocaust. Peretz Goldstein, for example, testifies to this. He was about to be sent to his death, and leaves in writing instructions for handling the book that he wrote about "The Dreadful Slaughters in the Town of Huszt"; with income from the sale of the book for one Polish zloti apiece, a monument must be built in memory of the murdered people from Huszt. The remaining balance should be handed over to the Polish Kapar family who had supported him and his family: "The Kapar family hid us in their house for a long time".[141] Gusta Berger-Ehrlich from the prison in Montelupich mentions in her letter the jailer in the prison who was kind to her, and she therefore requests "at least five Zloti for every day that I stay here. He and his wife, too, help me and do for me more than they're allowed to do".[142]

We learn from the letters that although the general atmosphere prevailing in Poland was one of anti-Semitism and joy at the Jews' misfortune, there were also Poles who extended help. The origin of most of the letters here are from Poland, where, as is known, the vast destruction of the Jewish ingathering between 1942 — 1944 took place. These matters have been stated in the widespread research on Polish Jews during the Holocaust. Yet the experiences and fears, the fury and resolve, the weakness and compassion emerging from this compilation of letters enrich the research with the personal angle, providing it with authenticity and profundity.

Dilemmas

Quite a few of the writers of the letters agonized over difficult ethical dilemmas, whether with regard to a crucial family decision or friends in trouble, or whether in the relationships between the persecuted Jew and his non-Jewish benefactor.[143] The familial dilemma is properly expressed in the letter of Pinchas'l, a boy of 17, whom we have mentioned above. The letter is intended for Pinchas'l's older brother and written in a most emotional tone. He describes how a friend of the family, called K.S., came to their home in Budapest, beaten up and seriously injured, after clashing with the Nazis. This friend suggested to the family to take Suraleh, Pinchas'l's sister, to a secure location. Suraleh jumped for joy and wanted to join him immediately, but the mother blocked their way claiming that the Nazis would catch them on the way. Suraleh was determined — she wanted to live. The mother then suggested that if Pinchas'l would also join them — she would agree, and Pinchas'l wrote in his last letter that he had decided to stay, because he could not abandon his parents. What a dreadful dilemma to burden such a young boy. The dilemma between the chance to save his sister but at the price of forsaking his parents, is like decreeing the death sentence to one or the other.[144]

The dilemma confronting the Jew at times was one faced by those gentiles, who were ready to conceal Jews, thus endangering their own lives. This is how Melech Goldenberg acknowledges the help that he received from his friend, "He saved me […] he frequently endangered his life for my sake".[145] Feivush writes of "a gentile who wants to take me in, despite the fact that by doing so he will suffer the same fate".[146]

These examples offer a glimpse of the difficult dilemmas and courageous decisions of the Jews faced with crucial and personal life and death decisions. It is difficult for us, observing from the vantage point of decades after the events, to judge and take a stand on what was the "correct" decision, but it is possible to sense the ethical burden and the dilemma weighing on the conscience of the victims, and admire the courage they found to solve these dilemmas.

Acceptance and Rescue

It is possible to conclude from the letters that the forms of acceptance of fate differed, even as the circumstances were different. Some accepted what was coming when they understood that their fate was decreed, when only a step stood between them and death. When reading these letters today we can understand this emotional state and even identify with it. But there was another type of acceptance, which originated from anxiety over the future, by Jews who were not in imminent danger of death, and this motivated them to write. In this letter the religious tone is emphasized to some degree. The reader senses that the words are written with measured thought and not out of shock from the current event. So for example Julius Joseph writes to his son that just as his life had been lived with dignity — so too will he go with dignity to his death. Although he has reservations in his letter about the "holiness of the letter" — the father is certain that every event has a deeper meaning, and he ends the letter with the traditional priestly blessing.[147]

In 1941, Regina of Hamburg wrote before her deportation to her daughter Ilsa. In contrast to the letter of Julius Joseph, who expressed faith in a supreme power but had reservations about the ritualistic aspect of the religion of Israel, Regina writes a letter of acceptance expressing devotion to the commandments of God. "If only you will aspire to Torah and commandments", and "May you be inscribed and sealed for a happy and long life among all those loyal to Israel". The mother requests and hopes that the pain over her death will pass by in order to focus on more important issues. Regina was aware of the upheaval in world order when parents bury their children, and she writes, "children should bury their parents, not parents their children", in the sense that life should go on as usual. Her wish takes us back to the young boy, 14-year-old Chaim of Pustkow bemoaning his impending death.[149] Indeed, this was a time when life was not as usual.

These two letters, written in 1941–1942 by German Jews, testify to a measured and balanced prevalent mood. Regina's letter shows the inner world of the religious and educated Jews, who together with observing the commandments were also knowledgeable about general Western culture. She reinforces her farewell words with a paraphrase from Shakespeare's Julius Caesar: "If we meet again, I do not know. Therefore for eternity bear the wish of farewell, for eternity be well for me, my Ilsa, Manfred, Frantza. And if indeed we meet, for your lives — we will smile. And if indeed we do not meet, this parting is sweet for the mouth". She quotes Don Carlos in Schiller's play: "Ho Queen, life was so beautiful".[150] This attitude and style were typical of German Jews and were not widespread in farewell letters of Jews from Eastern Europe.

Together with acceptance of the bitter fate, optimism and encouragement for the next generation emerge. Sophie Heiman writes from the Noe camp in France in August 1942, appealing in this tone to her husband and children. She expresses the hope that she will live to see her dear ones when she is in one piece and healthy, and encourages them not to lose hope and to have faith in God. She is more devoted than ever in her faith that God will protect her and also, in the future; but if her fate is decreed to die, it is necessary to accept this with the awareness that this is the will of Providence. She ends with words of encouragement. Not to lose courage and always hope for the best.[151]

The three letters share the concern of parents for their children, with an acceptance of the fact that they themselves have already lived their lives. But when children turn to their parents, another tone is evident — perhaps because they cannot accept the fact that they have reached the end of their road. They look for a way out and request the help of their parents for rescue in any way. In a letter written in June 1941 from Angeles[152] in France, Helen writes to her parents, Henia and Yisrael Rappoport. A desperate call for help emanates from the letter: "Maybe dear Father has someone in America or another place, with whom you can make contact to get us out? […] Do whatever is possible to enable us to have this chance". Helen and her sister are sent to Auschwitz — never to return.[153]

The spiritual aspect is particularly prominent in the theme of acceptance: Most of the writers place their trust in the will of the Creator, and their religious belief strengthened them on their road to the awful end.

Faith and Undermining Faith

> One day when we came back from work, we saw three gallows rearing up in the assembly place, three black crows. Roll call. …The three victims mounted together onto the chairs. The three necks were placed at the same moment within the nooses.
>
> "Long live liberty!" cried the two adults.
>
> But the child was silent.
>
> "Where is God? Where is He?" someone behind me asked.

At a sign from the head of the camp, the three chairs tipped over. ...

Behind me, I heard the same man asking:

"Where is God now?"

And I heard a voice within me answer him:

"Where is He? Here He is — He is hanging here on this gallows..."[154]

These chosen lines, from Night, the renowned book by Elie Wiesel, center on the religious dilemma confronting Jews in the Holocaust. As stated, the sense of acceptance and the willing acceptance of the judgement come to light from the last letters. Perhaps this relieved the victims, and the reader senses the profound faith of the writer. Yet in the last letters an undermining of faith and skepticism appear more than once. Elie Wiesel tells of disappointment from Providence: "Where is He? Here He is — He is hanging here on this gallows"; because after all when God is hanging a boy — doubts do arise.

There were two ways of coming to terms with Providence from the abyss, and one must not prefer either one. The person condemned to death who was devoted to his faith in God, despite everything, awakens in us awe and admiration, but even the response of Jews whose faith is undermined and plagued with skepticism, is a human response. Faith was expressed, for example, in prayer, like the one in the letter from Budapest in March 1944 of a father to his son, Henry Adler in Michigan: "You Who is in every place and also with our beloved grandchildren, with our beloved children, with my beloved wife, and with myself [...] Disrupt the evil intention of our enemies every time and every place".[155]

Sometimes man, during his daily life, hides behind the will of God in order to flee a personal decision or from helplessness that paralyzes his steps. Yet in the Holocaust the condemned showed acceptance of their situation from lack of an alternative: They threw off their burden at the Almighty knowing that there was no escape and all ways were blocked; because there was no way out, they viewed the atrocities befalling them as the will of Providence. With this belief, they reinforced their hope or their acceptance.

The following four letters were written in this spirit. Yosef Hagar of Lesko[156] writes in his farewell letter of the deportation of "men, women and children"; 3,000 people will stay for labor near Linesk, and the rest will be sent to be slaughtered. He rules that if it is decreed in Heaven, every Jew must accept it with love as an atonement of sins, for him and for the entire people of Israel.[157] A father from Holland expresses his unwavering faith in the Almighty: "The kindness of the Lord wanted it like this; I accept His will with equanimity and faith. I think about how much kindness He has granted us […] I trust in 'for your salvation do I long, O God'!"[158] In a similar way a father from the town of Kamionka[159] parts from his daughter whom he had never met in a letter signed with the initials A.D. He writes that in the world only evil exists today, but this is the will of the Creator.[160] In a postcard sent to Mrs. Rena Gutman in Budapest in May 1944, Mrs. Prager wrote that Rena's relatives were put on a railroad car "and only God knows where they will be taken […] We will place our trust in God in Heaven".[161]

Sometimes the ability to resist drew its strength from the faith in Providence or from general religious sentiments, and this was termed by the editor of the book "History of the Jews of Konstanz" — "heroism from faith". This resistance is expressed in the letter of an elderly woman, 84-year-old Rosa Weil, from the Gurs[162] camp in France. Under difficult conditions, she even maintained a sense of humor: "The hygiene is unbelievable, but we, the Jews, have clean blood and we overcome everything". The letter is intended for her daughter, and she stresses to everyone that there is hope in her heart and they are courageous, with no sad faces around: "so they won't be happy with our humiliation". She requests from her daughter: "Don't worry, God does not abandon His own […] God sends us a good messenger in every situation!"[163] The willing acceptance of the judgement appears here together with a firm belief in the Creator, as a support and emotional reinforcement. With the willing acceptance of the sentence, the believer annuls himself before the Creator's will, but actually this devotion to the Creator reinforces his existence and his power to cope with the dreadful events around him, and he draws strength from this. The two conditions — one can be termed "theological" and the other "psychological" — do not express despair or fatalism, but a human way of trust and faith.

For some people, their faith in God was undermined. The undermining was a response to the skepticism towards the Creator who was perceived as being responsible for the horrendous atrocities that gnawed at the foundation of faith. "Do you still believe in God?" cried Maya to Shmuel in May 1943.[164] Rosa Timberg of Berlin also doubts the existence of God in light of the dreadful suffering.[165] In a relatively small number of letters, the writers did a severely critical reckoning with the Lord; for example, a parent declares that he does not believe any more and therefore avoids blessing his son Yehoshua with the blessing ""May God safeguard you".[166] It is difficult to reach conclusions about the general public, but it can be assumed that there were some Jews whose faith was undermined, but they usually did not place themselves or their fate at the center. Perhaps because of this we find only a few expressions of atheism. We can presume that the enemies did not succeed in destroying the faith of the Jews in the Almighty, but these are only assumptions.

Resistance

When the Jews endured in the camps, the underground or anywhere within the enemy's grasp reach of the enemy, the element of resistance is embodied. This resistance has diverse facets: a collective Jewish resistance, that Yehuda Bauer defines as "any collective activity that was taken with an awareness that it was against the laws, the activities, and the known or implicit intentions of the Germans and their accomplices whose goal was to harm Jews".[167] This definition includes resistance with or without ammunition, and it is mentioned in the letters.

Referring to the revolt in Warsaw (April 1943), members of the National Committee wrote in November 1943 that "We want the Jewish people and the entire world to know that like a hero, our youth defended its life and the honor of our people".[168] On April 27, 1943, about a week after the revolt broke out, a telegram from Poland arrived in the Home Office in London with an excited call for financial assistance to purchase ammunition and to save lives. It says among other things: "We are fighting with weapons for our life and for the honor of the survivors of the Jewish people".[169] But most of the last letters emphasize the personal unarmed resistance with various motivations. Esther the daughter writes to her parents and her brothers in September 1942, that she is going to an unknown destination; but she is going courageously and in good health.[170] This was a common form of resistance, motivated by a sense of optimism. This feeling perhaps stemmed from the fact that Esther, like many others, did not know what was awaiting her, and she therefore still hoped for good.

The revolt in the Warsaw Ghetto as well as the fighting of the underground were methods of endurance and resistance with clear goals facing the rebels and fighters, enhancing their motivation. This resistance can be termed "organized resistance". In the letters another type of resistance is revealed: unplanned resistance, taking place in an unexpected situation. Even those that withstood the test did not know from where they drew strength. In a shocking letter Chulda describes this resistance: She escaped with her parents from Lvov to Brzezany, but also there they did not find shelter from the actions and pogroms. She decided to go to Midowa without identifying signs, escorted by a Christian acquaintance, and she was imprisoned. "Miraculously" she left prison, but the actions had continued outside. In one of the actions their hideout was discovered, but they managed to release themselves with bribery. She writes her letter awaiting the termination action. "Now we are also on death's door, which is worse than the others, because we are waiting for it with our complete awareness [...] I write on and on, but still haven't been able to relate even a fraction of what has happened to us during this whole time. After all I cannot count all the heart spasms before each impending action [...] and I particularly cannot describe the dread of the horror of death. And despite this, we still live, we haven't gone insane yet, we don't cry and don't shout. We are alive, as if all that is going on around us doesn't affect us. Until the last moment of our lives, we laugh and sing. And only sometimes, when reality becomes too lucid, we forget the laughter".[171] It seems that here, unconsciously lies one of the explanations of the source of the strength to endure, it is a natural resistance originating from the force of survival, whose source or meaning was not understood by the victim himself. This explanation emphasizes a principle that the Nazis did not take into account, despite the calculated planning of murder — the principle of the natural inclination for life. As an inherent trait, it does not require special motivation.

In the farewell letter of Sarah and Yechiel Gerlitz (of Bendin, Poland) to their daughter, the mother writes: "I would like you to know is that your mother walked with an upright posture, despite all of the humiliations that we suffered from our enemies, and if she is sentenced to die, she will die without condemning, without crying, but she will put a scornful smile on her face while facing her executioners". The father adds: "I believe with complete faith, despite everything, that we will all overcome and return our hearts to each other".[172] This resistance is one of emotional bravery, of human pride, that is not willing to surrender to humiliation, neither prior to death nor at the time of death. This is a resistance that is aware of human dignity versus those who behave in an anti-human way. It is obvious that not every person was able to reach such personal elevation in these difficult moments, but the resistance born of an awareness of human dignity was resistance of the spirit.

Leopold wrote to his parents, probably after the deportation from Westerbork, that it is obvious to him that now his materialistic deterioration has started (he calls this "materialistic proletarianization"), but with all this his spirit is firm. He compares himself to a hedge-hog protecting itself from the hostile surroundings by rolling up. It is important for Leopold to maintain his spiritual independence; in this he sees his ability to endure the hardships. He adds that a day will come when he will shift from passive struggle to active struggle for the sake of "our Jewish people".[173] This awareness of resistance expresses personal strength, but it also contains an idealistic prin-ciple; that in the future his role would be that of active assistance, so that the "tragedy which now befalls the Jewish people, specifically, and the nations of the world, in general, will not repeat itself". All of the incidents have a common denominator: maintaining the human image in the face of totally dehumanized barbarism.

Suicide

From the memoirs of the Holocaust survivors in Europe it emerges that suicide was not the way of the masses of the people of Israel during conditions of distress. The overwhelming majority preferred to suffer in order to survive the present travails and live to the point beyond them, derleben on eiberleben.[174] Yet there are letters that include the element of suicide, with various motives, backgrounds and locations.

The letters express various inner feelings according to the person-ality of each writer. It is natural for a person to fears the fateful step of suicide; this fear is expressed in Mika Liubin's letter, where she admits that she had attempted suicide a few times, until finally she does not have the courage to end her life. She expected death by the enemies "without fear" as she says.[175]

Another motive that is repeated in the letters is the motive of heroism. The motivations for heroic acts differed from each other. Teacher Zlata Brizitz, a native of Lodz',[176] tried to end her life by slit-ting her throat, but she did not manage this and recovered. Her end proves her intention: She was a member of the underground, while her husband had joined the Red Army. The son Josek was caught by the Gestapo and killed. After she was saved from the suicide attempt, she was tortured by her captors in order to extract information — but she refused to talk, and was about to be executed.[177] The Polish friend of the Fohorils family handed over to Dr. Reuven Shugar, a lawyer in Tel Aviv, information about the heroic act of Manak Fohorils, Shugar's brother-in-law, in the spirit of "Let my soul die with the Philistines". When the police tried to remove him from out of the bunker, he shot the policemen and then his family and himself.[178] In a similar spirit, Avraham Zeitz and Feivish Kamlazi of Konin, gave their lives, notifying that they were planning to "behave like Samson".[179]

Although there were a few who had contemplated suicide, they avoided it for different reasons. Religious conscience stopped Moshe Akar, in his escape, from killing himself.[180] Anna Trauman was afraid that she could not endure the difficulties of deportation because of the frailty of her body and she decided to commit suicide with poison. After she took the poison she wrote: "I hope to die conciliated with the world and in hope of kindness and love".[181] Also Elsa Klauber considered the possibility of ending her life if she would feel unable to withstand the suffering[182].

It seems necessary to emphasize the incidents that were mentioned as heroic acts, as acts of resistance with clear awareness and choice on the part of the heroes to voluntarily march to their death. Despite this, the phenomenon of suicide was not common among Jews. This is backed up by the statement of Meir Dvorz'atski that the "obstinate vitality to suffer and see death eye to eye and not to commit suicide was the way of the overwhelming majority of Jews during the Holocaust".[183] And indeed the tragic cases described here do not reflect on the general public; here the aforementioned urge for life is reaffirmed. The will to survive was stronger than anything, and perhaps this is the explanation for the relatively low number of people committing suicide.

Another reason for the revulsion of many to end their lives was the rule of religion. There were certainly many — even if they did not state this in writing — who were deterred from suicide because of the ideal of the sanctity of life, one of the principles of Jewish tradition. Life is a gift from God and we do not have any right to tamper with the order of creation. In the Mishna, in the Ethics of Our Fathers, it says: "Against your will you were born and against your will you live and against your will you die". The Talmud explicitly says: "One who commits suicide has no part in the World to Come".[184] These words are intended for a person living under humane conditions. But when the individual is torn away from a framework of humane standards, when the world has turned into an abyss, when he has sunk into a "black void"[185] — does this Talmudic saying have relevance? After all, according to the feeling of the Holocaust victim, even in this world he has no part?! Indeed most of the letters show the desire to live in this world, with a yearning for a sane and humane world.

The motif of commemoration emerges from all the last letters, and a sense of mission is added from the last letters written by the people of the underground. Because of this sense of mission, the letters of the underground differ in their content and essence from the rest of the letters. Sometimes the text is more like an informative report, suppressing the personal aspect. It must be remembered that the partisans and the underground *the underground* people had to maintain confidentiality in their letters and reports. Hannah Senesh writes in the letter to the member of the kibbutz secretariat who handled her mission: "We are accustomed to our friends' activities becoming known in public; we all experience together the successes and the difficulties. But you should know that in order to satisfy the friends who want to know about our destiny, we could pay very dearly for this. Every word of appreciation and publicity — you realize what this means".[186] From here we see that personal matters, news and impressions of the underground members were not always expressed in the letters.

Another difference that stands out between the letters and reports of the fighters and other last letters, worthy of emphasis is: The substance of their mission, the goal of the fighters, even when they realized that they had reached their end, offered meaning to their lives and anguish. While other writers expressed the feeling that their lives had lost all purpose and their existence was bereft of importance or meaning.

All of the last letters presented in this book, including the letters of the underground, are in fact memorial tablets commanding one to remember and perpetuate the memory of the victims, their personal experiences and their inner world. Yet the commemoration of the underground people is not always personal, because it was not always possible to identify the victim and the commemoration deals frequently with anonymous individuals and nameless groups. Commemoration of these anonymous figures is actually a "historical commemoration": We identify with their historical acts more than with the personal destiny of the anonymous writer. The letters are divided into two sections: The first was written by members of the undergrounds in the ghettoes and camps, and the other was written by Jewish fighters outside of the camps. The intention is not to record the history of the underground, but to disclose, in these written messages, the fighters' inner experiences, both the common ones as well as the unique ones.

We have preserved the last letters of the Bund members operating in the underground in Warsaw and Vilna. Among them is the last letter of Shmuel Zigelboim, one of the heads of the Bund, who managed to flee from Poland and arrive in England. The letter was written a day before he committed suicide on May 12, 1943, and was directed to the exiled president and prime minister of Poland. According to Zigelboim's testimony, 300,000 Jews remained alive out of a total of 3,500,000 Jews in Poland and approximately 700,000 Jews deported there from other countries. Zigelboim demands from the Polish government to do an extraordinary act for the sake of the Jews. In his letter the personal tone is prominent: He states that "I cannot live and be silent at a time when the remnants of Polish Jews, whom I represent, are being murdered". He regrets that he was not privileged to fall as his friends in the underground, but "I belong with them, to the grave of the masses". He presents his death as a deep objection against the apathy of the world, which observes and does nothing, and he gives his life for the Jewish people in Poland. A sense of self sacrifice for the sake of rescuing the public prevails in this letter.[187]

Mordechai Anielewicz ("Malachi"), the commander of the Jewish Fighters Organization and the Warsaw Ghetto revolt, left a last letter written on April 23, 1943 to Yitzchak Zukerman (Antek).[188] He describes what is happening during the fighting and writes about the scouting companies that went out in search of weapons, which they urgently needed. The letter expresses his sense of mission: "I feel that great things are happening, and what we dared to do is of great and tremendous value". He turns to his friend, one of the fighters in the ghetto, in hope that they will yet see each other, but he declares that the dream of his life has become a reality — armed Jewish resistance and revenge have turned from theory into fact.

In the letters of the underground and the writings of the Bund members and pioneers from other movements, personal expressions are mixed with a tone of national Jewish mission. Anielewicz's letter to Antek is typical when he writes of the "the dream of his life", the goal and the ideals. The issues have greater significance on reading the words of Yitzchak Zukerman, one of the surviving commanders of the revolt. Zukerman claims that the rebels saw themselves not only as Jewish pioneers fighting the Nazis, but also as representing the entire world, as the first group that rose up against the Nazis at a time when there was no sign of hope or rescue.[189]

The letters from Hrubieszow and Grabowiec present the existence of a connection with the commanders of the underground in the Warsaw Ghetto, such as Yitzchak Zukerman. One should note the puns in the letters.[190]

In contrast to the image of the underground partisan fighters as rough people who supposedly do not express their feelings, a totally different picture emerges from the letters of Mordechai Tannenboim-Tamaroff,[191] the commander of the revolt in the Bialistok Ghetto who fell in 1943. Tannenboim is characterized as a cultured fighter with a sensitive and refined poetic soul, traits that were disclosed in the letters of others, too, like Hannah Senesh. Tannenboim addresses his letters to Bronia Vinitzky-Kalibenski, who was the signaler of the Jewish Resistance Organization on the Aryan side of Bialistok.

Tannenboim had a great love of flowers; they appear in many letters, and are mentioned also in the codes of the underground: "a small home of your own, definitely a home entirely of your own".[192] "If I ever visit you — I will bring flowers".[193] In another letter is a lively and charming description of flowers. It is amazing how such a romantic description merges with the dark reality of the underground messages: "I must write you now about my flowers. So many, so many! [...] An assortment of field flowers resembling the lily [...] golden irises [...] During the night they blossomed in their full glory [...] On the floor [...] an enormous bouquet of the acacia plant".[194] He explains his great interest in flowers: "Do you know why I deal so much with flowers, why I write about them so much? It is the law of contrasts. Precisely because conditions are so, etc., etc. — I love them so much. For the future generations — for psychological assessment. I don't have a sausage [weapon] yet. The assumption is that it will be tomorrow. If I get it — I will notify you".[195] The need to nourish the soul with beauty, with the invigorating, with the symbol of life represented by a flower which is counterweight to a "sausage", a tool of destruction, shows us a lot about the character of this Jewish fighter. Amidst the requests and orders of weapons, the following request is inserted: "Please buy for me peony and dahlia flowers — but dark ones, the color of blood. Fresh flowers — which I can keep for a long time".[196] "When I don't have flowers — I'm so sad, it's so strange — because of Wanda".[197] These letters are an instructive example of the inner world and the experiential aspect of the writers.

Hannah Senesh also reveals her poetic soul with the terror of

death hovering over her. In her last letter to her mother she mourns:
One--two--three…
Eight feet long,
Two strides across, the rest is dark…
Life hangs over me like a question mark.

One--two--three…
Maybe another week,
Or next month may still find make here,
But death, I feel, is very near.

I could have been
twenty-three next July;
I gambled on what mattered most,
The dice were cast. I lost.[198]

Today's readers of these letters stand in awe of the combination of poetic refinement with physical resistance and courage.

The combination of physical bravery with a poetic soul are evident also in the letters of an especially unique Jewish fighter, who also paid with his life: Jup Westroil of Holland, who was shot in 1944. He left a letter where he mentions a fellow in arms who was caught and committed suicide under torture of the Gestapo so as not to inform on his friends. Jup Westroil expresses the conviction that he would endure and not reveal names. He was shot in August 1944 in an attempt to escape from the concentration camp where he was imprisoned.[199]

When reading the letters of Liana Berkovitch, daughter of a Jewish father and a Christian mother, who was sentenced to death for her membership in the underground, the differences between Christian and Jew are blurred. The letters to her Christian mother are a monument to the suffering of a person as a person, of a mother constantly worrying about her baby. The father of the baby, Remus, was executed because of his underground activity. The baby was born in prison. Liana, devoted to her Christian tradition, requests that her mother take care of Yirena (Eirka) and baptize her in the Greek-Orthodox church. Jews and Christians who were caught resisting the Nazis faced the same destiny, and the road to their end was similar: Jews who were caught as underground members went with equanimity and pride to their death, as Liana Berkovitch did, "calm and in control of myself and I'm not afraid of death", and requests only that they should take care of her little Eirka.[200] She too, as is seen in the set of letters, does not worry about her own fate but about the fate of those who come after her. The human concern beating within the person, Jew and non-Jew, blurred the differences and made it a certificate of honor for all of the victims in general and for the underground people in particular.

The revolt in the Warsaw Ghetto, the uprising of other ghettos and the role of the Jewish partisan movement have removed the image of the passive Jew in exile — claims Israel Gutman at the end of his book: The Warsaw Ghetto Uprising.[201] The letters of the underground people, that incorporated all of the organizations, shed light on the non-passive figure of the Jewish fighter. The words of the fighters, members of the underground, reveal their personal sentiments and feelings during their operations, and they complement Gutman's insightful statement as a researcher reaching a comprehensive conclusion.

We presented here various themes that characterized the last letters. We must add and outline one method of writing that typified some of these letters. Some of them were written in coded language, sort of like a code that the addressees would comprehend.

coded language This was not a technical method of writing, but rather a style of camouflage used to describe the true situation, and to relay information or accurate developments in the situation and mislead the censorship. Obviously, this method also served to inform the outside world about events in the occupied countries, the underground movements and the camps.

Frequently, the writers would use Hebrew words. In order to notify that it is unnecessary to write letters, it said "Michtav [Letter] doesn't want to be here; Sakana [Danger] also doesn't want to", in the letter of Yakov Kashashiv of Bendzin, in August 1943.[202] In a different letter Gertrude Eisinger, imprisoned in Birkenau,[203] requests to relate that she is hungry, by using coded language: "Aunt Lechem [Aunt Bread]" does not visit her.[204] From the destruction site in Birkenau news comes in about the murdered people: "[Send] regards from me Mr. Kaddish", or "Magda Goldberg works together with me, and the others with the first Kaddish". Another Coded language, no less terrifying, was also written from Birkenau: "Frau. Halal [Mrs. Slain] is very diligent here. Back home I didn't like it when she would be in my house, but here I'm with her all the time, and I've already befriended her…"[205]

The difficult situation in the Warsaw Ghetto was related in coded language by anonymous writers. In one letter it says that on July 15, 1942 the writer "got sick" — meaning that the deportations and murder had started; she had to go "to the hospital", which means a safe place; about her physical condition she relates that "the diet was poor and the different attacks threatened my life every day", and she hopes to get help from her people: "We impatiently await the promised help of our Uncle Ami [Uncle My People]".[206] Names like Kilajon — "when Kilajon [Destruction] comes — and Mavetzky [from Mavet — Death] — "they are by Mavetzky [Deathsky], that's why they don't have time to write you" — were common in the lexicon of the coded text.[207] Helina writes about her Aunt Mavetia [Aunt Deathia) who is liable to visit her and requests from Uncle Dror (Uncle Liberty) to make sure that Aunt Alya (Aunt Aliyah — Immigration to the Land of Israel) will rescue them.[208]

Zvi writes from Sosnowiec,[209] in October 1942 about his bitter disappointment from the ability of Geulah [Redemption]: She learns all year, he writes, but when she takes exams — she fails. Aunt Tikwa [Aunt Hope] is struggling, with her last strength, but the physicians do not give her much hope.[210]

In October 1942 Riva Nisdovska of Bendin writes to Natan Schwalb in Geneva that "Herr. Gierusch [Mr. Deportation] is staying with us and brought with him also Herr. Mawed [Mr. Death]. And then we hope very much for "Hatzalah [Rescue]".[211] Josik[212] writes from Warsaw, in October 1943, to the "Beloved Aunt Moledet [Aunt Homeland]". He relates that 38,000 people are at the location. Last week friends went to "Haganski" [Defenski]. "The last days were very hard for Ami [My People], who has meanwhile taken sick. We paid a lot to Dr. Mavet [Dr. Death]; the children go to him regularly and we cannot do a thing against this".[213]

In February 1942 an anonymous person writes about the sick and even the deceased people from a disease that "Yosef the Righteous had for 12 years [Imprisonment]".[214] In a series of letters written between the years 1942–1943, the mother and sister of Emil Bromer, a Jewish brigadier who was taken into German captivity, write about the atrocities affecting them and his fiancée in Zborow.[215] In April 1943, they report on "a thorough cleansing. Our grandfather's factory was working at full force. About 1,500 pairs of shoes (mainly for women and children) were destroyed". In May she describes the events in April as "a big storm that uprooted big, young trees with their roots". Also in June "an awful storm lashed about destroying the entire city. Only those that found 'shelter' from the thunder, as we did, were saved".[216]

The circumstances forced the writers to use coded language. But it is obvious that these dark messages constitute authentic descriptions of the situations and personal testimonies about the horrific events of the Holocaust. They also teach us how the Jews found a method to deceive their enemies by transferring from the vale of death news of historical value, despite the tightening of the Nazi noose. The method they employed, coded language, can be seen as yet another method of resistance, in the spirit of the aforementioned definition of Bauer at the beginning of the chapter Resistance under Trial. Through these circumventive and deceptive methods, the true intentions of the Nazis and their acts of torture and destruction were revealed.

Zwi Bacharach

Endnotes

[1] From: Primo Levi, **Survival in Auschwitz: The Nazi Assault on Humanity**, translated from the Italian by Stuart Woolf, New York 1971, pp. 22–23.

[3] Balzac, **The Great Book of Quotations**, p. 366.

[4] Letter 1, Avraham Tori, **Day by Day Ghetto**, Jerusalem 1998, pp. 604–608.

[5] Letter 2, Yad Vashem Archives (YVA), O–48 B/5–2–6, S.N. 5330.

[6] Ringelblum Diary, quoted from Ruta Sakowska "The Two Types of Resistance in the Warsaw Ghetto: The Two Roles of the Ringelblum Archive", **Yad Vashem – Collection of Research** 21 (5751), p. 175.

[7] Letter 3, Ruth Sakowska (ed.) *Archiwum Ringlebluma: Konspiracyjne Archiwum Getta Warszawy*, Warsaw, 1997, letters 140–145.

[8] Letter 4, YVA, 3–ל, O–48/66, S.N. 10517.

[9] Letter 5, Sakowska (ed.), *Archiwum Ringelbluma*, letter 103.

[10] Letter 6, YVA, O–48/66–G–1, S.N. 10087.

[11] Letter 7, YVA, O–48 B/5–2–2, S.N. 97/68.

[12] Letter 8, Sakowska (ed.), *Archiwum Ringelbluma*, letter 41.

[13] Saloniki — a port city, the second largest in Greece. It was occupied on April 9, 1941 by the Germans. 50,000 Jews had lived there. On February 25, 1943, the Germans began to transport the Jews of Saloniki to Auschwitz.

[14] Letter 9, Chulda Archives, 8/128.

[15] Byten — a town in the Belarus region.

[16] Letter 10, Dadl Abramovitch (ed.), **The Byten Ledger: Der Aufkom on Untergang fon a Yidische Kehilla**, Buenos Aires 5714, pp. 550–551.

[17] Zaslaw — a forced labor camp used as a concentration camp near Sanok, in the Zhashov (Reisha) region. In 1942 some 10,000 Jews were transported from the camp to destruction in Belzice, and many more Jews were murdered by shooting.

[18] Letter 11, Nathan Mark and Shimon Friedlander (eds.) **The Yizkor Book for the Martyrs of Liba"i**, with no mention of place and year, pp 381–388.

[19] Tarnopol — a city in western Ukraine, where 18,000 Jews had lived.

[20] Letter 12, **The Encyclopedia of the Exiles** c, Jerusalem 1955, pp. 403–412.

[21] Letters 13 and 14, The Central Zionist Archives, S26 1419.

[22] Moletai — a city in the Otin region, eastern Lithuania.

[23] Letter 15, YVA, O–48/B5–2, S.N. 3697.

[24] Shavli — a city in Lithuania, when the Germans occupied the city 6,500 Jews had lived there. Only 500 of them survived.

[25] Letter 16, YVA, O–48/B5–3, S.N. 2807.

[26] Letter 17, a letter from Zamosc, see Sakowska (ed.), *Archiwum Ringelbluma*, letter 58.

[27] Bedzin — a city in Poland in the Upper Shelsia region, just before World War Two

27,000 Jews had lived there.

[28] Ponary — a mass murder site near Vilna. It is estimated that between 70,000 and 100,000 people were killed there, mainly Jews.

[29] Letter 18, **The Zaglambia Ledger**, Tel Aviv 5733, pp. 541–542.

[30] Letter 19, **There Was a Town: Memorial Book for the Kehillos of Beresteczko, Bermelia and Surroundings**, Haifa, 5721, pp. 18–23.

[31] Letter 10.

[32] Letter 20, the testimony of Pesach Bezradki in "The Struggle for Life", Nachman Blumenthal (ed.) **The Yizkor Book of Miechow, Rascheintz and Kashoinzh**, Tel Aviv 1971, pp. 205–206.

[33] Magdeburg — a city and concentration in Germany, west of Berlin

[34] Letter 21, YVA, 1–ג, O–48/B S.N. 7940.

[35] Letter 22, YVA, O–30/111.

[36] Letter 7.

[37] Letter 23, Yad Vashem Archives, B/48–2, S.N. 6055.

[38] Letter 2.

[39] Borislaw — a town in the Darohovitch region in Galicia, where 10,000–11,000 Jews had lived.

[40] Letter 24.

[41] Letter 25, Sakowska (ed.), *Archiwum Ringelbluma*, letter 139.

[42] Letter 26, Moreshet Archives, D.1.5601.

[43] During 1941–1944, Kishinev was the capital of Bessarbia, included in Romania. The number Jews there was estimated to be about 60,000 in 1941.

[44] Letter 27, YVA, B/44 3–b, and also O–11/46.

[45] Letter 28, *Letzte Briefe zum Tode Verurteilter aus dem europaischen Widerstand*, Munich, 1962, pp. 252–254.

[46] Letter 29, YVA, O–48 B/66–2, S.N. 6801.

[47] Letter 12.

[48] Rimanow — a city in Poland, in the Lvov district. In 1940 displaced Jews went there from the surrounding area. The total number of Jews in the city is estimated at 3,000. Those that were fit were sent to labor at the Plaszow labor camp in 1942. But most of the Jews were sent to the Belzice extermination camp. It is estimated that 300 Jews survived from Rimanov.

[49] Letter 30, Ben–Zion Firer (ed.) **Book of Rimanow**, Tel Aviv 5746.

[50] Letter 31, **The Book of Stari-Sambor: Testimony and Remembrance Chapters**, Tel Aviv, 5740, pp. 232–233.

[51] Druya — a city in Poland, with 1,800 Jews constituting the majority of the population. When the Germans came, a ghetto was built. In 1942 the Jews in the ghetto were murdered, except for a few who managed to escape and joined the Partisans and the Red Army.

[52] Letter 32, Mordechai Neistadt (ed.), **The Book of Druya and the Miur, Dravisk and Leonopol Kehillos**, Ramat Gan 1973, pp. 95–100.

[53] Zolkiew — a town in eastern Galicia.

[54] Letter 33, **The Book of Zolkiew (A Glorious Town)**, Jerusalem 5729, pp. 579–584.

[55] Letter 34, Yeshayahu Austriden (ed.), **Book of Chortkov**, Haifa/Tel Aviv 5727, pp. 271–272.

[56] Letter 35, YVA, O–48/48–4.

[57] Letter 36, Central Zionist Archives, S26 1295.

[58] Theresienstadt — a city in northwestern Czechoslovakia, where the Germans established a model ghetto. About 140,000 Jews were deported there, and it had a rich communal and cultural life. At the end of 1943 a Red Cross inquiry committee visited the ghetto.

[59] Letter 37, YVA, S.N. 13491.

[60] Letter 38, Sakowska (ed.), *Archiwum Ringelbluma*, letter 42.

[61] Letter 39, YVA, O–48/66 3–n , S.N. 9832.

[62] Letter 6.

[63] Letter 40, Lohamei HaGetaot Archives, EVIII 3608.

[64] Letter 41, Massua Archives, 378.

[65] Letter 42, Sakowska (ed.), *Archiwum Ringelbluma*, letters 15, 17.

[66] Letter 43, **Only a Legend Remains from Jewish Krakow**, Tel Aviv 1986, pp. 69–73. For the complete form of the letter (untranslated) see: YVA, 2–13/48, S.N. 5998.

[67] Letter 44, Massua Archives, 1613.

[68] Letter 45, YVA, O–15/27, S.N. 3807.

[69] Belzice — an extermination camp in the Lublin region.

[70] Letter 17, a letter from Warsaw, Sakowska, "The Two Types of Resistance in the Warsaw Ghetto", p. 160.

[71] Letter 17, a letter from Zamosc.

[72] Erich Fromm, *The Revolution of Hope*, New York, 1968, p. 13.

[73] Letter 46, YVA, O–40/10, S.N. 7020.

[74] Letter 47, YVA, O–48/5–1.

[75] Gorlice — a town in Galicia.

[76] Letter 48, Ein Hanatziv Archives.

[77] Letter 49, YVA, 4–B/44, S.N. 6179.

[78] Mauthausen — a concentration camp in upper Austria. The number of prisoners going through this camp is estimated to be 199,404.

[79] Letter 50, YVA, O–75/239, S.N. 7717.

[80] Letter 51, YVA, B/54–2, S.N. 8012.

[81] Letter 52, **Letters from Nowhere: Last letters of Jews from Countries under Nazi Occupation**, Jerusalem 5748, pps. 42–42.

[82] **The Great Book of Quotations**, p. 553.

[83] Letter 16.

[84] Letter 53, YVA, O–48/113–2–6.

[85] Letter 54, YVA, B/6a–3.

[86] Letter 55, YVA, O–48/B 5–3, S.N. 18156, see also: **Letters from Nowhere**, p. 101.

[87] Letter 56, YVA, O–48/B 5a–1, S.N. 7154.

[88] Tractate Brachot, 10a.

[89] Letter 57, **The Leshitz Book in Memory En Omgabrecter Kehiller (a destroyed community)**, Tel Aviv 1963, pps. 277–278. The original is in the YVA, B/5–3, S.N. 18/56.

[90] Letter 43.

[91] Letter 15.

[92] Letter 11.

[93] Letter 58, YVA, S.N. 13476.

[94] "Occupation with the deceased is not only occupation with the corpse of the deceased, but rather with his memory and the vacuum left by his death among the mourners. The cyclical ceremonies connected with the memory of the deceased, the tombstones and monuments put up in memory of the deceased, are an attempt to preserve a continuation of the relationship with the deceased. Although in the future the deceased will be forgotten from the mind and the mourners will return to regular life […] But the psychological overcoming of mourning does not cancel the need to continue the memorial, among other things, by observing the annual day of death, prayers for uplifting the soul on the anniversary and on other days designated for this ("Yizkor"), saying Kaddish, the naming of children and grandchildren after parents and other family members", Nissan Rubin, **The End of Life: Burial and Memorial Ceremonies in the Sources of Our Sages**, Tel Aviv 1997, pp. 153–154.

[95] Henry Abramovitch, "Death", In Arthur Allen Cohen & Paul Mendes–Flohr (eds.), *Contemporary Jewish Religious Thought*, New York, 1987, p. 133.

[96] Letter 23; See also letter 59, Yalkut Moreshet, an anthology of "last letters"; Aron Erlich, letter 60. *Par-dela Les Barlreles*, Paris, 1986, pp. 197–198.

[97] Letter 61, *Letters from the Shoah*, p. 4.

[98] Letter 62, YVA, S.N. 13520.

[99] Westerbork — a transit-concentration camp in Holland.

[100] Letter 63, YVA, O–40/10, S.N. 6709.

[101] Morgen is an ancient German measure of area.

[102] Letter 53.

[103] Letter 64, YVA, B/44–2–2, S.N. 5079.

[104] Dabrowa Gornicza — a city in Poland, in the Kielce region. Just before the war it had 6,000 Jews. In the autumn of 1942 a ghetto was built in the city. In 1943 its last Jews were deported to the extermination camps and the enforced labor camps.

[105] Letter 65, **The Book of the Kehilla of the Jews of Dabrowa Gornicza and Its Destruction**, Tel Aviv 5731, pp. 427–428.

[106] Letter 66, Erlich, *Par-dela Les Barlreles*, pp. 166–167.

[107] Letter 67, YVA, S.N. 13008.

[108] Letter 68, YVA, O–48/66–1–2, S.N. 8162.

[109] Letter 30.

[110] Letter 69, **Lukow**, Tel Aviv 5728, p. 345.

[111] "Hasag", a factory for armaments, Czestochowa — a city in Poland, in the Kielce district. In 1941 a ghetto was built and 36,500 Jews were transferred there. In October 1942 the process to liquidate the ghetto had begun: those fit for work were sent to enforced labor camps and the rest were transferred to extermination in Treblinka.

[112] Letter 70, **Czestochowarer Yidden**, New York 1947, p. 199.

[113] Letter 71, Erlich, *Par-dela Les Barlreles*, p. 165.

[114] Letter 72, the Bet Lohamei HaGetaot Archives, 1524 איר.

[115] Letter 73, **The Book of Austra (Volhynia): A Memorial Monument to a Sacred Kehilla**, Tel Aviv 5744, pp. 245–247.

[116] Letter 74, a letter from March 14, 1941, Menachem Meir and Friedrich Reimes, **Are the Trees Blossoming by You?**, Jerusalem 5761, p. 73.

[117] Letter 74, a letter from April 20, 1941, ibid. pp. 76–77.

[118] Letter 74, a letter from April 22, 1941, ibid. pp. 77–78.

[119] Ibid.

[120] Letter 74, a letter from June 4, 1941, ibid. pp. 79–80.

[121] Letter 74, a letter from August 16, 1941, ibid. pp. 86–87.

[122] Letter 74, a letter from November 8, 1941, ibid. pp. 89–90.

[123] Letter 74, a letter from August 10, 1942, ibid. pp. 102–103.

[124] Letter 75, YVA, O–48/44b–3, S.N. 6949.

[125] Letter 45.

[126] Letter 56, a letter from April 2, 1943.

[127] Pressburg is Bratislava.

[128] Letter 76, Central Zionist Archives, S26 1419.

[129] Kovel — a city in Poland in the Warsaw district. Just before World War II there were 1,225 Jews there. The Jews were sent to labor camps in the Poznan district and to the Auschwitz and Chelmno extermination camps.

[130] Letter 77, **Letzte Briefe**, pp. 251–252.

[131] Letter 10.

[132] Letter 56, YVA, O–48/B 5–2–3.

[133] Letter 34.

[134] Letter 11.

[135] Letter 78, **Last Night a Holocaust… A Memorial to the Kehillos: Breslav, Opsa, Okmanitz, Dobina, Zamosh, Zaretch, Yassi, Yos, Slobodka, Palussi, Kiselubacezna, Rimshan**, Tel Aviv, 5744, pp. 300–301.

[136] Letter 79, Neistadt (ed.) **The Book of Druya and the Miur, Dravisk and Leonopol Kehillos**, pp. 114–116.

[137] Elie Wiesel, **Legends of Our Time**, New York, 1968, p. 193.

[138] Letter 11.

[139] Letter 34.

[140] Letter 75.

[141] Letter 80. **The Book of Huszt: A Yizkor Book**, Tel Aviv 1957, pp. 5–6.

[142] Letter 43.

[143] See the important article of Prof. Melech Westreich: Melech Westreich, "One Life for Another in the Holocaust: A Singularity for Jewish Law," *Theoretical Inquiries in Law*, Vol. 1, no. 2 (July 2000), pp. 341–367. He writes in the summary: "The Holocaust, as a civilized/humane experience, was unique in the physical sense or perhaps it was a black astrophysical void. In other words, in a situation when laws are no longer valid, even Jewish law (*Halacha*) stood back and would not be able to enter and enforce its

laws and rulings". This remark is important in our opinion since it confirms, within a discussion on Jewish law, that in a government that is devoid of law and order, a "black void" pervades and the individual is unprotected, and the crucial decisions, the choices and alternatives are up to his own ethical decisions.

[144] Letter 29.

[145] Letter 19.

[146] Letter 81, **The Konin Kehilla when It Flourished and Its Destruction**, Tel Aviv 1968, pp. 625–627.

[147] Letter 21.

[149] Letter 28.

[150] Letter 62.

[151] Letter 82, YVA, O–48/66, 3–צ .

[152] Angeles — France, on the coast of the Mediterranean Sea.

[153] Letter 83, handed over to Yad Vashem by Dr. Yael Peled.

[154] Elie Wiesel, "Night" in "Night Dawn Day", Northvale, 1985. Translated from the French by Stella Rodway, pp. 71–72.

[155] Letter 84, YVA, B/48–3, S.N. 6609.

[156] Lesko — a city in Poland in the Lvov district. During the first stages of the German occupation a Judenrat and Jewish police were established there. The Jews were employed in public works in the city. In September 1942, Jews were transferred to Zaslow, a labor camp was used as a concentration camp, and from there they were deported to the Belzice extermination camp. Out of the total of Jews in Lesko only four were left.

[157] Letter 85, YVA, O–75/540, S.N. 10512.

[158] Letter 86, YVA

[159] Kamionka — a town in the Ukraine.

[160] Letter 87, YVA, DN–28/111, 131/107.

[161] Letter 88, YVA, O–48/6a–2, S.N. 4719.

[162] Gurs — the first detention camp in France, built in April 1939. The detainees were sent to the Auschwitz and Sobibor extermination camps. When the camp was liberated in the summer of 1944, only 48 Jews had survived.

[163] Letter 89. Erich Bloch, *Geschichte der Juden von Konstanz*, Konstanz, 1971, pp. 171–172.

[164] Letter 90, Bet Lohamei HaGetaot Archives, 1624/תא.

[165] Letter 91, YVA, O–75/465.

[166] Letter 45.

[167] Yehudah Bauer, **The Holocaust: Historical Perspectives**, Tel Aviv 5742, p. 119.

[168] Letter 92, Central Zionist Archives, S26 1316.

[169] Letter 93, Central Zionist Archives, S26 1166.

[170] Letter 94, S.N. 4132.

[171] Letter 95, Avraham Becker (ed.) **The Memorial Book of Husiaton and Its Surroundings**, Tel Aviv 5736, pp. 299–307.

[172] Letter 96, YVA, O–33/146–2–3.

[173] Letter 97, YVA, B/O–48 5–3–4, S.N. 406.

174 Meir Dvorzhatski, "Resistance in Daily Life in the Ghettoes and the Camps", **The Holocaust of the European Jews: Background — Events — Significance**, Jerusalem 5733, p. 282.

175 Letter 98, Z'vulun Foren (ed.), **The Memorial Book of Yuroberg in Lithuania**, Jerusalem 5751, pp. 451–452.

176 Lodz' — the second largest city in Poland. Just before the war there were about 225,000 Jews in the city, about a third of the entire population. On September 8, 1939, the city was occupied and annexed to the Reich. In April 1940, the ghetto was closed up with 164,000 Jews. The number of survivors from the Lodz' Ghetto is estimated at 5,000–7,000 people.

177 Letter 99, *Letzte Briefe*, pp. 257–258.

178 Letter 95.

179 Letter 81.

180 Letter 53.

181 Letter 100, YVA, B/48 1–ב , S.N. 7190.

182 Letter 61.

183 Dvorzhatski, "Resistance in Daily Life in the Ghettoes and the Camps", p. 281.

184 Tractate Gittin 57.

185 See the remarks of Prof. Westreich, in the above endnote 143.

186 Letter 101, a letter to Yehuda Berginski, **Hannah Senesh, Her Life, Mission and Death**,

Tel Aviv 1966, p. 224.

187 Letter 102, Yitzchak Arad, Yisrael Gutman and Avraham Margaliyot (eds.) **The Holocaust in Documentation: A Selection of Documents on the Destruction of the Jews of Germany and Austria, Poland and the Soviet Union**, Jerusalem 5738, pp. 258–259.

188 Letter 103, ibid, pp. 250–251.

189 Israel Gutman, *Resistance: The Warsaw Ghetto Uprising*, New York, 1994, p. XIX.

190 Letter 104, **Testimony** Booklet 7 (1992), pp. 129–131.

191 Letter 105, Mordechai Tannenboim-Tamaroff, **Pages from the Blaze: Chapters of a Diary, Letters and Writings**, Jerusalem 5718. There are 23 "letters to Bronca". We chose to present five of them here.

192 The meaning here is an isolated house that may be of use to the underground.

193 Letter 105, a letter from Monday, 6:20, ibid, pp. 123–125, letter 1.

194 Letter 105, a letter from Saturday, 11:15 p.m., ibid, pp.132–133, letter 7.

195 Letter 105, a letter from Monday, June 7, 1943, ibid, pp. 144–145, letter 14.

196 Letter 105, a letter from Thursday, June 10, 1943, ibid, p. 147, letter 15.

197 Letter 105, a letter from Tuesday, 10:20 a.m., ibid, p. 153, letter 18. Wanda is Tama Schneiderman, the signaler of Dror and the Jewish Resistance Organization, who was sent in 1943 by Tannenboim from Bialistok to Warsaw. She was caught and sent to her death in Treblinka.

198 Letter 101, the last note to the mother and the poem "In Prison", **Hannah Senesh: Her Life and Diary**, Hakibbutz Hameuachad, 1966. Translated by Marta Cohn, 1971, Valentine, Mitchell and Co..

199 Letter 106, **Bet Lochamei HaGetaot Reports**, 1(8) (January 1955).

[200] Letter 107, **Letters from Nowhere**, pp. 14–17.

[201] Gutman, *Resistance: The Warsaw Ghetto Uprising*.

[202] Letter 108, the Massua Archives, 3875.

[203] Auschwitz-Birkenau — an extermination camp in eastern Upper Shlesia in Poland where approximately one million and a half men, women and children were murdered.

[204] Letter 109, YVA, B/24–2, S.N. 3751, the letter of Gertrude Eisinger.

[205] Letter 109, the letters of Leah Weinberger, Ella Mandel and Alice Balla.

[206] Letter 110, "Beyond the Wall", Central Zionist Archives, S26 1155, pp. 1–17.

[207] Letter 111, Chulda Archives, 6/149, 19.

[208] Letter 112, "Mail of the Holocaust", Massua Archives, 308.

[209] Sosnowiec — a city in southwest Poland. Just before the Nazi occupation there were 28,000 Jews in the city; most of them were sent to enforced labor camps. In the spring of 1943 the ghetto was built in the city, and the Nazis started to liquidate it a few months later and deport the Jews to Auschwitz.

[210] Letter 113, Chulda Archives, 7/171, 203.

[211] Letter 114, Chulda Archives, 7/171, 202.

[212] Josik was the head of the JDC in Warsaw.

[213] Letter 115, Chulda Archives, 9/171, 346.

[214] Letter 116, Sakowska (ed.), *Archiwum Ringelbluma*, letter 26.

[215] Zborow — a city in Poland in the Tarnopol district. An open labor camp was built in the city that enabled the Jews to have freedom of movement. An enclosed labor camp and a ghetto to which the Jews in the region were deported were also built. In August 1942 a mass action took place and 1,300 people were sent to Belzice. In April 1943 there was another action, in which 2,300 people were killed by shooting. In June 1943 the Germans liquidated the open ghetto and started to kill by shooting the last ones in the enclosed camp. In June 1944 the Soviets liberated the city; only 25 Jewish survivors were found there.

[216] Letter 117, The Memorial Book of the Zborow Kehilla (Eastern Galicia), organized, collated and prepared for print by Eliyahu (Edik) Zilberman, pp. 75–84.

the Letters

Letter 1

Williampola, Ghetto Kovna
October 19, 1943
My beloved son and daughter!

I am writing these lines to you, my beloved children, at a time when we have already been here, in the vale of tears, in the Kovna Ghetto of Williampola for over two years. We found out that in the next few days our fate will be decided: The ghetto that we're in will be cut and shredded to pieces. Only God knows whether we will all be destroyed or whether some of us will remain. We are afraid that only the slaves capable of labor will stay alive, and the others will be condemned, probably to death.

We have remained here, a few of the many: Of the thirty-five thousand Jewish residents of Kovna, there are now only about 17,000; and of the quarter of a million Jewish residents of Lithuania (including the Vilna region), less than twenty-five thousand remain here in the country now. Five thousand, who were naked and destitute, were deported to grueling labor in Latvia in recent days. The rest were executed and put to death in cruel deaths by those who fulfill the will of the greatest Haman of all generations and times. Also many of the people close to us are not alive anymore: Aunt Hannah and Uncle Aryeh were killed together with one thousand five hundred residents of our ghetto on October 4, 1941. Uncle Tzvi, in our hospital with a broken leg, was saved miraculously. The rest of the patients, together with the physicians, nurses and patients' relatives who happened to be there, were killed or burned alive in the hospital that was set afire on all sides by soldiers, after the doors and windows were nailed down. This left no exit or way to escape from the fire.

In the province, except for Shavli, no Jews are to

be found. Uncle Dov and his son Shmuel were probably executed together with the entire community of Kalvarija. Our ghetto, due to internal and external reasons, has lived an exile (*galus*) existence with slavery and grueling labor, with hunger and nakedness — in relative calm (most of our clothes, our portable articles and our books have been taken from us by the regime already two years ago).

The last slaughter, the largest one, cost us ten thousand victims at once. It was on October 28, 1941. All day, the entire congregation stood "under the rod of the ruler: Who is to life and who is to death." "I am the man whose eyes have seen" those taken to die. I myself stood early in the morning of October 29th in the midst of the camp as it was led to the Ninth Fort to be slaughtered. With my own ears I heard the awful symphony of the crying, howling and screams of ten thousand people, elderly, youth and babies, that rent the Heavens. No one has heard anything like this throughout the ages! During this time, together with the many martyred, I disputed with my Creator, and with them I called out of a torn heart: "Who is silent like You, my Lord!" And in my attempt to occasionally rescue, soldiers have hurt me, and I have received severe beatings. Wounded and streaming blood, I was taken out by order of the guarding officer. And when I fainted from weakness, I was carried out of the camp on the hands of friends. In the ensuing confusion a small band of thirty to forty people were saved with me. The "smoking embers rescued from the fire."

We were located in one of the vales of murder in the East. About two years ago, before our eyes and facing our windows, many, many thousands of Jews from south Germany and Vienna passed by with their property and large packages to the Ninth Fort, situated a few kilometers away from us. They were all killed there in extreme brutality. As we found out later, they were certainly lied to. They were told in their homes that they were being brought to Kovna to settle in with us in the ghetto.

I have been the head of the ghetto since the day it was founded. The community elected me, and the regime confirmed me as Chairman of the Committee of Community Elders. Together with my fellow friend, advocate Leib Garfunkel, who was once a representative in the Lithuanian governing authority, and other friendly people, who tremble, worry and are fearful for the fate of the remaining survivors, we lead our mad ship in the heart of the sea, when daily waves of disaster and severe decrees hurry to swallow it. Thanks to my influence I have often succeeded in doing away with their verdict. Sometimes I have scattered the black clouds that hover over our heads. Standing straight and tall, I have stood watch, asking not for pity, but always defending our honor with faith and confidence in the sincerity and justice of our demands.

In the most difficult moments of our lives, you, my beloved, have always been on our minds and part of our thoughts. During long and dark nights, your beloved mother sits with me, and we both dream about your lives and future. Our souls yearn to see you again, to hug and tell you once more how attached we are to you and how our heart pounds when bringing up memories of you. And at what time or hour, day or night, my dears, do we not bring them up? As we stand on the edge of the pit, at a time when "a sharp sword is placed on our necks," only your picture, my beloved, is before us, and in your faces' appearance, I see it all. And you, my dears, how did you live through the past five years that were so difficult and full of calamities and disaster for European Jewry? I would not be surprised, even though you live far from the location of devastation, that you feel our pain, and are seized with sorrow and grief. You tremble at every rumor coming from the vale of tears, and in the depth of your souls you feel the horrendous tragedy that has no equal during our entire bitter exile.

Concerning me, not much can be said, I was ill last year [...] Even during the more difficult days of my illness I continued to bear the burden of concern for my community, and from my sickbed, I participated actively in the work of my friends [...]

It is about a half a year now that I am no longer ill [...]

About six months ago we received word from Uncle Hans via the Red Cross that you are well [...] We are sorry and feel pain, that while we sit here in the vale of tears, we have not been able to call you and tell you that we are still alive. We know how distressing it must be for you to doubt our existence, and how much strength and help you would have had if you would know with certainty that we are alive [...] I greatly fear the despair and apathy which can kill a person, and I pray every day that you, my dears, will not reach such a stage. I am very doubtful, my beloved souls, whether I will be privileged to see you again, to hug and squeeze you to my heart. Prior to my departing from the world and from you, my beloved, I wish to say again and again how precious you are to us, and how we yearn for you.

My beloved Joel! Be a loyal son to your people. Be concerned with your people, and don't be concerned with the gentiles [...] Try to settle in the Land of Israel [...] The power of faith is great, and it can transfer and move mountains from their place. Do not look either right and left on your path, my son, go straight before you. And if you sometimes see your people in a bad way, with their filth and sins, even so, my beloved son, do not lose heart. It is not them, but the bitter exile that is to blame. Truth, my beloved, should always be a guiding light, it will guide you and show you the path of life.

85

Concerning you, Sarah, my beloved daughter, read carefully the last words that I wrote to Joel. I rely, my lovely one, on your clear mind and intellect. Don't live for the moment and don't ask as you go on your way, for blooming flowers. They will wither and droop as fast as they've appeared. A pure life, a noble life, a life full of content is so full of beauty. The two of you should go together throughout life, attached and holding one another. No distance should separate you and no events of life should come between you.

Remember, both of you, what Amalek has done to us. Remember this and don't forget it your whole lives, and pass this on as a sacred will to the next generations. The Germans killed, slaughtered, murdered us calmly and in tranquility. I saw them and I stood among them when they sent many thousands of men and women, infants and babies to be killed. How were they then able to eat with appetite their morning *Butterbrod* [bread and butter], while teasing and mocking our martyrs. I saw them when they came back from the vale of murder, filthy with the blood of our beloved ones from their feet to the top of their heads [...]

The land of Lithuania is drenched in our blood from the Lithuanians themselves, those with whom we've lived for many hundreds of years. We helped them with all our might to establish, at the time, an independent state. Seven thousand of our brothers and sisters were killed here by the Lithuanians in the cruelest of deaths during the last days of June 1941. In the provincial villages — they, and no one else, executed entire sacred communities following German orders. With special relish they searched, on their own, in caves and up walls, in fields and forests, and took the survivors from there, turning them over to the regime.

Show no regard for them your entire lives. They should be cursed and ostracized, as well as their sons, for you and for all future generations.

I am writing at a time, when many people are broken, many widows and orphans, many naked and hungry, are stationed at my door requesting our help. My strength wanes. I feel as if a desolate desert is within me and my soul is departing. I am naked and empty with no words in my language. But you, my dear beloved, you will have insight and understand what I wished for you and wanted to tell you at this time. For a moment I close my eyes and picture the two of you standing before me. I hereby hug and kiss you and I tell you until my last breath that I am your loving father.

Elchanan [Alex]

November 11, 1943

I am adding some lines.

It is about two weeks since we went from regime to regime. Our name was changed and now it is called the Konzentrationslager Kauen N.4 instead of the ghetto, with new clerks and attendants. Our vial of tears has not yet been filled. On the 26th of the previous month 2,709 people were led from our ghetto. According to the news that came in, the elderly and the children were separated from the camp and are certainly not alive anymore. Those that are capable of work were led to Estonia for grueling labor.

On the 5th of this month, all the children under the age of 13 were taken from Shavli together with the elderly men and women. They told them that they're taking them to Kovna and they were certainly all put to death already. About three thousand people still remained there in the city.

We are awaiting our fate in a very short time.

I place these words, together with some other documents, in storage and pray that they should only reach you.

We have definitely found out that the Germans are busy now with eradicating and wiping out any memory of their murderous acts. The bones of our martyrs will be burned now in the Ninth Fort and in all the other places located by the experts in this field, including chemists.

With love, affection and blessings,
Your father

Letter 2

2nd day of Shavu'ot 5704
May 29, 1944
My precious son Emmanuel,

Blessed is the Almighty, we are still alive today. On hearing about the terrible destruction going on among our brothers in most gatherings of Jews in the states of Europe in general, and the slaughter of the majority of Lithuanian Jews in particular, you must have certainly despaired of us when thinking of us. It is with luck that we've survived until now — we were rescued from the talons of the predatory beast immersed in our blood, and this beast is still not satiated. The enemy still continues to brutally trim our saplings that remain like smoking embers rescued from the fire, and we don't know how we'll end up. Our eyes are lifted to Heaven and we await rescue by a miracle. Whatever happens, one must anticipate — in times of danger. Therefore I have decided to leave at least some information for those remaining after us, so you will know what happened to us from a primary source. I have dedicated these lines to you, and from them you can estimate how many years we were in captivity and how long we suffered from the oppression of a cursed enemy, and his attendants, the angels of destruction.

During the entire period of our exile, we are here together in the ghetto, me, Mother, and Joseph, your brother. Aunt Bertha is also with us. Yossel and his brother Barris were caught by the Lithuanians immediately when the war broke out, and there are no tracks of them until this day. Also Dadik, the son of Martzi, was then taken prisoner and exiled to an unknown place, together with a group of boys his age. Meir, her [Aunt Bertha's] brother-in-law, and their daughter are in Shavli. I receive news of them from time to time. During the three years of our imprisonment here, great troubles engulf us. Our lives hang on a thread, and we are constantly in great danger. You will find many images of what goes on in our lives in the records that I'm attaching to this letter. As you will see, I have written enough for the time being, per my strength. I have pointed out in the book every important incident and powerful impression. In my opinion, the material that I have collected in my anthology is of historical importance. For this reason I made sure that it would not get lost. I gave it to an archive in a secure place, in order to protect it for future generations. My writings may reach you one day; if only this should come true — then my efforts will have been rewarded.

My eldest and firstborn son!

I amuse myself with the hope that I myself may be privileged to publish my records in my lifetime. But on the day, God forbid, that my luck betrays me, then you will have to complete the task. And therefore, I give you insructions of what you are to do after my death.

First of all, find an expert proofreader, an educated and decent person, who can arrange all the material for printing […]

Secondly, regarding the real estate property retained in Shavli. In this matter you must go hand in hand with my brother Lipa. He will certainly take the necessary steps to return our estate to its owners. You must consult with him about anything dealing with this. You may decide, that one of you will travel there to Shavli. Then don't forget, to claim our apartment from the landlord […] damage for objects, furniture, household items, books and the large storage of food that Mother had left in the house before she traveled to Kovna. The entire property adds up to a large amount, it is necessary to demand it from him until the last penny. As I heard, he occupied our apartment immediately after she left home, and everything is with him. Mother traveled to Kovna to stay with me a day before the war, and the next day on June 22nd, 1941, the war broke out and she didn't have a chance to return home. We mention you on every occasion and at every time. Our ideal is to be privileged to see you face to face in the Land. Perhaps you have already managed during the three years to start a family? The time has arrived for you to have a family life. I sometimes dream in my fantasy that you have a delightful child, a beautiful boy, talented and clever, with beautiful eyes. If only we are privileged to embrace sons of our sons in our arms.

We wish you success in whatever you do. May it be that you have no shortage or wandering in your life, that in your days Judah and Israel be redeemed, and that they be rebuilt and live in security. You should enjoy the best of everything and satisfaction for your place in the Land of the Fathers. Be a Jew in your tent and a person when you leave. I have trust in you that your behavior makes you worthy of your parents.

I hug you from afar, and kiss you warmly in my imagination, your father who loves you as he loves his own being, and hopes that you will fulfill his wishes precisely.

Mother and Joseph hug and kiss you with love.

Nechemia

Williampola Concentration Camp.

Letter 3

Plonsk, December 16, 1942

Please toss the note in the nearest mailbox.

It is now morning. We are in the railroad car with the whole family. We are leaving with the last transport. Plonsk is cleansed [of Jews, the German expression]. Please go to the Bam family, on 6 Niske and send them regards.

Yours truly,

A note thrown from a train taking a transport to the Auschwitz death camp. It was written by an unidentified Jew to his family in the Warsaw Ghetto.

◆ ◆ ◆

Legionowo, [December 16] 1942
Additional payment of 18 gr' (Legionowo)
Warsaw
Nalabecki
47/19

Please kindly toss this into a box.

Today we left Plonsk, our whole family, and all the Jews traveled. Be aware, that we are traveling to a wedding [in other words, to annihilation].

See you again!

David

A note thrown from a train that was transporting a group of Jews to the Auschwitz death camp. It was written by a Jew named David to his family in the Warsaw Ghetto.

◆ ◆ ◆

Warsaw, Praga, December 16, 1942
Additional payment of 18 gr'
L. Paz'igoda
Warsaw, Mila 46

Please kindly toss this into a box.

I'm in the Praga station, writing a few words to you. It is unknown where we are traveling.

Be well.

Leah

A note thrown from a train transporting a group of Jews to the Auschwitz death camp. It was written by an unidentified Jewish woman named Leah of Plonsk to her family in the Warsaw Ghetto.

◆ ◆ ◆

Czestochowa, December 17, 1942
My dears!

We are now passing Czestochowa, therefore I'm writing a few words. We have passed Warsaw also. We are traveling to work. Think positively. I'm not giving you my new address, because I don't have it yet.

Parting with kisses,

Yours, Gittel

We are en route for the second day.

The train station. A note thrown from the train taking a transport to the Auschwitz death camp. It was written by an unidentified Jewish woman named Gittel of Plonsk to her family in the Warsaw Ghetto.

◆ ◆ ◆

Czestochowa, December 17, 1942

Dear Sir

Roguzak

Warsaw

19 Zamenhoff St.

For P. Rothblatt

My dear,

We are with the whole family at the Czestochowa Pass, we don't know where we're traveling.

With best wishes, I kiss you

Guta Fuchs

A note thrown from the train taking a transport to the Auschwitz death camp. It was written by a Jewish woman whose name was Guta Fuchs of Plonsk to her family in the Warsaw Ghetto.

◆ ◆ ◆

Thursday, Czestochowa, December 17, 1942

To

E. Bogatti

Warsaw [...]

My dear!

We've been en route since yesterday morning. We were inside the train for a few hours in Prague. I am here, we are here, in Czestochowa in the train station. We are probably traveling to a labor camp, to Tarnowskie Gory or to Auschwitz. I have great heartache because of my tragedy with Lonia and Henio. Will I ever see them again?

I feel very saddened.

Mark

A note thrown from the train taking a transport to the Auschwitz death camp to relatives in Warsaw.

Letter 4

December 16, 1944
Dear Magda,

I cannot describe in what emotional state I write this letter; for eight days we've been locked up in a railroad car. Out of 77 people — 65 men and 12 women — 14 have so far escaped, and I don't know whether to do so myself.

Imagine that at about 8–9 in the morning they release us from the railroad car to relieve ourselves — and this happens near the cars, because it's impossible to move away even one step. Then they again lock us up and until the next morning they don't open the railroad cars for us, no matter what happens. And, so, many of those here relieve themselves in the car.

Once a day we get one slice of bread with a morsel of canned food, and this was only since Tuesday — until then we didn't get a thing. The heart nearly passes out for a sip of water, and I cannot even describe the kind of people here. A decent person gets completely lost in all the muck here.

My Magdushka, I am terribly miserable. When I think that they will take me and that I'll never see you again and be with you, I'm close to insanity. If only the Lord helps so it's over fast because such a life cannot be tolerated. How shocking and awful what goes on here at night! Our days somehow pass by, but already at 5:00 in the afternoon it gets dark and a person curls up over his bag. Until 7:00 the next morning he cannot even budge. I think that in a day or two we will also have lice, because I heard that some have already found...

My Magdushka, since last week when I came from home I wasn't even able to wash up once. I can rinse my mouth from time to time, but for this I must give up my daily ration of water, and instead of drinking I prefer to rinse my mouth.

So that... my Magdushka, it's impossible to tolerate this much longer... to humiliate people to such an animal level. It is almost inconceivable. If I myself were not here, I wouldn't be able to believe it.

And to top it all, it's winter and it's snowing, and I am absolutely without a home, so alone in the world.

I think that I will try to escape because if I fail and get caught — then at least death is certain.

My Magdushka, my heart is torn just thinking about Father. I arrived here and he remained alone at home, poor thing. I don't even know where he is or what happened to him.

I am very worried about him and I have no one to discuss this with who can understand me. Because the loved ones of 90 percent of those staying in the cells have already been taken, and they hope to meet with their relatives "outside."

But I know that here in [Budapest] my whole world exists. Everyone who is dear to me and everyone who symbolizes life in my eyes... and the two graves in the cemetery [graves of the mother and daughter of the writer of this letter] that perhaps now... I will have to leave here forever.

I'm going absolutely mad, my Magdushka, I am ashamed of myself. What has become of me, day and night I sit in a corner and weep.

I only wonder how my eyes aren't drying up, my Magdushka, but sometimes I still feel that I wasn't so bad that the Lord would hurt me, tearing me away from you forever. Perhaps it is also possible, that from the path... somehow... we will be directed back. In some way, the good Lord will help us and they will not take us "outside."

The one and only request that I ask of the Lord, is that we should all be together as before, and I hope that the good Lord will help me attain this.

My Magdushka, take very good care of yourself lest something happens to you, my little sister. I don't feel that this is a parting letter because the Lord is good and He will not abandon us.

**I kiss you with love,
Blanca Levi**

The letter was written in the winter of 1944 in the train that deported the writer to Bergen Belsen.

Letter 5

Treblinka, October 5, 1942
My dear wife!

I am in Treblinka since August 31, '42 and I'm healthy. I'm employed as a carpenter in the workshop of the camp. How is your health? Also write me whether our parents are healthy.

Regards and heartfelt kisses from me to everyone,

Yours, Hersh Lapek

Hersh Lapek wrote this to his wife in the Warsaw Ghetto. Perhaps Hersh was not alive when the letter was delivered. It is known that the Germans in the extermination camps allowed the victims to write letters to their families before they were murdered.

Letter 6

July 31, 1943

My dear,

Thank you from the bottom of my heart for the shirt. The threads and the needles that you've sent me will be very useful to me. But really, don't trouble to help me, because in any case it won't bring about anything, to my sorrow.

You ask, my dear, about the pharmacist. Unfortunately, he hasn't been around since the month of May. An even more difficult blow befell us last Thursday. As a result of the liquidation [actions] of the companies used by the Wermacht, we have lost our dear Lidush. What is going on in my heart and what I went through that night are hard to describe! Anyhow, I can expect the same thing to happen to me. And I am well aware of this. It may take a day, or several days, and perhaps even longer. Unfortunately, there is nothing that I can possibly do about this matter. I have no place — or cause to run to. And in addition, at the beginning of the week, I received a beret hat from Lodek, and on Friday, 100 Zloty; and on Thursday evening they led him, with the entire division, by way of Pilichovsky Street — to the sands, instead of to his sleeping board ... the smell of burnt bodies and bones remained in the air until the next day...

I am ready for my last road. I have no debts and obligations. I own nothing and I will leave nothing after me... There will be just a slight smell of fire. Someday, at a not too distant time, when you are fortunate enough to reach a better future, you will be able to locate my tracks in the form of documents which you will find with Mrs. Gosh in Brezowice. It is hard to act against fate. Over there is also the last letter from my dear mother. Perhaps God will allow us to continue our correspondence (on Wednesdays and Saturdays). Perhaps destiny will have us meet again and we will survive this disaster. But for now I am parting from you. I am aware of my future and the impossibility for me to change it. I wish you are privileged soon to reach the long awaited goal. To you, my dear, I am very grateful for the motherly treatment that you have given me since the beginning of my stay in Lvov. You will remain the sole representative of our family. All the others have gone, one by one, and I will be forced to finish this march and tread courageously in line, on the way to eternity. I write this letter following my dear mother's example and part from you.

I give no advice or instructions, because I don't regard myself entitled to do so. Meanwhile, I will live a few more days (this is what I assume), write me something and I will answer you. The uncle feels very well. On Thursday he returns to sleep by me. He even offered me a loan: I refused. I no longer need anything, except perhaps a miracle.

I expect news from you. Powerful kisses and wishes.

I'm not a writer of rhymes

I'm only parting and wishing

A lot, a lot of happiness.

Letter 7

Dear Moshe… Baila…

May you all be healthy and we will make an effort for your sake. Please pay the person who sends you the letters. We are fasting for two days and are going to be slaughtered. The date of our death (*yahrzeit*) will be the 28/9 of August [sic]. Please be meticulous about this. Father is not at home, and who knows, he's certainly dead for a long time. We are standing dressed, all of us, with my dear children and waiting. We are all in the Study Hall (*Bet Midrash*) and until death, we have had enough, and we have wished it for ourselves more than once. Already on the eve of the New Moon (*Rosh Chodesh*) of the month of Av, they lined us all up in a row to shoot us and a miracle happened. Today, if only a miracle would happen and the Almighty would have mercy on us. But if they shoot us, He will deliver our letter to you. Moshe — the little ones are yours. So, be healthy and be strong. We Jews will be the sacrifice for the sake of your redemption.

Tzipporah

Letter 8

Lublin, Sunday, March 29, 1942

My dear sister,

It is difficult for me to respond to your two letters because you must have heard about the deportation of Lublin, continuing already for 14 entire days. No one knows when this will end. Fifteen thousand have already been sent away — fathers, mothers without the children, children without parents, naked and barefoot. I went with nothing. I left everything behind. There was no place for me to hide a thing, and I also didn't have where to bring anything. About one thousand dead people, we shouldn't know from this, perished in a tragic way. I am still hiding in a dark cellar in Lublin, for 14 days already I haven't seen the light of day. Today, Sunday, I went out to the street. I walked to the post office. Perhaps some money came for me. I was left without a penny. In the cellar I subsisted, together with my cousin, on bread and water, that a person provided us.

Already today I have nothing and we don't know when it will be over. It's as if Lublin has completely died. M.Z. is with M. All the children with N. were caught and sent away, it's not known where. It is impossible to describe what happened in Lublin. If they catch me, I don't even have 50 golden coins to take with me for the way. It's necessary to go to P. and together with him try sending me something urgently, so I will have some money ready for the way. If only I stay alive. In Lublin they say that it was all caused by B.K. [probably Henrik Becker, the chairman of the Jewish Committee, an unfounded charge], and because of him the tragedy happened. I cannot write more. I look like a dead man, from hunger. What I did succeed in saving will certainly get lost since no one is sure if he is alive the next day. They took the patients out of the Jewish Hospital and out of the Hospital for Contagious Diseases. They don't know where they took them, and the hospitals closed down. Terrible things are happening in Lublin. Remember what I await, this is possibly the last assistance for me, since my life is not safe. Not one single person in Lublin is safe. Go directly to P. and show him the letter. Tell him that in Lublin a fire blazes over the heads of the remaining survivors. Help me while it is still possible.

Meanwhile I am very cautious. If only I succeed also in the future. I didn't get the 100 golden coins that you sent me once with someone from Lublin. And I surely won't receive them now, since he won't find me. I also don't know with whom you sent it. Send money to the address [...]

Friendly and heartfelt regards to you. I kiss you from the depths of my heart. If only we can see each other again and correspond with each other,

Daniel

Letter 9

Athens, 14th of Av 5703

Dear Brothers,

The first response to our appeal to our brothers in free countries came to us with your letter of the 12th of Tammuz of this year. Many thanks to you, my dear brothers, that you heard our voice and rushed to our assistance. May God be with you. May He not forsake your sons.

We ask your forgiveness for the style of this letter, since we don't really know your language. And now I am presenting you with the history of all that has happened to us in recent months. In June 1942, 8,500 Jews of Saloniki were sent to hard labor. In November, the Saloniki community completed the job for a fair amount that was sent to the Germans until February 1943. In March 1943, they forced all the Jews of Saloniki to put the Star of David on their garments, to leave their homes in the city and assemble in the ghetto. On March 14, they suddenly took three thousand people from the ghetto, the elderly, youth, women, boys and girls, and put them in closed railroad cars meant for cattle. After the first train's journey, they took another three thousand people, and so it continued with the third and fourth trains, and more, so that by the first of June, the last of the Jews were deported. A total of 53,000 of our brothers were deported, and now no Jew remains in Saloniki and the cities of Macedonia. Until this day we do not know where they sent them and what is their fate. It is impossible to describe to you the conditions of their journey. We are afraid that only twenty percent of the passengers will remain alive when they reach their destination.

We do not have the spiritual strength to describe to you the many troubles that we have undergone between March and June of this year. The congregation of Israel has witnessed awful days of mourning. All those that have fled the decree came here to Athens tired and naked. They number about three thousand. The Jewish community of Athens has done all that it can to ensure their lives, despite concerns over their own fate. But our enemy is very cruel and who knows what will happen to us at the end.

Now, not one single Jew remains in Saloniki. "Alas — she sits in solitude", "a city and center of the Jewish nation!" Houses of prayer were lost, our cemetery was destroyed, our libraries, our Torah scrolls were destroyed, all the community ledgers were burnt and our property was taken.

We are approaching you with a request to make an effort to do the following for us:

    a. Make an effort to find out what happened to 53,000 of our brothers who were deported to Poland and Czechoslovakia. Send them, somehow, food, clothing and various medications.

    b. Cry out so your voice will be heard in the entire world and seek the "embers rescued from the fire."

    c. For those refugees who came here without money, food or clothes: Make sure that the International Red Cross will give them bread and food certificates, as it gives our Greek brothers in Athens with all the associations, and the Chief Metropolit at their head. Stand beside us in our hour of need and do whatever is within your ability to come to our aid.

It is impossible to give you an address to forward money here since it will be of great harm to our entire community. Please send us whatever you want with the messenger who is giving you this letter. You will be able to learn our address if you ask these friends of ours: Ask Irmon Nigrin, 12 Nebi Yadniel St. in Alexandria who his dear friend is — his family is in Athens, and he will give you my address. Also ask our brothers, Mr. David Floratin, Asher Malach and Leon Recanati in Tel Aviv. All the best to them. Three hundred and fifty Jews of Saloniki are Spanish subjects and traveled to Spain via Germany 12 days ago. You will be able to learn from them all the details about the decree that befell our community.

And now, our upright brothers, farewell to you. Our hope is not yet lost, for with the last of the Jews remains the last of our hope.

◆ ◆ ◆

Athens, 21st of Elul, 5703

Dear Friends,

Today we received your letter and also the packet of money. Many thanks to you. At this moment, great mourning befell the city of Athens, too. Now that the Germans took over authority from the Italians, they called in the Chief Rabbi half-an-hour ago and told him that here, too, they would do all that was done to the Jews in Saloniki. We have nothing to write you. From today onwards, we don't know what will be the end of us. Perhaps when your reply comes, we will be in Poland.

If you are able to save us, hurry and do not slumber. The danger is immense. Tell this to all those from whom we await rescue.

Immediately demand from the Greek radio in London and Cairo that they tell our Greek brothers in Athens what their duty is in troubled times like these. They should stir up interest and appeal (?) for us in whatever way they can. If you want, send us more money. If we're no longer here, we regard this man as a trustworthy person who will return to you.

Plenty of peace to you and to all our brothers in Zion. Do not abandon us. Perhaps our rescue is close. Our hope is not lost.

Letter 10

Mr. Wincet, Arange, P.S.A.

July 31, 1942

My dear Moishkele and all my dear ones,

We are now after a horrible slaughter. On 25.7.1942, mass slaughters took place here, like in all the other cities. 350 people survived. 850 were killed and died a dreadful death at the hands of the murderers. They threw them like dogs into latrines. Live children were thrown into pits. I will not write a lot. I think that there is yet to be a person that can tell about our suffering and the blood-bath. We have so far succeeded in being saved, but for how long? Every day we await death and meanwhile we mourn our close and dear ones. Your family, Moishkele; is no longer, there is no trace of them. But I envy them. I will end. It is impossible to write and cry out about our agonies. Be well and the only thing that you can do is to take revenge against our murderers. A drop of revenge against them. I kiss you strongly, strongly. I part from all of you before we all die.

Zlotka

◆ ◆ ◆

My dear father!

I am parting from you before my death. We want to live very much, but what's to be done — they don't allow it. I am so terrified of death, because little children are thrown into the grave when they're still alive. I am parting from you forever. I kiss you strongly, strongly.

Yours, Yuta
A kiss from Garda

This letter was written after the first slaughter in Byten by Zlotka Wishniatzky and her 10-year-old daughter Yuta, to husband and father Moshe Wishniatzky, who was in the United States. The letter was handed by the aforementioned woman to a Christian, with a request to forward it to the United Sates after the war. She felt that she would not be able to behold peace. After the liberation, K. Masluski, the farmer from the village of Kochanowe, handed over the letter to the brother of the woman that was killed. The brother was a partisan in the forests and was saved. Zlotka and her two children were killed in the forest on January 20, 1943.

Letter 11

January 25, 1943

My dear, one and only sister Rivka,

I have no patience and I already have no human sentiment to write. I'm only writing out of hope that you, the only one of our entire family, will remain alive, and therefore I want you to know when to observe the memorial days. I ran away today from the Zaslow Camp and I am with a gentile, and will leave this letter for you. To my regret, there is nobody to hide me, since everyone fears for his own life. I don't want to give details, since no human being can describe it. If chroniclers ever describe what we went through, don't imagine it like that. The greatest poet is not capable of describing even one-thousandth of the reality. I myself am not capable of relating everything that happens here in one day. I'm forced to say that this was some nightmarish dream, but to my regret it is entirely true.

So, until this day, all that you have remaining of the entire family is just me, the only one. Ten days ago they took away from me the only solace that I still had. Together with others Jews in the camp, they also took Hinda, Shaul and Melech. We remained in the camp a total of 70 Jews out of 15,000 from the entire Snokai Region. I requested to go with everyone and do away with this life already, and I got beaten up for requesting. They told us that they would send us to labor in Krakow, but my assumption is that they will terminate us also after we clean up the shacks in the camp. Therefore, I use this opportunity to leave you this letter. I have no will to live already. But you — you and your children should know to revenge the pure Jewish blood that was spilled. You must educate your children in the spirit of arms and hatred towards the German people. I turn to all Jews from there: Don't look for business or job advancement, just take up arms, murder everyone you come across (from the German nation), people, women and small children, because that's what they did to us. The greatest writer is not talented enough to describe their cruelty towards your brothers. Therefore you must be intent on revenge only! Revenge! Revenge! Our Hinda started to keep a diary, but it was impossible to continue. She left a letter for you which I'm enclosing. So, be well and have the strength to live, because we have suffered the troubles for you, too. I send you regards and kiss you, your children and husband. Do not cry a lot. When my time comes, I will go in song to unite with my family. The memorial day of Father, Mother and Losha: They were shot in Zaslow on the day after Yom Kippur, on Tuesday at 10:30 a.m. in 1942. Rachel was shot in Zaslow on 25.10.42. Shalom died a natural death, of pneumonia on 6.11.42. Today, 10 days ago, that is on 15.1.1943, more than 2,000 Jews including Hinda, Shaul and Melech left here on the last transport. I leave this letter with a Christian woman and give her 25 dollars for it. I wish you a long life with health and happiness.

Asher son of Yitzchak Schwartz

A letter from Asher, the son of Yitzchak Schwartz of Linesk to his sister Rivka Ginzburg-Schwartz in Haifa.

Letter 12

Tarnopol, April 7, 1943

My Dear One,

Before I depart from this world, I would like to leave some words for you. If you ever receive this letter, I and all of us here, will no longer be alive. Our end is coming near. We feel this and know it. We are all doomed to death like all those innocent Jews, who have already been executed. Those who remained, who survived the mass slaughter, their turn will also come in a very short time (within days or weeks).

It is a terrible matter, but it is the entire truth. To our sorrow, there is no going back or refuge from that horrible death.

I could tell you so much, but how is it possible to describe all the nightmare and anguish that we are experiencing. The pen cannot relate the tragedy of our people in this blood-drenched country; the agonies and destructive cruelty to oppress human beings, to agitate them, chase, degrade and finally kill them. At the beginning we were squeezed like lemons, our blood was sucked till the last drop, and finally we were thrown into the sewer ditch. At the beginning our hearts were torn away, we were robbed of all our human emotions and human instincts, and after turning into beasts working in a mechanical way, we were slain en mass. You cannot grasp this, you cannot feel what we ourselves felt. A person who thinks in a normal way will never believe that it's possible to withstand these tortures, and that in the twentieth century atrocities like these are possible. I'll try to tell you briefly about our fate since July 1941.

Already at the beginning of July 1941, close to five thousand people were murdered, among them my husband. David left his house on the seventh of July 1941 (12th of Tammuz) and hasn't returned since. He volunteered to be a member of the Judenrat that was about to be organized. Despite my opposition, he saw it as an obligation for himself, as a candidate for the rabbinate, to offer his services. He wanted to be a advocate of his people. Six weeks later, and after five days of searching, I found him among the many bodies that were brought from the brick works (the killing spot) to the cemetery. From that day, life has ceased for me, has lost all its meaning. Even in my youthful dreams, I couldn't have wished for myself a better and more loyal husband. I was given two years and two months to live a life of true happiness. And, it's strange — exactly two years and two months [have passed] (May 7, 1939, the wedding day until July 7, 1941, the parting day). There is no point in prolonging the words about the agonies of my soul, about the bleeding of a wounded heart, at a time when you must bury with your own hands the person most precious to you of all your loves, the man who understood my spirit, a beloved and loyal person. How is it possible to describe to you that we were already so exhausted from the many searches that we were "happy" when we found "our" corpse among the many abandoned corpses. Can we relate all this in words?

Here is a woman who in one day lost her husband, the second lost her only son and the third lost everyone — both husband as well as children. Is it possible to describe the overflowing extent of sorrow and pain? And this was the fate of thousands.

And so, David is no longer. And he is blessed that it is all beyond him and that he did not have to witness two years of horror. The bullet of death still awaits us. At first, I was convinced that I wouldn't recuperate after his death, I thought that I wouldn't be able to live without him, but oh, what a tough creature is man! I continued living. How?

It's hard to say. The deep and bleeding wound has no cure. How difficult and sad it is to remain alone, and it's precisely because I was so pampered by my loyal husband, and I have gotten so used to our calm and tranquil home. However, on we go with life.

In September 1941 we were sent to the ghetto. Imagine that we were surrounded by fences and allowed to enter the Aryan neighborhood only with permits given to workers. A large gate guarded by German or Ukrainian guards was the border. Food items were smuggled into the ghetto with great challenges and fear. I received a position in a German firm in September as a secretary-typist. As luck would have it, the office was in our former home. The dining room is used now for an office. A desk stands in place of the piano. Instead of playing the piano I now start to "play" on the typewriter. I mustn't complain. My job was good. The employer as well as my fellow workers were good, and their attitude towards me was fair. They treated me like a human being and not like a Jewess. Father and Bobby got work in the same factory.

At the beginning the ghetto was very depressing, but slowly one also gets used to these conditions of life.

The winter of the year 1941/42 was very harsh and cold, and it was really hard to survive. People died of starvation and cold en masse. But despite the pillages, searches, the intensifying hunger and the cold, people went on with life. From time to time they sold their items, the white clothes etc., and they somehow managed. Until March 1942. Then the nightmare started again. A genuine Eve of Bartholomew's (March 23, 1942). From the Judenrat, a "quota" of seven hundred people to murder was demanded. What, you disbelieve that this is true? Indeed, it was like this. Our brothers, the policemen, they were the ones who took the people to their death. The gathering place for the victims was the former synagogue. There it was warm already, so that the "wretched" ones wouldn't suffer from the cold before their death. Also bread and jam were served to them and later they were put in freight cars and led to Janowska. Everything was ready and prepared: graves, machine guns, and it's all done with. How awful that night was! But this was only the beginning. And again silence for some time. Silence — if it can be called silence. The persistent nightmare of the enforced [labor] camp, the never-ending fear of tomorrow. And yet we still continued living, with the distress and the dread.

In July 1942, Tzila [the writer's sister] was sent to a labor camp in Jagielnica, because she didn't work. Her situation wasn't bad.

On August 31, the "great action" started. Three thousand victims were required. It's not known exactly how many of the living perished, two thousand five hundred or more.

We then lost our beloved, good and devoted mother. This time the murderers used a new trick. The workers and their families received special stamps from the police on their work documents. Supposedly, no "action" would apply to them, since this time again the action was supposed to include those who were not fit for work and children. Again our Jewish police looked for victims in apartments and hideouts. Bobby and I went to work. Mother and Father stayed at home — after all, the "stamp of life" was in their hands. They didn't allow us to go through the gate and they led Bobby and me to the place of disaster. We were convinced that we would be gone. But we weren't there for a long time; we escaped and this success brightened us up. Many were shot there. With luck I arrived at the office. I had a lot of work then. I sat in the office and outside thousands were awaiting death. How is it possible to describe all this to you? In the afternoon I learned that Father and Mother were seen in the square, and I had to continue with work. To help — I couldn't. I thought I would go mad, but one doesn't go mad. In the evening our friend came to work, the German that rescued forty people from among the workers of our firm, among them also our father. Mother could not be saved: women, especially those that didn't work, housewives — they could not be saved. I did not know whether to mourn and cry for Mother or to be "happy" that at least I had a father who was saved. Can one grasp this? Doesn't the mind and heart tremble? No, nothing happened to those that remained alive. Only the victims are those that are gone...

August 31 was awful. Thousands were compressed into the closed cattle cars. Women, men and small children, the elderly and young, all were loaded in the cars and transported to the special slaughterhouse for people called Belzice. Some say that they were poisoned there and some say that they were put to death by electric shock. How they were murdered there is not exactly known. I would like to add that the family of David was terminated long ago. The same thing in every place, in large cities and in remote towns. The same thing exactly. An order was an order in every place. Well, we went on with life without Mother, that good, faithful and devoted soul. Oh, how she is missed every step of the way!

In October, Tzila returned from the Labor camp in Jagielnica. Meanwhile the daily worries continued and the difficult struggle for a meaningless existence. And again it was necessary to move. The ghetto was reduced, since the apartments of those murdered were vacated. We moved this time to 22 Shpatitzkich. By coincidence three of the houses (20, 22, 24) were in the area of the ghetto. We went on living.

On the 3rd and the 5th of November 1942, the "actions" again started. People were taken out of all possible hideouts, from all especially prepared underground bunkers and taken to be killed. Again it was our police who took the young people to "the interior" [sic]. Entire families, houses complete with their tenants, were wiped off the face of the earth.

The fifth of November fell on a Sunday. And again it was necessary to move. At 11:00 a.m. the ghetto was surrounded by surprise and the devil's dance started anew. I was lucky: Without knowing about the "action" I left exactly ten minutes before the ghetto was surrounded. It seems I am destined to leave with the last convoy.

And again, after a short time, we were forced to move to a new place, to vacate streets and to crowd in even more. In the course of time we became so used to it all, that we were like dummies. We didn't react at all when we lost those who were closest. No one cried. We ceased to be human beings. We were like stones without feeling. There was no news that made an impression on us any more. We went silently, even to die. The people in the square where we assembled were reserved and silent.

In January 1943 we went from the firm to the labor camp. We were subject to a regimen of barracks. Men separately and women separately. It was forbidden now to appear in the street alone, but as work groups accompanied by a policeman, and this, only in the Aryan neighborhood. We became labor prisoners. Father and Bobby lived in the men's division. Tzila and I were in the women's division. I forcibly brought Father to the camp when he was sick with a kidney infection. I wanted to be together and go towards death together. And that is how we lived in the camp. Many acquaintances escaped to the big cities, equipped with "Aryan" papers. Many were caught, and perhaps only several succeeded in escaping.

From January until April 1943 it was quiet. We again continued with life and became accustomed to our troubles and the inspection campaigns that took place in the camp, etc. In April it all began again. A small number of people in the ghetto were dragged out to the middle of nowhere and murdered. Twenty people. On Monday again, fifty people, etc.

◆ ◆ ◆

April 26

I am still alive and want to describe to you what has happened since April 7th until today. The widespread opinion is that now the turn has arrived for "everything." Galicia has to be free of Jews ("Juden-frei"). First of all the ghetto will be terminated until the day of the first of May. In the ghetto today there are seven hundred people.

In the last days again thousands were shot. Now they use a new method. People are led to death in an "official" manner. Previously this was called "Umzidlong" (resettling). Not now. The last events were again horrendous. The gathering place was in our camp. Here the victims taken out by the Jewish policemen from their hideouts were sorted and led to death. We, in the camp, could "watch" from the windows of our rooms and see everything. Oh, these sights, these images! How can they be described? We ceased to be human beings, we became beasts, we lost all human sentiment. Sons brought their parents to the execution place, fathers brought their sons, women tried to escape by leaving their babies. And again another spectacle. Children joining their parents, although they could have saved themselves for a certain amount of time, as they were fit for labor. One sees the square filling up with a growing number of those doomed to death. This time the graves were in Piotrkow, prepared ahead of time. The victims were forced to leave their outer garments on the spot. Men were stripped to the undershirts and led on foot to be slaughtered. After all, it is very close. Why fuel the cars, why bother the train? What a pity! After all, it is simpler to get rid of this harmful material on the spot. And when the people were transported by train, individuals succeeded in escaping from the railway cars, and now there is no such possibility. In my opinion it is an easier death than traveling for two to three days with the awareness of going towards death. It is certainly terrible. At least now it is done at a quick pace.

In Piotrkow it appears like this: they undress before the grave. Kneeling naked, the men wait for the shooting. The rest stand by ready and await their turn. Meanwhile they must arrange the slain in the graves, so that the place will be used to capacity. The situation does not continue for a long time. After half an hour the clothes of the thousands of slain are in the camp.

The nerves have no strength to bear all this. If someone had told me ahead of time that I would be able to bear so much anguish, I would never have been able to imagine such a thing. From where does one get strength for all this at a time that they know that it's all in vain? There is no rescue. It is a pity to mislead the heart to think that it is possible to escape from this mass slaughter. We have no hope. We live from day to day, or more correctly from hour to hour.

On the ninth of April, 1500 people were murdered, after that it was quiet for two to three days, and again it all started anew. Without end. Today we are still only seven hundred Jews in the ghetto.

I must add that after the "actions" the Judenrat received a bill of thirty thousand golden coins, that it had to pay for "used bullets." Interesting, isn't it? We, the people of the camp, have to go after work into the apartments of the slain and snatch the items. How disgusting, how terrible it all is! Remnants of an entire people. These empty apartments, these desolate streets, this dead city. Oh, how painful it is, and why does it have to be like this? Why can't we shout, why aren't we able to acquire arms and defend ourselves? How can we see so much innocent bloodshed and not say a thing, but just wait for death to come and take us too. It's so horrible. We think of bursting violently, but there are no violent outbursts.

Life — if this can be called life — and the world knows that we are dying like this, and nothing happens. Nobody wants to help us, there is nobody that wants to rescue us. So miserable, miserable, we must descend to the abyss. Do you think that we want to end up like this, to die like this? No. No. We don't want to. Despite everything that we experienced. The opposite. The instinct of life is greater now, and as death gets nearer, so the will to live is stronger.

We want to live so much! We would like to see with our own eyes the avenging of the millions of the victims for our immense, inestimable suffering.

Unfortunately we will not live to see this day of revenge.

My dears, you are obligated to take revenge, you must do something to take revenge against this overflowing measure of injustice, of these inhumane atrocities.

The truth is that revenge is not at all possible. Whatever happens is insignificant, as nothing and as nil compared to our fate, for what has been done to us cannot be grasped.

I cannot continue, I cannot write more. And if I fill up a few sheets, you will not understand anyhow. I will therefore finish. My beloved David is laying in a cemetery, my mother, I do not know where. A transport to Belzice. The place of my burial I will not know — Piotrkow or Zagrobeck, Zrodzhin. I don't know if you will ever come here by chance after the war, ask our acquaintances where the last convoys from the camp were headed.

It is not easy to part forever. World, we are going to die already with laughter on our lips.

Be well, have success, and if you can, when the day comes — take revenge!

Mushiya

Letter 13

Prague, May 20, 1943

— Here remains only a small part [of the Jewish population that lived in Czechoslovakia]. In the entire country there are 10,000 Jews. There are six times more in Theresienstadt (60,000). Of them over half are from Austria and the German Reich and also children and a few elderly from Holland.

According to regulations [in Czechoslovakia, regarding the Jews] it is forbidden to buy meat, milk, white flour, cakes, eggs, fruit, vegetables, fish, cheese, sweets and jam. We must also get used to not smoking. Our children don't attend school. It is forbidden to convene for prayer in a quorum (*minyan*). Despite this, our situation is better than that of the majority who were transferred to Poland. We can't receive any news from them. However, what we hear saddens us very, very much. In Theresienstadt only a small part remain of those that were deported over there from here [Prague]. The majority was deported further. The death rate in Theresienstadt is high, especially among the elderly.

[Heinz Valazar]

Letter 14

Bratislava, 21st of Iyar 5703
To the Mizrachi World Center

— With deep sorrow we notify you of the extent of the tragedy of European Jewry and of Slovakian Jewry in general. About 60,000 Jews, who made up 80% of the Slovakian Jewish population, were deported last summer to Poland. According to news coming from there, from eyewitness reports and accounts from witnesses who were told, most of them fell there sanctifying the name of God among [the nation of] Israel, as did the rest of Polish Jewry. The elderly, women and young children were killed and murdered in a cruel way. — Only a small remnant remains of Slovakian Jewry.

Previously, that is, until the liquidation and the split of the Zionist Organization in Slovakia into factions and parties by the wicked regime, the number of members of all parties was numerous and considerable.

—

Members who remained, like all other Jews here, remained only thanks to their supposed financial worth or due to the fact that they are members of the "Jewish Center," the Judenrat and its clerks.

—

The situation of the Jews in our country is not safe. The danger of deportation, of death, always hovers over the heads of the Jews like the sword of Damocles.

Letter 15

My Dear Sister and Brother-in-law,

I am writing this last letter of farewell before my death. I will leave this letter with a Christian, who will send it to you after the war. I am writing to you about our tragic death, a death that overtook all of the town's Jews — they were shot for seven days in the month of Elul. I together with Yudka and Saraka and Itzik ran away. We were confused when we ran and we lost one another. They shot at Zelda and at — together with all the Jews. All the Jews of Moletai are buried in one grave in back of the yards of Moletai, near Lateka. I lie in a pit with Yudka for 16 weeks. We suffered in a dreadful way…

I am writing this letter as a prisoner in jail. We are counting the minutes until they come to take us and execute us. In a few minutes.

◆ ◆ ◆

They caught Jews in the yard of 8 Anmisel. Abba Shniplisker was there with his family. They came here from the "afterworld" — that is, they suffered hunger and cold. We left unclothed, it was still warm before Rosh Hashanah, and now we are ten days into Tevet (1941). It is very cold. At the end we were forced to register, but they caught us on the way and tomorrow they are going to shoot us. I don't know whether they will shoot us in Moletai or in Utena. We haven't found them yet, because they shot them. 21.12.41 […] Ella Gutz went to Shavli. There is not one single Jew in any town. Today we see how the world looks without Jews.

◆ ◆ ◆

I prepared a tombstone for Father. I will try at the police to get permission to transfer the tombstone to the cemetery, accompanied by a policeman. Perhaps there will be a possibility to visit the graves of our parents and the martyred slain people of Moletai. Mother doesn't have a tombstone, because it was too early. I had not yet finished saying Kaddish. Be well. These are my last words. Your brother who perished and his son Yudel Nutlevich. Today is 21.12.1941 and it will be our day of remembrance.

This is the address of the Christian with whom we are leaving the letters. At the end of the war he will send them to you. If you would like to answer him, write to him in Lithuanian: [...]

◆ ◆ ◆

My Dear Uncle and Aunt,

This last letter of farewell, I am writing to you from prison, condemned to death. A barbaric murderous arm condemned me, victims innocent of any crime.

Thousands and thousands of people have fallen. The blood of those slain will not be silenced. It hurts to leave this wonderful world. Before we even began to live, we fell, me and Father together with our family. You won't know where our corpses will wind up. I end my letter, live in happiness and enjoy the beautiful world.

Your devoted nephew, who perished, Yudel Nutlevich Moletai, December 21, 1941 from prison — a few days before death

Children from Labaner [Labanoras] were shot in Nova Schweintzin on July 22, 1941. That is, the Russians deported all the people of Labaner, and Chaimke Boches. It is unknown whether they killed him or not. It would be more correct to say that they killed him.

Yudka had a photo with him and he is enclosing it.
Tomorrow we will be transported to execution in Utena, December 27, 1941.

Letter 16

We confirm that on July 7, 1944 an order was given to evacuate the Shavli ghetto.

We would like to publicize our names for the sake of future generations:

1. Shmuel Minzberg son of Shimon, from the city of Lodz, Poland, with his wife;

2. Reisele, nee Sachs, of Vaiguva;

3. Faigale Sachs, her sister;

4. Friedele Niselevitch of Vaiguva, the daughter of Nachum Tzvi.

We don't know where they're transporting us. In the ghetto, 2,000 Jews await the order to go. Our destiny is unknown. The mood is terrible.

B"B of the Kingdom of Israel
Shmuel Minzberg

Letter 17

[Warsaw]

[...] We sat in a dark and cold cellar in Chelmno. After a day of backbreaking work burying those murdered, we would fall on the layer of thin straw and cry. Monik Halber, a boy of fifteen from Izbica leaned on me and sobbed: "Oh Shlomo, if only I would be dead instead of my mother and sister." And Meir Pitrovski, my neighbor in the layer of straw, said with tears: "I left behind at home my beloved wife and children, and who knows whether I will live to see them again. What will become of them?" [...] That evening one of the armed soldiers entered the cellar, stood in the doorway and threatened us with his gun and ordered us to sing. I don't know how I had the strength. With a trembling voice, I turned to my fellow prisoners and said: "Friends, stand on your feet and wear your hats, and repeat after me." The armed soldier hurried us impatiently. Everyone stood on their feet and I opened with the words of the prayer: "Hear, O Israel, the Lord is our God, the Lord is the One and Only" [...]

◆ ◆ ◆

Zamosc

The Honorable Mr. Wasser,

I can inform you that, thank God, I am healthy. I wish you the same, and to hear from you only good tidings. As for me, I am in a critical situation. I myself do not know what to do, because I would very much want to see Mr. Kohn, and this is my only aim.

The Honorable Mr. Wasser, the community's committee does not want to help me, therefore I truly request that my sir agrees to write immediately, because meanwhile

I have no work and not a penny. That is why I really request from my sir to send me some Zloty so that I can save my life. I received regards from my cousin in Lublin. They write that people went to the afterworld in the same way as in Chelmno. Imagine my despair. I have no more strength to cry. This is probably my last letter and I am about to go the same way and in the same manner as my parents. Honorable Mr. Wasser. My sir, give me advice about what I should do in order to see Mr. Kohn, and if not — I will never see you. And I would greatly wish to see you again, urgently, and relate what I went through. In general, to tell everything. There is a House of Eternity [cemetery] in Belzice. It is the same as in Chelmno; I received regards from my cousin who lives in Rawa Ruska. I haven't seen her for a long time. She was in Rawa Ruska from where she went to the afterworld. My grandfather in Bilgoraj also died on me, so I have not one person from my family. Imagine, my sir, the grief that I am experiencing. It is not only I who imagine that I will shortly meet with Mr. Chaim Reuven Izbitzki, and I would definitely prefer to see you. How is it by you, my sir, what is your wife doing and so forth, and how is it with all our acquaintances? Kisses to you all.

Shlamek

Regards from all our acquaintances, and I remain with much appreciation. He is cold [the murderer] just as in Chelmno, and now we are in line. The cemetery is in Belzice. He already froze the towns mentioned in the letter.

I end, and kiss you all.

Shlamek

Shlemak escaped from Chelmno but perished on April 11 or 12, 1942 in Belzice. The first section is taken from his testimony in Warsaw before Mr. Wasser, before he went ahead with his escape. We chose to bring both the testimony and the letter because together they comprise his last words.

Letter 18

Bedzin, July 17, 1943
To Vania, Mendel, Ze'ev and all friends wherever they may be,
Dear Friends,

Following a lengthy anticipation, only today we received the messenger and your letter with immense joy. To our sorrow, your messenger was a little late in coming. For years we have dreamt of the opportunity to tell you about our lives and our war.

During the year and a half of the war we have established a tremendous training enterprise. And besides this, the youth movements are a lot stronger and more pleasant than in regular days. But a year and a half ago, to our regret, all regular activity ceased. After a period of organizing the ghettos, systematic annihilation started. At the beginning it was done in Warta, in the Lodz and Posnan districts. About eighty thousand Jews were poisoned there with gas — in official language this is called "Aussied Lung." In Lodz itself a small gathering of Jews, numbering some forty thousand, remains enclosed. Without doubt, they are starving and perishing from hunger and tuberculosis. At this moment, we have no news from there. The place of destruction is called Chelmno.

After this, came the annihilation of Lithuanian Jewry by shooting in Ponary. Altogether twenty thousand Jews remained in Vilna, Kovna and Shavli. We have no news from there for some months, probably because they're "Judenrein." We prepared for defense, but to our sorrow, without success. In the area called "Government" [General-Guvernman] — Warsaw, Lublin, Tschneskova, Krakow and the environs — there are no more Jews. Their annihilation was done by means of gas in Treblinka, near Melikinia. This is a well-known place of annihilation. Not only for the Jews of Poland, but also for Jews from Holland, Belgium, etc.

The nice chapter in our war was in Warsaw. Tzvia [Lobatkin] and Joseph [Kaplan] organized the defense together with the children [meaning the various Zionist youth organizations]. Awful battles took place in the ghetto. To our sorrow only a few hundred fell among the enemy — eight hundred. The result was that all the Jews were annihilated and the ghetto was destroyed without a remnant.

In the area of the "Government" there is no more Jewish settlement, except for three enforced labor camps — Trawniki, Poniatowa and Prokocim. They number up to thirty thousand people. In a few weeks there won't be one single person alive from them either.

In Warsaw, several thousand Jews survived illegally among the gentiles on the Aryan side. Among them were Tzvia [Lobatkin], Yitzchak Zuckerman. Galar [Eliezer] of the Ya'ari family [Meir Ya'ari, from the heads of the national Kibbutz movement of "Hashomer Hatzair"], nobody remained. Tussia [Altman], Hancha [Plotnitzka], Leah Perlstein, Joseph Kaplan, Mordechai Anelevitch and hundreds of people are no longer alive. From the Reiss family [Workers of Zion Tz.S.] only Sack [Joseph], Graiek [Shalom], and Levin [Laizer] remain. From the Samak [Kaplan] family only Bloch [Eliezer Lipa] remains in the labor camp, and Kirshenblum [Menachem]. Of the Altar [Victor] family only a few individuals remain.

The Ukraine and Polsia are Judenrein.

In Bialistok, about twenty thousand Jews survived in better conditions. The Lublin district was totally annihilated in Belzice and Sobibor. The last Jewish settlement, which until now had relatively fair conditions, is Upper Eastern Shelsia. Three weeks ago seven thousand Jews were deported. They are being annihilated in Auschwitz. They are killed by shooting and fire. In the next few weeks our district will be without Jews. When you receive our letter, not one of us will be alive. On the basis of the passports that we obtained via Switzerland, only a few people were arrested [to a detention camp for subjects from abroad]. None of us were among them. Today the authorities are causing great difficulties and they don't put people in the detention camp anymore. We didn't receive any news as of now about all those that were sent on the last transport. On the contrary, today we know for sure that the transport went to Auschwitz. Immediate intervention by the sponsoring government is extremely urgent. I'm not sending you the required material, since you can get all the pictures and data from Natan [Schwalb] and from Zilb [Dr. Avraham Zilberschein].

All the regions that I've written about, I myself visited, and I was eyewitness to all the actions of annihilation. Hershel [Spinger] is still here, but don't write to his address, because he has a dispute with Authoritowich [the authorities]. I myself don't live with him in complete harmony. We are looking for a way to get to Hungary and request that you help us in any way possible.

Do all that you can. I doubt that you can help us in time, because we near our final days. All the youth movements today don't even total several hundreds, including members of our kibbutz and the children's kibbutz — unofficial kibbutzim. Our hope to meet with the Homeland [the Land of Israel] will not come true, to our hearts' sorrow. Heartfelt regards to Taben [Yitzchak Tabenkin], Eliezer [Grabitzki], Bendarski [P.Bandori], Ya'ari [Meir], Kolodni [Moshe Kol], Goldstein [Yitzchak], Pinchas [Lubianker - Lavon] and all the relatives.

We are writing this letter in great haste, because the messenger's time is tight. We have no more energy and patience to write everything to you, about that which we most require and about that which we would most want.

We bless you from the depths of our hearts.

Frumka [Plotnitzka]

Hershel [Springer]

Tzvi [Brandes]

Koz'och [Israel]

Shlomo L. [Lerner]

Letter 19

Brody, April 30, 1942
To My Beloved Sister and Brother-in-law!

When this letter reaches you, I will long not be among the living. Yet I wish to explain the events to you, and to the extent that I can focus my thoughts, I will describe our lives until the last moments. And all that I can describe to you in writing will not include even one-hundredth of one percent of all of what we really went through.

Fate had it that I should remain alive until this day, eight months longer than all the Jews of Beresteczko, since I managed to flee the pogrom to Galicia, that is to Brody, in days when quiet still prevailed there. In the continuation of the letter you will understand how this happened. In my description, I will start with the first day of the German army's invasion into Beresteczko.

The war broke out on 22.6.1941, on Sunday at dawn. And on Monday 23.6 at 12:00 noon, the German army was already in the city. Perhaps I would have fled to Russia, but immediately on Sunday night they drafted me and Moshe to military service and we were sent to the front. Obviously, on the way to the front we were already surrounded by Germans, and we managed to retreat, without falling into captivity, which means death by starvation. As was proven later, hundreds of thousands of prisoners died of starvation; and when the prisoner is Jewish, it becomes that much easier...

And when we arrived safely home, a saga began that involved moral suffering. While the army passed through Beresteczko, they would take men for work on the roads and other types of labor, and the wages for this labor were blows. *And here, like found like.* The Ukrainian nationals, grandsons of Patelyura and Taras Bolva, who have frequently filled our pages of history with pogroms against Jews, joined up with the "dear" barbaric German government. They cooperated with the Germans and helped them a lot, after being promised an independent Ukraine. And since the German was powerless to give anything, and since he needed the Ukrainians' help, they had to be rewarded with something. The German gave them freedom to rule over the Jews. And the lives of the Jews became chaotic. They began to rob the Jews and to wage pogroms against them. About a month after the war broke out the SS or the Gestapo, the special force that carries out pogroms against the Jews, came to Beresteczko. With the help of many Ukrainian policemen, they assembled about three hundred Jews, men aged 14–65 near the palace, under the excuse that they were about to take them out to work, and the Jews dug for themselves at this spot, a large pit. Everyone was put to death by shooting and buried in this pit.

I was also honored to be among these men, but due to the fact that all the soldiers knew me, since we would fix their bikes and do other jobs for them, they took me out and hid me.

I will write about our family's experiences during this entire period later on. Although compared to others we suffered less, due to the fact that we all had friendly relationships. This way we had special rights, that others couldn't enjoy. But all about this — later on.

I must stress that among the three hundred buried near the palace are members of our family: Chaim Teitleman (Maya's husband), Uncle Berel Vabrik with his son Chilik. Aunt Chatzel remained alone and lived with us the whole time. Also Motik Greenspun was among the three hundred near the palace.

Then three months passed with backbreaking work, flogging and theft. Although since the establishment of the administration, some order was introduced. According to this administration, there was permission to carry out pogroms against the Jews, but to steal and rob was only allowed individually, when others didn't know about it, since the right to steal was reserved only for the Germans. Nevertheless, all this was still the lesser of two evils.

Four months passed, and they first began to assemble Jews in the ghetto in Beresteczko, before it was done in any other place in the area, thanks to our 'good' neighbors. They carried this out one-hundred percent according to the Nuremberg Laws. The Jews of the city were forced to go to the synagogue square. On one side was the river and the border, and on the other side, along the streets going towards the market, they put up a high wall of two and a half meters, with only one gate set as an exit. A Jewish police was organized. Its privilege was to get blows from any Ukranian policeman, all the more so from a German. A Jewish council was established (the Judenrat), made up of six people. They were assigned to supply the Germans with whatever they required, whether the Jews had it or not. And every time, contributions amounting to hundreds and thousands of rubles. Also a Ministry of Labor ("Arbeit-Ammet") was established, assigned to send people to work, wherever this was needed: from washing floors to uprooting trees in the forest. For all this they paid what the Judenrat received as a government wage: flour for bread that was rationed at 14 deco a day per person. Besides the 14 deco of bread a day per person received by every Jew, they were forbidden to buy or sell. Aryans were forbidden to enter the ghetto. Jews were forbidden to leave the ghetto alone. Jews would go out to work as groups directed by Jewish police, and they were forbidden to enter a Christian home. Also on the way back from work, Jews walked together. Whoever left the ghetto alone was shot dead. And if, on the way back from work, someone managed to buy an onion, and in a search they found it on him, he was beaten in such a way that he lie sick for three months, and in addition he was fined for two thousand to three thousand rubles. Yet all this, one had to accept with love, because he could have been shot dead.

You can imagine the situation in the ghetto. Nevertheless they could buy everything in the ghetto, because there were Christians who supplied, of course at a great expense, and only the wealthy could buy. And in Beresteczko few were wealthy, many died of starvation, mainly the old, and also from the filth due to the crowding, since four families would live in one room.

The Jewish artisans enjoyed special rights. They lived in the marketplace, that is the quarter between the Zinger building and the Gedalia Sakolski House until the Staritchana Bridge (Starichaner Brick). Although they were not surrounded by a wall, limits were also imposed on them as on all Jews in the ghetto. They were forbidden to buy and sell, going out on the street was forbidden, other than to their workplaces, and they were equipped with special permits. The workers were all organized in workshops according to their professions. The workshops were concentrated in the Ratuss. They received wages for their work and could have even reached the amount of 300 rubles a month, an amount sufficient to buy five loaves of bread. The lives of the artisans were much easier, since they were not surrounded by a wall, and they could exchange advice.

This is how life went on until the middle of the summer of 1942. And despite great suffering, a considerable percent could have stayed alive until after the war and lived to see an improvement, if only they would allow it. But to our sorrow, this wasn't so. On one of the days of September 1942 (I can't remember the exact date, it was a Saturday night), 200 police surrounded the artisans' quarter together with the ghetto, without any possibility to escape. Until Wednesday of that week, it became forbidden to leave the houses. Behind the Rentchina (rentzina), on the way to Smolova (Smalawe), 400 gentiles dug during this time, two large pits — each one was 18 meters long, eight meters wide and four meters deep. On Wednesday, they started to take people out and shoot them. Each and every person was forced to undress naked, go down into the pit and lie flat. In this condition they shot him. The clothing of the people and everything they had, were sent to Germany if they were in fair condition; and the items that were very used were sold to local residents.

So the Jewish problem was solved.

And later, when I happened to meet a Ukrainian from Beresteczko, I asked him: "What does the city look like now?" He responded: They already got used to it as if Jews had never been there. This was his answer, and I had to hear and be silent, for what could I tell him? He wouldn't see things my way, since he doesn't want to understand at all. After all, he inherited the Jews. For a few rubles he bought his clothing and his bedding, and he was pleased.

Indeed, we didn't imagine this to ourselves, because until now the Germans didn't annihilate Jews in any country. Until three months ago, Jews in the entire Poland, with certain limitations were able to sit freely and not in a ghetto, except for Warsaw, Krakow and Lvov, which had ghettos. Now they are implementing the same plan there, with one difference for the time being: the healthy men with professions were put in barracks, they work and receive enough food that they already forget themselves in drink [sic], but for the time being they're not killing them. And even, if we had known about what would be done to the Jews, we wouldn't have been able to get help, because there was no place to escape. In the entire Europe, the Jews received the same regulations. When the German army crossed the Polish-Soviet border, at Mashivituvka, they killed the Jews in every single spot. And indeed we knew this, but we assumed that they were taking revenge against the Communists. After all, in their eyes it is obvious that all Jews are Communists — that's how we explained it to ourselves. And it seems that when the war continued for a longer time, without them being able to put an end to it within six weeks, as they had planned, having passed through Europe with a gallop, capturing it easily, they thought that here it would be the same. And since they were unable to do this, it is obvious that the Jews are guilty of everything (even if Germany wins, the Jews would be guilty of everything). They started to change the policy towards Jews and terminate the Jewish problem in each and every country in a systematic and extreme way.

I've already stressed that our family didn't suffer financially or morally like other Jews. This was due to good connections with the local authority and the hoodlums in the area. Likewise, because I and another Jew worked in the Electric Institute, and other experts weren't there, they allowed us and also Moshe to remain in our apartment in Firstut (Firstadt) and we had permission to walk about the street day and night, also after curfew hours. The Aryans kept on coming to our apartment and workshop, we made profits, and we took everything for ourselves, of course, so that we were able to buy everything as in the good days, and we could even offer help to our relatives in the ghetto. This is how it continued until two months before the pogrom. After that we were also ordered to move to the artisans' quarter, and this is where we have lived until recent days. And, of all our good friends, not one came to warn us a in advance of what was going to happen. We assumed that something would happen, after news came in from other cities in Volhynia. In many cities they liquidated the ghettos, yet they left the artisans' quarter. With us too, they prepared certificates for artisans and their families a week before the pogrom. Therefore, we thought that they would leave the artisans' quarter alone, but this didn't come true. We were deliberately misled, and also in places where the artisans' quarter remained, they later liquidated it. I myself didn't rely on the certificates, and when I learned about what happened in other cities in the area, I quit staying overnight at home and I would sleep at the Electric Institute. Also during the night that the ghetto was surrounded, I slept at the Electric Institute. And early in the morning, when I learned the latest news, I hid, and after hiding for several days and finding out that nobody remained alive, I crossed the border to Brody at night.

You must be wondering, which border? I must explain to you, because the border exists now between Galicia and Russia as it did in 1913: Strzemilcze, Antonowka, Mielnice. This border was set mainly because there is no bread in Galicia, and so they wouldn't have to transfer bread from Volhynia to Galicia, because the Germans take everything for themselves.

And when I came safely to Brody, the second part of the saga of my suffering began. On the Friday that I came to Brody, I learned that they were planning an "action," as they call it: During one day 3,500 people were deported by train to Belzice. There, they say, a special electric bridge was installed, on which they lifted the people, killing them with an electric current. When I learned about the "action" they were preparing, I immediately went to the person who sends you this letter, and he led me to one of the villages, to an acquaintance of his. I gave the person the 2,000 rubles that I had, and I remained there all day. When I later saw that quiet prevails in the city and that I didn't have extra money

137

to pay, since I didn't have time to get more money ready; I had to sell everything — but the matter was not resolved. I came to town after the "action" without a penny to my name, and with an increase in expenses, three times more than by us. I couldn't get work. The Christians didn't take Jews to work, and the hunger afflicted me. I was forced to go to acquaintances for food. After a week passed I installed a "mini-mill" for grinding flour, since the mills didn't grind flour for citizens. I had started to earn a little and I was able to eat potatoes until I was satiated.

But this also did not last for long — when I awoke at dawn and heard shooting in the street, I understood that they were again conducting an "action" against the Jews, and the place where I stayed overnight was not a good hideout. They took me out of hiding and bought me to the gathering place. I didn't have the sleeve band with the Star of David, they could not recognize on my face that I was a Jew. Therefore I was lucky until now, that I could walk about the street without them noticing me. I decided to run for my life, because from here they were surely taking me to death, and perhaps I may succeed in being saved. My words became actions. When I passed down the street and many people came near to watch the game [sic], I managed to leave the line without them noticing, and I mingled among the people who were about to watch the goings-on. I remained standing and saw how they were being led. This is the fourth time that I was saved from death, but I haven't come to the end yet.

After the second "action" that went on for two days, in which 4,000 people from Brody were taken, they put the ghetto up after a month. I decided that whatever would happen with me, I would not enter the ghetto. And with the help of the friend sending you the letter, I managed to do this. He found a gentile, who for a decent payment arranged a hideout underground. In consideration of a man that I brought along who paid him a hefty sum, he let me in for free. That is how I evaded [being caught] until today, that is, until May 1943, and now I face this question: What else can I do? I don't have money. The people dispersed each on his own; whoever could take care of himself, did just that. We were sure that the war would be over this winter and we hoped that in March we would be rescued, but it seems that the handful of Jews had no luck in remaining alive. "The God of the Jews has gone abroad," the Germans would tease, and the truth is that everything ended up badly.

From the duration of my stay in the pit, I have nothing to describe. It was like this: Imprisonment for 5 months in an awful jail, where it was forbidden even to cough. In addition to this — the cleanliness and other pleasures. But all this is nothing compared to the will to stay alive and take revenge. Revenge and only revenge. Oh, I so very much wanted to stay alive until after the war and take my revenge. To immerse in their blood as they immersed in ours. After this I have no desire to live, because anyway this life is of no value. I have gone through so much and seen too much in life. Just to take revenge — that is my single wish. I am extremely concerned, that the evil intent of the murderer will succeed and no person will remain to pay him his reward.

I assume that you read in the newspapers about what's going on with us. They certainly don't tell the entire truth, and it's possible that they don't know the complete truth abroad. When reading a German newspaper or listening abroad to the radio about 130 thousand Jewish workers sent from Poland to the Ukraine, no person abroad would understand that it wasn't 130 thousand, but four times 130 thousand Jews [sic], and these were sent to the afterworld. Therefore it is hard for you to sense all that we're going through. I also read at the time about the suffering of the Jews when Hitler came into power in Germany. I read the newspaper after work while I was drinking a cup of sweet tea. While reading this, I perhaps groaned in commiseration, I finished my tea and went out for a stroll. Many Jews in America and England feel now like I had felt then. It scares and worries me, that nobody will remain to punish the murderer. It is obvious that those suffering from them will know how to properly punish them, but to my sorrow, I am doubtful if we will live to see this. Therefore, I call upon the Jews who will stay alive after the war: take revenge in all ways and at every chance that you have! We must pay these two nations with blood for blood! And if there is only one percent truth in the German's shouting that the Jews control everything, that they do everything, that they're guilty of everything, if the Jews have the strength to do something in whatever place, the first thing to do is to take revenge against Germany, to try to wipe it out of the world, as they wiped out the Jews of Europe.

I decided to write you the letters now, because I must leave Brody now, and at night I return as a thief or murderer, when nobody sees me. After all I am a person condemned to death, running away from jail and hiding wherever permitted, and everyone who meets him is allowed to kill him, without being punished. I am forced to walk home since I left there some objects of mine with Sascha and with other friends. I will take and sell them, if they agree to return them to me. They may want to inherit me and hand me over to the regime, and then I'm gone. And if they return something to me, I will be able to exist for a certain amount of time. My way is strewn with dangers. It is ninety-nine percent certain that I am going towards death, and only one-percent possibility of staying alive, but I have no other alternative. Perhaps I will manage to meet partisans located in our forests. This is the best way out for me. As for my remaining alive until today, I must thank the friend who is forwarding you my letter. He saved me like a most loyal brother. I would have to be grateful to him for my entire life. And if I don't stay alive, you thank him, because he frequently endangered his life for my sake. If only [the war] would go on for a short time, he could still advise, but to my sorrow the war must go on another year, and in order to live another year, I need a lot of money. If I had money, I would be rescued.

I am ending the letter. I related everything briefly, according to my ability. There is not even one-percent of what we went through in this letter — I wrote the leaves — and my eyes —

The letter was written by Melech Goldenberg and sent to a relative in the United States by a Christian friend. The relative forwarded the letter to Melech's sister in Israel.

Letter 20

My Dear Brother-in-law,

Don't feel bad about the prohibition of transferring food packages, I still have enough of a stock of staples, which I won't be using anyhow. You should know, that the Warsaw Ghetto is gradually being liquidated, and these days are the last days of my life. They are already cleansing [from Jews] Novolifia St., and I am expecting to be deported to Treblinka at any moment. Perhaps it is better like this, than tortures without any chance, the end should come and be done with. Do you hear, Pesach! This is my last letter to you! Be well, for eternity, forever and ever.

Yours
Chana

◆ ◆ ◆

To My Friend, My Beloved Pesach!

The end of the destruction that we've been expecting has started, we are now face to face with reality. The ghetto in Warsaw is being liquidated. Accordingly we see that the Jews of Warsaw have pushed off any illusion about their destiny, and that the only goal is the annihilation of Judaism. This awareness has caused those remaining to integrate in unity about an idea and sacred goal: That is an uprising against the Nazi beast. If we are condemned to die, at least it should be with respect.

For this purpose, a fighting organization was established in the ghetto. Many of the members of the printing worker's union are in it, with Chairman Lazar Sklar at the head. I advise you to behave likewise also in Meichov. Probably by you, it won't be feasible since the Jews have not yet reached the necessary awareness. More recent news to tell you: Chierniakov committed suicide.

One clear day, we received news from our friends outside of the ghetto that the German murderers are scheming against the Jews of Warsaw. We decided to hinder the implementation of the plan. When Chierniakov returned from the Gestapo to the Judenrat offices, three members armed with pistols entered. We closed the door and with drawn pistols we said to him: "We know that you just came back from the Gestapo, that you received an order to provide ten thousand Jews daily to the deportation square and send them to Treblinki for annihilation."

"Therefore we are presenting you with a condition and warning: either you refuse to carry out the order or we shoot you on the spot." After reflecting for a few minutes, he requested a delay until the next day to give an answer. And the answer was indeed given!!! The next day we were informed about his death at his own hands. Regarding Chierniakov's death, specific elements wanted to make him into a national hero, but we know that Chierniakov and heroism are an oxymoron. Yes, he was a hero compared to Jews who went like sheep to the slaughter, but he served the Germans faithfully. It is possible that during his last moments, he was convinced of his bitter mistake, and perhaps he understood, indeed late, that after implementing the Germans' mission, his fate would be like that of the rest of the Jews.

[Mottl Bornstein]

Pesach Bezradki received these two letters on the same day.

Letter 21

Magdeburg, June 27, 1942

My Dear Arno,

The last letter that I received from you was from November 1940. It was a letter to Mother on the occasion of her birthday and it arrived at the right time. Mother was very pleased with the sincere words that you found for her, and we were all happy together with her. And indeed there is no better mother than her on this earth, a mother like you had, and many tears flowed because of you. But Mother is also a very courageous woman, even today. The aches and suffering that Mother has known until this very day have earned her the name "one full of pain" already a long time ago. But Mother is always prepared to fight off whatever makes her tired, and time after time she grabs hold of herself in order to cope with life, a shining example of being devoted to duty and of the power of action. Mother has been working for nearly two years at the sack factory of Max Behr. Two months ago she had an accident. She fell in such an unfortunate way that she was confined to bed for seven weeks, and as of now she hasn't yet recuperated. But we are hoping that soon all will work out. As I've already told you at the beginning of my letter, your last letter was from November 1940. We are therefore without any news from you for a year and a half, despite the fact that America joined the war only a year later. We have no explanation for your silence. We can't assume that it's because of your negligence. But if this was the reason, despite all, we forgive you at this time.

I do not know when this letter will reach you. Perhaps the events of the war brought you also to strange lands. It just might, might be that you must actively participate in the war. And you will learn to recognize the atrocities of war, that are the same atrocities everywhere, here or there, with supposedly cultured nations or uncivilized nations — they have their own reasons for waging wars. I am writing you this letter in a difficult hour. Because I must assume that it will be the last one in our lives. We do not want to complain about this, my dear son, but to carry on with dignity that which fate has destined for us. I like to imagine that we bore our life with dignity, and we would like, if it won't be possible otherwise, to accept death like this.

Yes, perhaps we should thank Providence for providing us with so many more years. We were able to go on with life without a doubt, while hundreds of thousands of suffering brothers have long ago come to a bitter and hasty end. Perhaps it will calm you to hear the truth, that during all the long years that you're not with us, we haven't suffered from any distress. We always had work and bread to eat, and we lived without any disturbance. The year 1942 drew a finish line here also. The possibilities of life here have been limited greatly by countless edicts and laws, and you cannot take one step without bumping into a mine. Work is becoming more difficult for us because of the countless illogical prohibitions, like traveling on the electric tram to work, no matter how far it is. The most modest form of relaxation is impossible, because it is forbidden for us to tread on lawns and to visit the cinema. Not to mention the matter of nutrition. Now, as a final event, deportation to Poland awaits us, there we'll find our graves. But you must know, that also at this time, we are always with you in spirit. I was always very happy when I heard from you, during your childhood years, that your father is your best friend. We would go out to walk in the beautiful forests near Moser, and you would grasp my coat sleeve tightly. Now eight years have passed since those times! As difficult as it is for us to part from you, we are not sorry that we sent you beyond the great lake. Because

145

thanks to this, you escaped different things here. Today you are 21 years old and have become a man. Therefore, bear your destiny and cope with it like a man! Don't let the fact that destiny has harshly hurt your dear ones demoralize you. Because mankind as a whole was hurt and beaten severely! Fight and be happy at heart. Don't think that by doing this you are doing an injustice to your dear ones. You can be sure that with us, despite the suffering, happiness hasn't disappeared. Your dear sister takes care of this. While you were still under our protection, you were a good boy, and you were worthy of all of our love. You had an honest and decent nature. And we hope that you didn't change in this way. Stay decent in deed and in spirit! Stay away from all filth, whatever its color! Learn well and always earn your bread! Today a wave of hatred against Germany is going through the world. Don't allow this wave of hatred to sweep you away. Because we are not the only ones decreed to suffer! Also millions of good Germans had bad fate. If you swim with this wave of hatred against Germany, you will thus hurt your parents' friends, who kept up friendships with us until this very day, willingly risking to seriously endanger themselves. You forever owe thanks to my dear friend, Father Radka and his family, from whom you will receive this letter and some other things. You also mustn't forget Paul and Aunt Lizchen. They all donated contributions to make our lives more bearable. And I give you another good piece of advice: Be a good citizen in your country, but don't get involved with politics. I am today of the opinion that Jews who are involved in politics are the gravediggers of their people. I have never greatly considered the religion of letters. Nevertheless I think that there is nothing that happens by coincidence, that behind everything that happens, deep meaning is concealed, and the shortsighted cannot observe it. Our destiny, therefore, was also given to us already in the cradle. We cannot dodge this destiny, no matter how much we fight it. We must go along the path that was charted until its end.

Between us, my dear son, lands and wide oceans are sprawled out. Perhaps we will never see each other again. But with all my spirit I hug you and place my hand on your head and offer you from afar a father's blessing, the blessing that our forefathers have blessed their children long ago: "May God bless you and safeguard you. May God illuminate His countenance for you and be gracious to you. May God lift His countenance to you and establish peace for you." Amen.

With love and loyalty,
Your father Julius Joseph

Mother will yet write you separately. The attached curl is Mother's, I cut it in the year 1919.

Letter 22

To Mrs. Spira Hilda, Sydney Australia
From Annie Shado, Vienna, 22 Wallensteinstrasse
September 15, 1941
To My Dear Children!
Beloved Hildush from the depths of my heart!

Using caution which is perhaps overdone, Mother and I have decided, if this is God's will, that if we don't reach a situation when we can see you again, then we will part from you in this way. We are living in the stormiest of all times, and we don't know what each day brings. Therefore, my dear Hildush, I am informing you that I have left our property with Gertel's mother, with the Shen family and Mrs. Yelenik, and also with the last boss of Hans, and with the daughter-in-law of Aunt Johanna (Otto's wife). A small remainder of our savings is in my account in Bank Landerbank A.G.

I reminisce with a heavy heart of the time that you were still with us. My dear Hildush, you have always been a good daughter to your parents. May the Lord reward you for this and give you happiness. Love each other as you have seen us do, until your last breath.

Always remember that the relationship between the husband, wife and child is the deepest relationship on earth. May it be that God will allow us to see each other soon.

I bless you, kiss you and hug you warmly.

Your loving father,
Fredric

◆ ◆ ◆

To the Unique, Dear and Kind Hilda,
And to Dear and Kind Hans,

I am writing this letter with a heavy heart, in the event that Providence beckons us and we will not see each other again, Heaven forbid. I would like to part from you, my kind and dear children. I do not have to emphasize, beloved Hilda, that for me — you were everything, my joy and life!

I am thankful, my dear Hilda, for all of your love. And thank you too, dear Hans. Continue to be pleasant and kind to my beloved daughter. Gertel's brother or Fraulein Rosa will collect the things from Mr. P. and send them to you at a proper time.

Remain healthy and happy!

God, the Almighty, will protect and guard you, and shine His countenance upon you.

Hugging and kissing you warmly,

Mother

Letter 23

The C.M.C. Military Prison
February 21, 1942
My Dears,

I am living the last moments of my life, a short life but quite stormy. You've done everything for me; and all I've caused you was trouble, with the height of it ending in tragedy for you. Before my death, I regret one thing only — that I did not live to reach the day that perhaps I could have been useful to you. And I stick to my belief that a friend in need is a friend indeed.

If there is anyone who interprets my death as a heroic act — I tell you this: We have no need for heroes — specifically that —. It's strange that I'm the one who is encouraging you, but I do this because I know you so well. I myself find comfort in the thought that you will take care of our parents as necessary. Help them! This is my last cry. Listen, these are the last words of one who is about to die! For them it is small comfort, it is necessary to put an end to the reliance with which they lived until now. Sell all my belongings and send the money home, and if it's possible — bring them to you. I trust you, please don't disappoint me. Call your first child Dan, if it's a boy, and if it's a girl — Francesca.

Copy this letter and send it to Buzau, etc. The letter is for everyone — cousins, grandparents, etc.

Dear Parents and Sister,

Hope! Courage! Courage! And again courage! These are my only words, and they say more than enough.

In my last letter I wrote you: "I would be happy if I knew that you were in good health. Take care of yourselves, and as such you give me comfort."

Health to all of you and ... long life

[Adolph] Michaelovitch

Letter 24

My Dear Avraham,

Excuse me for my generally behaving with everyone in such an idiotic way, without leaving any money. I will transfer it to you — but through someone. Dear Avraham and Maika [Meir], don't mourn. To our sorrow — fate wanted it like this. I must go the same way as my most beloved. I request of you, take care of my beloved children, find out about Della, is she still asleep, and kiss her thousands of times from me. Be well and take care of my orphaned children, I am going to eternal rest.

Mother and wife,
Frieda

I sent 200 Zloty via Buksdrei. Come to the gate, I will give you the —.

The letter was written in pencil on both sides of a paper note, dated March 16-17, 1943 in the city of Borislav, in the place used as a assembling place (the Coliseum cinema hall) before the execution of some 600 Jews in the "sixth action." The letter was given to Avraham Chamaides by one of the Jewish policemen guarding the place.

Letter 25

Plonsk, December 14 1942

Our Rozhinka, dearest of all,

You see, we thought that we would stay until Friday, but to our regret, today is already our last evening. All attempts to move in with you were unsuccessful, and there is no time at all for this now. In this situation we have to approve and accept everything with love. Yes, my one and only, only God knows whether we will see each other again. After all, we live in hope that we will see each other again. Already tomorrow we are going to the unknown, with complete awareness and tranquility. If we are sentenced to live — that is good, and if not — what a pity! We have already lost that which is most dear and important to us, so what can give us comfort. Our only wish was to see you again, our one and only, the most dear. Blessings to you, our dearest of all. I know that it is hard for you to recognize the fact that you have already lost us, but what can we do! This is what fate wanted and this is what must be. I am parting from you, holding you tight near my heart. If only we see each other again.

I love you with all my heart and miss you,

Salla

Try to be only with Joseph. It is nearly certain that the epidemic will start by you too, that is why I think that it will be better with him. Our thoughts are always in your direction, without stop, our most dear, little and only sister. Regards to Joseph and the Kirshenbaum gentlemen.

◆ ◆ ◆

Our Rozhinka, dearest of all,

It's apparent to us that we are already writing the last postcard. On Wednesday, at five dawn, everyone is moving. Spread out before us is our modest and prepared baggage, and the railway cars already await us in the station. Just the thought that we will sleep at home this one single night, and that tomorrow we are going to wander the world, makes the soul sad. Who knows where destiny will bring us, it is difficult to describe our life, what awaits us and what will be. So, Rozhinka, our dearest of all, we are therefore parting from you in a heartfelt way. Prevail and don't despair. Wherever we will be, our thoughts will always be with you, our dearest of all. Rozhinka, if only we would have one more time to see you, our most dearest of all, the one and only. What else is left for us after the loss of our dearest ones. Be well, our one and only, let us believe that we will live and we will still meet. I kiss you heartily and hold you tight near my heart,

Loving you,
Dina

Letter 26

Dear Leib [Frankfurter],

My last words, as you see. Probably my destiny has been determined, I have no way out. I decided this evening to report to the Gestapo. My beloved Leib, if you ever have the chance to see Zusha, tell her that I so wanted to live, but it didn't work out for me. And I've already stopped having an interest in it. I thought that for a few days I would be able to meet you and talk but I don't even have this luck. Others have greater luck. Leib, I have with me a few thousand golden coins, and also a decent fountain pen, and other things. They're not necessary for me. Write me if you're interested. I will leave them here for you. They will take them from me anyway. Today I am sorry that I didn't go to die with everyone. Because dying alone is much harder. I sincerely wish health to Anya, keep on going, and request from God that I will have an easy death. I wait for an immediate answer regarding the money.

Mina [Hibshman]

Letter 27

November 4, 1941
My Dear Clara,

I sent you a postcard yesterday that will cause you grief you when you recieve it.

I am writing you now due to this gentleman's good intentions, and request that you don't tell Mother the truth because it's awful, and I don't want the issue to affect her health, which is frail anyhow.

Dear sister, for some days already a horrible danger hovers over us. We are about to be sent on foot to the Ukraine ("in order to settle us there"... that's what they say). You can imagine our situation, when one must walk this route by foot, the days are so cold, with a little boy and with items that can be taken, that is, only food items for the way.

We were supposed to be sent in groups of about 2,500 people so that within four days nobody would remain here. The first group left yesterday, among them Rosa with the children. May God protect them. Yesterday our committee sent a representative and our departure was delayed for the time being for 24 hours, and we hope that it will be delayed another six months, that is, until the spring. At 6:00 we will receive the final answer and you can imagine our panic. Perhaps this delay will also bring back the group that was sent.

I request, my dear sister, answer me through this gentleman, perhaps he will still find us here, and perhaps these will be the last things that I will get from you.

My dear, the articles and money that you sent me helped me a lot and came at the right time. From the wool that you sent me, I made a thick scarf (triple knit) for the neck of Willush [Willie, Ida's 3 year-old son] because who knows how many days we'll be en route. With God's help, there should at least be fine weather. I request not to spread this news so that you don't have 'un-pleasantries' and so that harm won't come to this person with good intentions.

My dear, I request that you take care of Mother, because you are the only one that she has. Never do what we have done: Never part with her. How I envy you for the happiness that you have in being close to her. You remember that I used to accuse you of being a coward, of not being active enough, that a person must try to struggle in order to exist.

I'm not sorry about a thing, this is the life of man. The only thing that I'm sorry for is that my eyes will never ever see you again. I suffer plenty. Hope would beat within me that we would still see each other, but I have lost everything now. One more time, if only I live to see you one more time again, and then let the worst happen.

Adieu my dear, my dear Mother, good Father. You were the first ray of sun that warmed up my life. I didn't know how to protect this ray (my life), I left without turning back my head. I was too full of (vain) hope for the future to understand that I'm leaving happiness never to be found again.

You remember, my dear sister, that I felt confused during the farewell at home, when I said to you (in anger), "Why are you crying? After all I'm not going to die." Forgive me, my dear, I was foolish. I was lightheaded. I believed that "whatever flies, you eat." It seems that I was too young, so what use is there of apology?

I'm very sorry that I didn't understand when we parted the importance of the moment, that I didn't look at you enough to engrave your image deeply in my memory, to hug you strongly and not let go of you. Now in vain I turn my head, with no hope, because fate has struck our lives a horrible cruel blow, and as much as I try to go near you, we are harshly dragged and drawn away from each other.

I would very much want to be at your side (after all, we were already so close, we managed to get close), to lie at your feet, tired from the such severe hardships, and to find a resting-place and never part from you again.

I would lie a lot at night with open eyes and reconstruct in my imagination the moment of the renewed meeting with you. I would get drunk from this thought. I would finish it and again begin to daydream.

Now I don't hope for anything, God does not want us to meet again; it seems that I've sinned a lot.

Farewell, my dear sister, live in joy and raise your children in happiness and health. Thousands of kisses on their sweet eyes. Does Revelina [Clara's firstborn daughter] still remember me? If only it would be and with God's help you will shortly see Karol [the brother-in-law] and live happily without concerns and sufferings. Kisses to Father and Mother, that they should be well and live for better tidings.

Vili and Doba [the sisters of Ida and Clara] give you thousands of kisses and part from you warmly. Warm regards.

Clara, answer me please.

Yours forever, thinking about you
Ida [Goldisch]

PS My dear Clara, this is the second day that our departure was delayed for 24 hours. So there is hope for our rescue. So don't torment yourself over the things that I've written.

Ida, her 3-year-old son Willie and her sister Doba were deported marching to the Ukraine. The son froze from the cold during the journey and after a few days Ida got sick and died. Doba fled from the deportation convoy and was saved.

Letter 28

My Dear Parents!

If only the sky were paper and the world ink, I wouldn't be capable of describing to you my suffering and all that I see around me.

The camp is situated in a forest clearing. Already early in the morning they take us out to work in the forest. The soles of my feet are bleeding, because they took my shoes from me. We work all day, with hardly any food, and at night we sleep on the ground (they also took our coats from us). Every night drunken soldiers come and beat us with wooden sticks, and my body is already black from bloodstains under the skin and it looks like a piece of charred wood. Sometimes they toss us some uncooked carrots, or beets, and this is shameful and disgraceful: here fists fly in order to grab a little piece or a small leaf. The day before yesterday two boys escaped, so they lined us up in a row, and every fifth one in the line was shot to death. I was not the fifth but I know that I will not leave here alive. I part from you, dear Mother, dear Father, dear brothers, and I cry...

[Chaim]

Letter 29

Budapest, October 16, 1944

My dear brother,

Hello! Remember the conversation that night, I felt as one with you. If I had known that your life would end, I would continue living with half a body and half a soul. And you said that if I die, you would kill yourself.

Remember what I said to you; if you live — I would live within you.

I would like to continue my life with you and our family. Plans, ambitions and hopes are before my eyes. I yearn for the unknown. I would like to know, to live, to see, to do, to love... but now it is all over.

The Jews in the city have all vanished from the streets. There is no way to escape. Tonight, or at the latest tomorrow, will be our turn. At the age of 17, I am forced to confront certain death. There is no way to escape. We thought we would be the exception, but destiny does not allow for any exceptions. I have always sensed death's pull when I wrote to you in the past. I think that I've also felt that I would die young. It seems that destiny has cursed each one of us.

After Yisrael [the older brother, aged 19] came my turn, with Father, Mother and Suraleh [the sister] (I hope that you will survive). Farewell and forgive me if I've ever hurt you (for the first time, I sense tears in my eyes. I'm careful not to cry because of the presence of others). Because I loved you and I see you smiling (the vein in your forehead swells) when you think, when you eat, smoke, sleep, and I feel great tenderness, great love — and my eyes fill up with tears.

Farewell, live in happiness, all the best to you, my dear brother, much luck, love and happiness. Don't cry (I felt so bad when I heard you cry that night). Remember me fondly, and if another world exists (I've spoken to you so much about this — and now I will know! My song "What will happen to me?" pops in my head… I've felt it already then), I will pray that God help you in whatever you do.

Farewell my dear, my one and only brother! If you are interested in knowing the mood, I will try to describe it and our situation at home. The tragedy began yesterday, in the evening. At night, Jews that live in buildings 54 and 64 were already taken away. Puddles of blood were on the sidewalk, but in the morning it was cleaned. I was awake all night. R.J. and K.S. were here. Poor R.J. could hardly stand on his feet, he was so frightened. At first we hoped that the police and army would protect us, but after the first telephone call we understood everything. The morning ascended slowly, but the events of the day changed our situation into a hopeless one. K.S. arrived at six. He was about to faint after he fought four Nazis who beat him roughly. He barely managed to escape while alive, he walked and stumbled and trembled, and he could hardly speak after what he experienced and saw. I am writing quickly, who knows whether I will have time to complete it.

K.S. suggested taking Suraleh to a safe place. She jumped with joy and wanted to go immediately. But Mother stopped her and in a calm voice said that she's not ready to let her go since the Nazis are liable to capture them in the street. Suraleh cried and was hysterical. She wanted to go.

———

[Pinchas'l Eisner]

Five days after the letter was written, Pinchas'l was taken to Csomad in the Budapest region. From there he was transported with 17 more Jews to the nearby forest. They were forced to dig a large pit, they were told to undress and they were shot in the grave that they themselves dug. Mordechai, the brother, was imprisoned in a labor camp and found the letter when he returned home, after Budapest was liberated from the Nazis.

Letter 30

Dear Hilda,

We are at the train station. A kind train worker enables me to send these following lines. My last wish: Take care of my children and Mother. We were punished in a cruel way and suffer harshly, but we don't know for what. Goodbye. It's impossible to say: see you again.

From the bottom of my heart

Regga

◆ ◆ ◆

My Dear,

In a few minutes, we will leave the train station and travel to eternity. Watch over Mother. My husband and I were given the chance to remain, because we work, but our little son must [go] and we don't want to let him go alone on his last way and we're going together to death. We have made peace with our fate.

◆ ◆ ◆

During the night our hairs turned white, pray to God that He spare you this thing that we've experienced. This is the last message from us…

The writer and the addressees are sisters. The second letter arrived a day after the first letter, and the third came three days later from the oldest sister in Czestochowa.

Letter 31

Sambor, the ghetto, May 24, 1943
Beloved Manya,

I am struggling to focus my thoughts to write you a few more parting words.

Beloved Manya,

I will write you more or less about the course of my life, and what has happened to me during the days of the Germans. During the German occupation, our entire family was concentrated in one place. Our brothers didn't go to the front. During the first days there were awful pogroms. No writer has the strength to describe them. All this continued for a few days. We were happy that we remained alive... During the first action, on August 4, 1942, none of us was yet hurt. Imagine to yourself, they captured three thousand five hundred people and I have no strength to describe the suffering that they went through until they were murdered.

The second action began on October 17, 1942. Then the[bitter]cup was passed to us as well, and we were struck with a severe blow. Our most beloved ones were taken from us: Avramak and Laizer. During the first days we lived with the hope that our brothers would write us or return. You must be wondering why they were taken and not us. I will explain this to you.

In the first action, some people who worked were released. Therefore, immediately after the action, everyone tried to get a job since they reasoned that workers would not be taken away. Our brothers also went to work and were sure that they would not be touched, but this was actually to their detriment. Until this day, we live with hope that they may still be alive.

Manya, when you read this you will perhaps understand what it means to be fearful of the night and fearful of the day, and to live under heavy stress day and night. Also we've tried overcoming this awful blow and hope for a better tomorrow, even though our most beloved ones were taken from us. And when our lives were a mix of hope, fear and suffering, the third action, conducted purely by the Jewish militia, came on October 22, 1942, and in this one Mother was taken away from us. But thank God that they rescued her and hid her in the home of Mrs. Zawabska for a week. I will never forget her for this. Later on preparations started for establishing the ghetto. People were walking about like shadows, going into the ghetto had the image of entering a death trap.

Many people left the city based on Aryan papers and a few hid in Polish homes. We were powerless and we decided to enter the ghetto. On November 30, 1942 we walked to the ghetto.

After we stayed in the ghetto for two weeks, an action took place. But a miracle occured, the action was stopped and those that were caught were released. Only four hundred Jews remained in detention and some of them were released for payment.

A glimmer of hope of rescue, putting an end to the horrible suffering, was awakened in us anew. A feeling of change for the better started to nestle in the hearts of the Jews and they started to come out of hiding. So two months passed by when they supposedly let us live. But our illusions were quickly proven wrong. In February 1943, an action took place in which 450 people were captured, transported to Radlowice and brutally murdered.

Again people started to go about at their wit's end, because we didn't know what was liable to happen to us at any moment.

A few more days of quiet passed, good news arrived

from the front, and we thought that soon an end would come to our terrible suffering. The Jews started going back to work. I and my sister-in-law worked in the sewing workshop and again the hope that we would be saved began to nestle within us. But to our sorrow, our suffering increased.

Imagine to yourself, Manya, that an action took place again in April 1943 and 1,200 Jews were caught, from whom some two hundred and fifty were released. They held them all in a prison and then they were murdered in the Jewish cemetery and they all lie in a common grave, resembling flowerbeds set up for sowing in the spring.

Human beings?! Is it at all possible to describe such awful acts of humans to humans! I think that there would not be enough paper to describe these atrocities.

We were saved this time, and that is how we went again through six weeks full of tension and fear, and days and nights full of distress and panic. Six weeks later there was an action again and 750 Jews were caught. They didn't murder them in Sambor but they transported them in the direction of Lvov.

After this action, too, we remained alive, thank God. But to our sorrow, we are not able to comfort ourselves with the fact that we belong to this remnant that stayed alive. We have become living corpses. We are certain that this cruel hand has no limits and will not turn away from hurting us too. Now they already left us no hope, and they talk of liquidating the ghetto not only in Sambor but also in other cities, and there is no spring board for us to escape. Only a genuine miracle may be able to save us.

My most beloved of all Manya,

Since we already expect and sense the impending footsteps of death, I've chosen some photographs of mine and I am writing you a farewell letter. Don't think that we are full of despair, we must and we force ourselves to make peace with our fate. But I have no strength to describe to you our moments when our lives don't depend on us anymore. If you see death in front of you, then life appears to you as a precious treasure, that to your sorrow, you are powerless to get hold of.

Manya, don't think that we suffered from hunger during the war. Hunger wasn't the main reason for our suffering, our slow dying has tortured us many times more.

Manya, it is clear to me that when you receive this letter it will cause you terrible pain, which you may not overcome. Despite this I write you these words to give myself relief. You have always tried to do good with me, therefore I wish to part from you.

People are unable to understand us, because they don't have the ability to imagine to themselves human beings that are nothing but living corpses.

There is no rescue at hand because we are like a bird in a cage. If some miracle doesn't happen, we are all gone. I give this letter and photographs to Mrs. Zawabska and she will give you them after the war. If you receive the letter send it to Fruma.

Manya! I bless you heartily and kiss you. Wishes and kisses to your husband and children. I wish them great happiness, to Fruma and everyone.

Don't cry bitterly, we were not the first, what happened to everyone will happen to us. If only it should never happens to you, what happened to us. I kiss you for the one-hundredth time.

Faige [Krauss]

◆ ◆ ◆

Sambor, May 24, 1943

Fruma, the Most Beloved One!

Since I wrote to Manya about everything that happened to us during the German regime, it is unnecessary to write twice about what a person is like as he confronts death. Imagine to yourself how many Jews there were in Sambor, in Turka and its surroundings, in Dobromil and Felshtyn — they were all concentrated in Sambor. Perhaps we remained some one thousand people, a small handful from the cities, towns and villages that no longer have a living Jew in them. And this small handful remains without any way out...

My mother and I bless you all warmly and kiss all the relatives and acquaintances. This is the last time that we are in touch with you. We will not see each other again because death is in our midst. At any moment, the fuse of our life is likely to be cut off.

Don't forget us!

Dear Frumcha and Manya, we are parting from you forever.

Mother and Faige

Letter 32

A farewell wish before death from Fanya and from all members of the family. Our dear ones! I am writing this letter before my death, but I don't know exactly the day that I and my relatives will be killed, only because we're Jews. All of our Jewish brothers and sisters were murdered and died a despicable death at the hands of the murderers... I don't know who remained alive from our family and who will have the honor to read my letter and my proud wish before death to all of my beloved and dear ones tortured at the hands of the murderers. Dear Chayaleh! Dear Monuska! It is possible that you will remain alive. Live with wealth and happiness. We are all marching proudly towards death, since this is our fate. As far as we know, Blyuma perished already with her whole family. I cannot continue writing. All of the relatives are crying and weeping over themselves. I am leaving the letter with the best of our friends, who has done so much good for us until now.

Yours Fanya [Barbakov] and the whole family

We are all lying in one pit. We are definitely sure that you will all know the spot of our burial. Mother and Father can hardly hold out. My hand trembles and it is hard for me to finish writing. I am proud that I am a Jewess. I am dying for my people. I have not told a soul that I'm writing a letter before our death. But!... How I have the desire to live and reach some good in life. But all is already gone... Goodbye. Your relative Fanya in the name of everybody: Father, Mother, Sima, Sonia, Zusia, Rasya Hatza and in the name of Zeldaleh the infant, who doesn't yet understand a thing.

Druya

In the concentration camp, before we will be murdered by shooting, in hiding.

Tuesday, 4 a.m., June 16, 1942

Farewell to all.

Yours Fanya

God is just and His judgement is just. We have sinned. Our meager property is concealed at home. But we have lost our lives. It is all finished. Brothers from all countries, take revenge for us. We are being led like sheep to the slaughter.

Fanya

Fanya was 19-years-old when she died.

Letter 33

Dear Mundak,

I didn't think of leaving you this letter, but Mother doesn't let up, insisting that I write a few lines. I know that it will cause you extra pain, because our situation is so awful, and when you hear this you will shed more than one tear. Back then, at the time of our parting, I didn't believe that something like this would happen to us, and instead of receiving you with a greeting, we say farewell to you forever. The situation has no way out, we are all condemned to death (the Jews, of course), except that we don't know when the death verdict will be carried out, and it's anticipated at any hour and moment. The persecution continues non-stop, and we are pushed to the grave in pace and by force, also those who are still alive, literally speaking. Do you have an idea how terrible it is, to live and know that at any moment I and all my precious ones are expecting this? And we so much want to live — and see you. Not long ago, we got regards from you, and we were so happy! It must certainly be difficult for you to imagine that we couldn't find any solution whatsoever, but to our sorrow we didn't find a way! Only friends, non-Jews, could help, and as you know, everyone abandoned us in troubled times, and everyone remains indifferent. Indeed, if God has abandoned us, what can we say and speak of friends, who would endanger themselves when helping. That's the thing, we cannot delude our souls, and we wait our turn which will come, for death which will redeem us from these moral tortures. To be eyewitnesses daily to this mass tragedy, to see children yanked from their parents' arms, who run about the streets with no roof over their head; naked, and barefoot and weakened from hunger, who have seen before their eyes a father and mother murdered, or parents who don't know where their children have disappeared to, and they are desperate and insane with worry. The trains that transport thousands of Jews to their eternal resting place, and the few that jump off the railroad cars in order to save their lives and they're shot on the spot. All this causes us to be insane and we begin wondering if our head works like it should and if our mind is lucid at all, and even those of us who are strong collapse in their spirit.

As you know, our father was a person full of vigor and energy, an optimist who saw the entire world through rose-tinted glasses, and now nothing is left of all these traits. He has become so negligent and tired in his willpower, and he lost any desire to live, and he has wishes to die: However, the misfortunate one, he must work hard because of the increase in expenses, and at times we don't eat enough to satisfy us. Indeed, we are not the exception, the [bitter] cup was passed to all. And Mother has claims on God, that He is not doing a miracle, and she always complains about Him that He shocks with His afflictions. And she cries for you lest she won't live to see you again, and she cries for Zunya and wants to know what will happen to him? And this goes on and on, again and again. And also Zunya suffers terribly, he is very annoyed, but he is inanimate as a stone, too proud to complain in vain, and by nature he is introverted. He is so handsome and kind; if only you saw how he works and every penny of his wages he hands over to Mother. My heart is torn and broken from grief when I look at him, so young, talented and good hearted, and it all has to go down the drain. I'm amazed at myself that my heart doesn't explode in grief. And I, with very jittery nerves, I show the most restraint of all, I am more immune to the suffering, since I've already suffered a lot in my life, and death doesn't scare me so much. As it were, every stone will cry out and every blade of grass will murmur, but enough of all this. Most important is this that I tell you — that if we die, and

171

it seems inevitable — I would at least want that you take everything, so that the labor of so many years should not be lost. I leave for you all of the registration and marriage documents of our parents, that may be useful for you, and also a list of various items that I'm placing with acquaintances, and also your clothes which most surely are necessary for you. And if God helps, when I plead before Him, I will notify you in detail to whom I assign this mission.

Besides this I don't have what to add, I part from you with deep grief and my aching heart. I wish for you that fate will show kindness towards you and that our suffering will redeem you from all wickedness, and if, Heaven forbid, you don't find us, don't despair, show restraint and make an effort to live in tranquility. I advise you to sell everything and go far away from this cursed place.

Farewell and don't continue worrying, since, after all, time heals all wounds of the heart, and also your aches will lessen in the course of years.

And a heartfelt wish to you
Genya

The letter was sent in the last days before the annihilation of the Jews of Zholkiev, probably in April 1943. It was sent from Genya to her brother Mundak Lainer, who was taken to the Red Army. Genya was sure that he would stay alive and she therefore left the letter with the maid of the teacher, Teichman. In the past, this maid had worked for the Lainer family. After the liberation, the maid handed over the letter to the Lainer brothers, Mundak and Ziggy, who returned to Zholkiev.

Letter 34

The Muchawka Camp, December 26, 1942
My Dear Brothers!

It is extremely hard to write in this situation, with the feeling that any day I might lose my life to the German murderers.

I am going to die aware that you, my dear brothers, were saved from my bitter fate, and it is very possible that all of the agonies that I suffered here, I suffered on your behalf, too.

Remember after the war — avenge your sister's death, who wasn't privileged in her lifetime to see you again.

Your father died a natural death in Tluste, on the 28th of MarCheshvan 1942.

This letter will be sent to you by my friend, who fortunately stayed alive.

Come and sell your fields. Be happy and don't forget this one condemned to die when she was nineteen years old.

Be well.
Regards from Mother.

Devorah [Dohl]

Letter 35

Berlin, March 25, 1939
The night after Passover ended

"For it shall endure and your hope will not be cut off." (Proverbs, 23, 18)

We will see each other in our Land,

Mother

◆ ◆ ◆

Berlin, April 25, 1939

— And now, my dear daughter, I must tell you about a most desperate matter.

Last Tuesday I was invited to come to the Palestinian Bureau [the Immigration Bureau] and there Mr. Kopadlovski told me in a most explicit way, that we have no chance of receiving a certificate for Palestine. The whole matter was totally cancelled. The same thing that happened to us happened to all those that were expecting to receive certificates in Antwerp. [There were Jews in Antwerp, Belgium who didn't want to immigrate to the Land of Israel, and therefore they sold their certificates to those in Germany who were interested.] And so a dream came to an end.

I was stunned. I couldn't control myself and I burst out in bitter crying on the spot. Mr. Kopadlovski didn't know what to do with me. I slowly, slowly calmed down and parted from him. It seemed like the world stood still. I never thought this would happen; and this, after a nerve-wracking wait of about seven months, until September 1938, and after we invested our very last pennies in this. My daughter, all I can tell you is that I felt as if I was empty inside.

I immediately went up to the second floor, where

Recha Freier received people [Recha was a friend of the writer during her youth]. After waiting in the hallway for about an hour, Recha took me in for a talk. She listened to me, calmed me down and thought about what to do. Finally she suggested that I apply to the Aliyah Bet. I didn't know where the office was. I found out and got an appointment for Friday. The aged Dr. Ludwig, 70 years-old, received me there and with pleasant words he announced: "It cannot be done." I stood like a fossil. He wanted to spare the answer to my question "Why?" but I insisted and he briefly answered me: "Your husband is simply too old." At that moment, I was so angry that I wanted to slap the man, despite his age.

I left his room and again went up to Recha Freier since she had requested that I tell her what happened, but Recha was abroad for urgent Youth Aliyah matters. They suggested that I send her a letter which she would receive the following day. I went down the steps disappointed. I stopped, thought and decided to write the letter anyhow.

"My dear Recha, they rejected me. They said my husband was too old. But he is only 52. I anticipate your advice. Goodbye and best wishes."

Now I must wait about a week for a response.

But my child, what can I tell you, our fate is signed and sealed.

For days I've cried, day and night. Even Father had tears in his eyes from so much despair.

Our only hope and dream was to be in our Land together with our children, even if the conditions there are very strenuous. Now there is no choice, despite the fact that I'm a veteran and sworn Zionist, I must now try and get to Shanghai. From there I will never get to you. Because even if your brother Tzvi manages in the distant future to demand for us a certificate, I would not be able to raise the necessary funds to travel such a long route to Palestine.

Father is behaving towards me in a most dignified and noble way. He is pleasant to me and says gently: "My dear, don't be so sad lest you get sick." Since our money is running out and we won't even have enough for travel fares, I've decided to go to wherever we can possibly get to. My request is only that, your little nine-year-old sister will be able to reach London, to safe shores before that. We don't want to endanger her young life in wandering to insecure places; if something happens to us, such a little girl will remain alone in a strange place. But if she is in London, taking care of her will be a sacred duty assigned to you and your older brother.

It is hard for you, as a young person, to understand how heavy is our heart and how sad we are, for myself and dear Father. But you too can probably feel that we have a reason for total despair. Now Father is going around to travel agencies to check if we can reserve some voyage, wherever and whenever. Everything is already booked for months. We would be ready also to try and get to England as a couple of servants, because we can keep on going there until the day that we can come to the Land, but we have no idea how to go about this. Perhaps you can find out and help us.

Be well, my daughter, and write soon and in detail, because we would like to know all about your activities. You can react openly to this letter. Father knows that I told you everything; but in order to prevent him from getting agitated again, I will send the letter without him adding his section.

Stay well, my daughter, and never forget your parents.

With deep love,
Mother

The writer and her husband were deported to Theresienstadt in November 1942. The husband died there. She was deported from Theresienstadt to Auschwitz in May 1943. Their little daughter was sent to England before the deportation and was saved.

Letter 36

Budapest, 18th of Shvat 5700
January 27, 1940
From: The Polish refugees in Hungary
To: The Zionist Executive

The internal political situation that developed here in the last days compels us to take pen in hand and present you with our tragic situation. Our situation here is deteriorating from day to day and from hour to hour. The police have "gotten close" to us and have started to "show an interest" in us, an interest unlike anything until now. Hovering over us is the danger of closing us up in a concentration camp or the "Shof-Hoise," — the corridor to hell. We feel as if at any moment we are nearing the edge of the abyss, the edge of the abyss that swallows us. This is the attitude of the authorities to us. And now a few words about the attitude of Hungarian Jewry towards us. The truth is that this Jewry is not at all interested in us, and its attitude is one of indifference. The community here is completely assimilated and we will never be helped by them, even a little. The Jewry here lacks that Jewish heart, that which Polish Jewry can be proud of. The community is conservative, without feeling the changes that took place, changing reality. In short: The community sees the Zionist Organization as its own misfortune. And the Zionist Organization? This is the fly in the ointment. It is "Hungarian" and therefore it differs from our Polish organizations. The truth is that it has made efforts and attempts to help us, but its good intentions did not bring about any positive action. "The needs of the belly" are not the main ones. And Lipski, a member from the Land of Israel, stays here. He came here as our leader and patron and his duty was to take care of us and rescue us. We regarded him as a "messiah" on whom we pinned all of our hopes and future.

But here, too, we were totally disappointed. We don't know how much he did for us and if he had done much, why were his deeds useless? For us, the fact that the problem of Polish refugees is very acute and still remains so, not moving forward a hairbreadth, is enough. We gorged our souls with illusions and fictions [sic] until the bitter truth delivered us a blow, and despair began creeping in our hearts. We were left forlorn and lonely without one to help and support, abandoned to the waves that strike us from each and every side. The attitude of the authorities to us and of the Jews to us makes our situation here severe and harsher than the situation of Polish refugees in other countries. Indeed, we know well enough that we are living in emergency times with many troubles and calamities, and also the Polish refugees in Romania and Lithuania have it bad. But our condition is many times worse than theirs, and the honorable Executive, for all that, supported only them!!! Is the blood of Polish Jews in Romania and Lithuania thicker than ours? Is it because our bitter fate tossed us to the country of Hungary that we should be discriminated against? Why should our share be less than the rest of the exiled Polish? While the Agency's emissary, Mr. Greenboim, was in Romania, he didn't see it necessary to drop in and visit us, as if we didn't exist, or as if the country of Hungary is a Garden of Eden for us. And for this, our heart is sick and aching. Until this day we don't know why the honorable Executive didn't take us into account in the month of November when distributing certificates to Polish refugees? Also here we have a significant number of some two thousand people, of whom the majority is still in the concentration camp. And thanks to the Zionist Organization we still exist in freedom. It should be noted that we have among us a decent amount of pioneer material. And now that we received news about the new quota of certificates that the Agency obtained for Polish refugees, we awakened again and shook off our despair. We were certain that now after you were notified about the bitter existence of our lives, the honorable Executive would not skip over us and would budget for us the maximum amount of certificates, so at least a tiny part of us would find a solution. And in any case, the attitude of the authorities to those remaining here would improve when they found out, that emigration to the Land of Israel isn't just an empty phrase, because the issue of immigration to the Land is a decisive one in our free existence here. We hope that after clarifying our situation here, the indifferent attitude of the honorable Executive will change to a warm relationship, aware of our fate here, and will bring with it substantial and realistic help. In our opinion, the attitude of the honorable Executive until now was based on a total lack of knowledge about us and our situation. It is now more than four months that we are here and not one document of complaint was sent by us, and not one word of complaint has been voiced from our mouths. And now, in our writing this letter, replete with complaints, we are showing that we are up to our necks in water and this shouldn't be counted as a sin on our part. We await your answer impatiently and your substantial assistance, we bless you with the blessing of the rebuilding of Zion.

Sincerely,
The Polish refugees in Hungary

Letter 37

Sunday [undated]

Dear Louis,

I am hastily telling you that we must leave on Wednesday, first to Killesberg near Stuttgart, and on Saturday there will be a transport, probably to Theresienstadt. You can imagine how furious we all are. I can serve as a paragon — Hennele wanted to send me someone [to help] with packing. But yesterday I packed the small suitcase with my own hands; tomorrow they will take it away from here and also my mattress. On Wednesday, I'll have to tie, by myself, the down blanket and the two pillows — and this is difficult for me, we'll see already what can be done. Veigold was by me this morning and told me that my sister-in-law Fanny must also go together with Y.Y. She is planning to take pills tonight so that she won't wake up any more. Veigold believes that I'll see my children there, but I don't think so, unless they've left Riga. I have awful stomach cramps. I asked Dr. Seth and in his opinion it comes from tension, he recommended that the nurse make me a compress for the night. You have no idea what the situation is by us and what it all looks like, we are all desperate.

Yes, this is what is liable to happen to a human being, who would ever imagine such a thing. Perhaps there will yet be a miracle from Heaven, I'm always optimistic. Besides this, there is nothing to tell. I of course have a lot to do today and tomorrow, and I will be forced to give up many things.

And so, to you and to Emmy a heartfelt kiss
Your Sophie, who is very sad

Sophia Felheimer (nee Frank) was deported to Riga and shot there.

Letter 38

Chelem, the day after Passover, (Isru Chag) April 10, 1942

My Beloved and Dear Friend,

I received the money and I am sending a sincere thank you from all the family members. You have sustained the lives of us all, we had [money] for potatoes, even if it were only enough to revive the spirit. We will remember you for this forever. The festival of Passover went by with much fear and trepidation. It is impossible to describe our nights and days, what we're going through since the Eve of Passover. There is no security at any second — from the Angel of Death who is walking about the streets and one needs great mercy after — of L. in Rejowiec, [in Chelem panic spread because of news of a liquidation operations in Rejowiec that happened at the beginning of April]. May God the Blessed One say "enough" already to the Angel of Death and that we should merit salvation, if not… Who knows — already near Chelem, God forbid. Pray to arouse compassion for us, and if you can, save us — in whatever way that you can assist us, and in this merit may God help you and bless you with all the best.

Letter 39

Vienna, December 28, 1943

Dear Mrs. and Mrs. Netzl,

Again a year has started with its hopes and fears.

1944 is at the entrance…

I wish you all health, happiness and wishes for our lives in the future — May God protect us from a cruel destiny and keep us together, or lead us together — this is all that I hope for and for this I live.

How are you? Didn't you receive my letter from September? I would be very happy to receive your answer and your lines would give me happiness. Didn't you hear more details about the sad fate of my poor Ozzie? I truly request from you to do to the best of your ability to help him or see him in some way. You said at the time that you have acquaintances there, that through a personal connection you may be able to obtain — please, please may God reward you if you do this good deed and help — it is obvious that I will willingly cover any financial expense. Wouldn't it be possible to do this on Christmas Eve, or perhaps New Year's Eve — because from here it is impossible. Because I'm not present at the place and I don't know whether the situation is more or less convenient, so I can't take advantage of it (you know the address and the name).

My miserable brother is lying already for 14 months in a hospital, and he has lost 43 kilograms from more than 88 kilograms. Lately he is undergoing a treatment of force-feeding and again he is putting on weight nicely, but during the month of March he awaits complicated lung surgery, and then they will transfer him to Vienna. He has already had three blood bursts, an infection on the skin of the ribs, punctures in order to drain discharge, and a respirator for a whole year. All this at the age of 19, and he is the only son in the family — but we still hope that he will recuperate. I was and still am very chilled — but I had to immediately continue on further. My eyes got very weakened from so much crying, and therefore my vision is bad, despite the glasses.

Now I finish my lines and wish you, the husband, the grandson and his wife Edith, many heartfelt wishes and all the best. Always yours.

R. Rhein

If you ever come to Vienna, you should write to me 10–14 days before regarding a place to stay overnight. The situation is worse today, because there are many here who were evacuated from the bombings of the Old Reich.

Letter 40

Blessed be God,
After the Sabbath
The Month of Shvat

"Only I, by myself, escaped to tell you!" (Job, 1, 17), "but one who utters slander is a fool" — all of us. I remained alone and bereft of my home, my father, my family, my community, my friends. Everything that was said in the Torah portion of *Bechukotai* (the Reproof) has come true except for "but despite all this, while they will be in the land of their enemies", etc. (Leviticus, 26, 44)

"Are you finishing off [the nation] of Israel?" — *and this is not said in jest.* "If only my head would be water and my eyes a spring of tears, etc." I am brimming with gall, but our brothers abroad are free and complacent. When I came here on Tu B'Shvat 5703 (15th of the month of Shvat), some forty thousand were still imprisoned in Warsaw. Among them were my brother Shiffer, of blessed memory, R' Zevach, of blessed memory, Trukenheim and more. Also the brothers-in-law of the aforementioned. I pleaded in countless letters to our brothers abroad — via Chaim Yisrael, of blessed memory, to save them, but they went about their duty in a lazy and indifferent way. I showed them the way, our way. But there was no money to redeem the captives sentenced to death, and the opportunity was lost. And on Passover Eve, the Night of Vigil, *total destruction wreaked loose.* Even all homes on the Jewish street were burned. And now in the country ounce known as the "Council for Torah and Documentation" some tens of Jews are hiding. All of them, that is about four million — have been destroyed in strange deaths, and we cannot bless any more "the One who is good and benefits others *". The Jewish court will cancel this blessing, because they were not buried in Jewish burials.

Remaining are only those who are here, most without their families, bereft and alone. It seems to me that it is my duty to notify you about this, after all I was your secretary.

I received questions about family and relatives: From Dr. Kahane, from Yitzchak Levine, about his wife and so on. Don't ask! Don't ask! There are no others, only those that are here. And we are in great danger, too, the danger of death. If only you would not have the obligation to behead a heifer over us, too.** And you should not have to say: But we are guilty. You must do more than is possible so we can get more out by exchange, to the Land of Israel, and if not, to America. It makes no difference to us so long as you don't miss the opportunity. Because each and every day the danger is greater. Rescue those remaining, rescue! Hurry without neglect. I notified you my name, and this is my year and place of birth: 12.1.1895 Miakov. My wife's name: Gina, 1898 Warsaw. My daughter is Gittel Miriam, 22.1.1917, Warsaw, and this is enough for the wise. I do not know if I can request a life without a goal. I am not requesting this, but I think that you must try with all your might to exchange us. It is possible, because it has already been done.

◆ ◆ ◆

I wrote a few times without any response. We here are the tiniest remnant from the whole ingathering of the nation of Israel. Do what you can because the danger is great. Of all the "Agudat Yisrael Girls," and of all the "Beit Yakov" teachers, I alone survived, and my sisters who are in the Land must remember this and act without neglect. The one that wrote on the opposite page is Father. I also have a mother here — Thank God! Send certificates for exchange: Gutta.

Mitsha and Mendel! I survived from our entire family and it is through a miracle that I am here. Do whatever you can.

Saraleh G.

The first letter was written by Gutta's father.

Footnote

* This blessing was instituted by the Sages following the Roman Revolt and the attack on the city of Beitar (in the year 70) which claimed the lives of many Jews. The corpses of the victims were left out in the open and when they finally received a decent burial the blessing of "the God who does good" was added to the prayers. This was not the case during the Holocaust and therefore the writer asks that the blessing be revoked.

** The writer refers to the Torah commandment when finding a corpse near the city with no one to claim it or take responsibility. The leaders of the city gather and axe an heifer, claiming they are not guilty and thus absolve themselves of guilt.

Letter 41

Bendin, October 31, 1942
To My Dear Schwartzbaum Family!

I finally received a postcard from you. Thank you very much. Regarding Mulak, he would have preferred to see those others again. It would have been good for me. Who knows if it's not too late. Alf, please write to Oscar to remember me. I am healthy, but the condition of my Pela is not good. I will have my picture taken and send it to you as a memento, because I think we will not see each other. I request again that you write to Oscar. He can rescue me. Besides this, there's nothing new.

Regards and kisses
Gold Yisrael B.

We don't get packages at all.

187

Letter 42

To Mr. R. Gelbart
Warsaw, Novolifia #28/18
Ghetto Krosniewice, January 21, 1942
My Beloved,

I shouldn't write to you when I'm in such a mood. I know that my letter will cost you much health. I am sorry for you, my dear, but it seems to me that each letter of mine is my last letter, and this shocks me.

Just this moment I spoke to someone who came from Chelmno. He came to this place from Turek, Kolo, Dabie and Kolo [sic]. What's happening to them has happened to Aunt Pazhachakova in Kalisz. This isn't a falsehood. Ask [Yitzchak] Bornstein and Dr. [Israel] Milikovski. Go, my dear, because that is indeed the purpose of my writing. Don't be surprised that I'm so full of energy. Maybe we'll manage to do something for ourselves. Speak with Lozer. I know that I won't be able to go back to you, because it's winter now, therefore cry out. Maybe they'll help you for my sake — so I won't suffer leaving the world in such a tragic way.

Forgive me for writing like this, you realize that I'm hysterical. If only it would all be a lie.

Regards, Roz'a

◆ ◆ ◆

To Mr. R. Gelbart
Warsaw, Novolifia # 28/18
Ghetto Krosniewice, January 24, 1942
My Dear Shmuel!

Today you will certainly get some unpleasant news from me. Meanwhile we're here, and the same matter is getting extremely noisy, even when it's not in our area. They searched for them here [the escapees from Chelmno]. In contrast, they [the occupation regimes] promise us that the matter concerns that region, and we will remain here until April. I don't believe them and therefore I'm not calm and my heart shudders all the time.

I would shout with all my might, but where can I run? After all there is such terrible frost here and the children will certainly freeze to death. When the frost eases up — it will perhaps be too late. Meanwhile I have no other choice, but to sit and wait. Maybe this disease will stop because the whole matter is becoming so public. Write to me what they say by you regarding this. Did you convene? Why do you write so little, for a week I didn't get a letter from you. In general, I don't get a postcard from you more than once a week. You probably don't have time.

I am bad to myself, but we know in advance what awaits us and this is a great tragedy. It's better not to know and that the matter is unexpected. Then man, even as he is banished, thinks that somehow he will manage. I had convinced myself that I would manage in any place, and now such a tragedy befalls us. We are all desperate and awaiting the final separation. I can't describe the panic. I must work in this situation. Even if the work isn't done well, I still work, and maybe this is fortunate since sometimes I forget what awaits me.

Be well. I kiss you strongly.

Loving you, yours,

Roz'a

Regards to Reuven. Regards from Mauritz and Blima.

Roz'a Kaplan to her husband Shmuel in the Warsaw Ghetto.

Letter 43

Sunday, July 19, 1942
My Beloved Daughter!

What can I write to you during the last hours of my life, from the corridor of the afterworld. I have committed severe crimes towards you, my girls, and I myself bear my sins. Thinking about you makes me insane, although I'm not ashamed to admit that also for my own sake, I don't want to die. I want to continue to live! I still want to experience something, I want to see you, Vladz'ia, at your husband's side. I also want to help Agussia get some place. But of what help is my will? The circumstances are critical, and the most awful part is that it's not hard to get me out of here. But nobody comes, and I can't communicate with anyone. Officially, I am allowed to write some words only once a week. I don't have false hopes anymore.

Considering that after my death your lives must continue and move forward, because this is the calling of life, I would like to give you, Vladz'ia, some instructions and worldly explanations. I'm convinced that someone will help you find solutions for Agussia's education. I know that if Poldi returns, you will take care of her. And if, Heaven forbid, something happens to Poldi, in my opinion, you should complete your studies and education in order to achieve an independent position. Learn in the Polytechnion! Your experience as a draftswoman will help you and give you an independent position even with the most devoted husband.

After completing your studies, get married. Don't be angry with me for writing this today when Poldi is alive, and we earnestly want him to come back, but in the future I will not be able to give you advice, and you know that I have a wise outlook on the lives of others. And if Agussia lives with you, then it should not be passed the age of 15 or 16 years. Later on she should live with strangers. Don't laugh, Vladz'ia! I'm giving you sound advice. You mustn't have at home a younger woman! But give her all the warmth possible!

For the near future, until the end of the war, I'm not giving you any advice, because life does not always go according to plans. Work if you can. A bright ray of light brought me a package yesterday addressed in your hand-writing. For the first time since Monday, I washed myself and took off my clothes at night.

Here, I leave you this letter with the jailer, the watch, the pen and glasses. He received instructions to give over all of this after I leave. The jailer must get paid at least five Zloti for every day that I stay here. He and his wife, too, help me and do for me more than they're allowed to do.

There's no doubt that it must have been the doing of Dravik's wife.

And she even had the *chutzpa* to come to me the next day suggesting that I give her an authorization that I owe her money, and that she would take for herself my furniture, and in exchange, she would take care of Agga! This is really the height of hypocrisy! Lucky for her, they didn't let her in, because I can't guarantee my actions. She also told this to the jailer's wife: that she had gone already to the supervisor, and that she knows well those from Zabierzow, etc. etc. I write you all of this so you will know what to do when the war ends. Although nobody will give me back my life, revenge must be taken against this cursed venomous snake.

I have a lot more to write, Vladz'ia. About my deep love for you, which may not be apparent, but you shouldn't have any doubt about it, Vladz'ia, even though I've pre-tended.

Regarding my stay here I'm not writing. This gang is beyond the wildest imagination. It's a shame that I can't

191

tell you about it. By the way, I'm treated nicely here. All together there are 17 prisoners here and only 6 mattresses and 5 blankets. Since the first night, I have a blanket and mattress just for myself. Although this is in exchange for a daily loaf of bread, and its price costs more than accommodations in a luxury hotel, it's good that at least I have this choice. For money, you can get everything here, because the jailer's wife goes shopping and you can even get lunch from Mrs. Philipovska, including fruit and vegetables. But, as you can guess, I don't have an appetite. I force myself to eat so I won't starve to death, because maybe some miracle will happen and I will get out of here alive. I have always believed in dreams and therefore maybe this time some miracle will happen to me also. The rest of the space in this letter I leave for a few days later, which I will receive as a gift...

◆ ◆ ◆

Sunday afternoon

So, the end is coming closer. The jailer told me now that they're taking me tomorrow. They know everything already. It's hard for me to concentrate. My nerves are stretched to their limit. I have the feeling that if they come to take me, I won't be able to control myself.

Goodbye to you, my beloved Vladz'ia and Agussia! Don't think that I'm a bad woman. During these last moments, I am quite miserable. Forgive me for the injustice I'm doing to you against my will. I'll pray for you in the afterworld.

Regards to all of my acquaintances and friends. I can't think calmly about Agga. I'm parting from you, my girls!

I leave a letter for Zaimba, the director. Bronya's keys.

The key to the box. Documents of the children and a photo of Elinka. A watch, pen, glasses and a pencil.

I'm taking the pencil with me. Maybe a miracle will happen.

A blanket, towel, pajamas that you can get by the jailer. Please pay him. They both tried making things easier for me. The chest is by Mrs. Bobovikova. Marussia was paid. She is an honest woman, she gave me food.

◆ ◆ ◆

Monday morning

Is there anyone in the world who understands what it is to sweat to death? Every moment of waiting, and the shudder at every murmur?

◆ ◆ ◆

Monday evening

A day that I received as a gift. Nobody understands the heartbeats and the straining of the nerves at the sound of each step in the corridor.

◆ ◆ ◆

Tuesday, July 21, in the morning

I am still here. Deprived of any ray of hope. Absolutely alone. All the prisoners have visitors, no one comes to me. I wrote to Mary. I was forced to buy from a friend the privilege of writing, and I waited yesterday for an answer. Meanwhile there was nothing. I read daily the "Gunietz" newspaper and look for some ad for me. Nothing. Did everyone despair already?

Wednesday, July 22 in the evening

I'm still alive.

◆ ◆ ◆

Sunday, July 26 in the evening

Today a week passed — the time that was set by the Gendarmerie for me to hand over the address of Z. the engineer. There is no ray of hope. I am totally abandoned. Tomorrow is probably the fateful day.

◆ ◆ ◆

Tuesday morning

The nerves continue to be stretched.

◆ ◆ ◆

Thursday morning

I'm still alive. I really don't know how to control my nerves.

◆ ◆ ◆

Friday morning

Not a thing. If it goes on like this, the bugs will eat me up. I am bitten and scratched until it bleeds.

◆ ◆ ◆

Tuesday, August 4 in the morning

And so, it seems that it's all over. Last night the

officer came to me — from Zabierzow. As I predicted, I immediately broke down and told him everything except for the address of the engineer. And after all, the address was of special importance to him. Now I'm waiting, but it's clear that after admitting my origin I cannot hope for good. But now I don't care already.

Probably on August 4, 1942, Gusta Berger-Ehrlich was executed after admitting that she was Jewish.

Letter 44

Vilna, March 2, 1941

Hello, Elsa,

The day before yesterday I sent you a letter, and today I'm sending you a postcard. I want to make sure that maybe you will receive a "last" postal item from me. The letter was written when I was very angry; today I am calmer. Yet, I do not know what tomorrow brings.

In any case, I am ready for everything. I was supposed to see you soon. And now? The worst of it all is the lack of knowledge of when I will return and see you. In any case, this postcard will be my farewell to you. Be well, Elsa, and keep on going. I remember you. If something happens, I would want there to be somebody who would remember that someone named D. Berger had once lived. This will make things easier for me in the difficult moments. I do not care so much about my family, because I gave up on them long ago. I sent with Leiblitz and Tova Mantok pictures for you, take the pictures from them. Remember! I thank you again, Elsa, for everything. Please don't worry and be strong, I will manage. Send regards to all those coming from Vilna. Special regards to Giza.

Farewell,
David Berger

◆ ◆ ◆

Dear Elsa!

Precisely because of these troubled times, I am writing a few words. I believed that I would be able to see you. I accept all that fate dealt me. I am calm. Be well.

Manya

Send regards from me to everyone, and warm regards to the group.

This postcard was sent to Elsa Gross in Petach Tikva, Israel.

Letter 45

April 20, 1944
My One and Only Dear son!

We are standing here, ready for the way, after packing our most necessary articles, in order for them to take us shortly with all Jews of the city to an unknown place for an unknown purpose, under orders of the Hungarian government. They gathered all Jews of the area and placed them in the brick factory —. They number approximately 10,000 people, and among them are Grandmother and Aunt Malevene. The Jews of the city gave them food for a few days, but now, when we're ready for the way, there is no one to care for us - - -

◆ ◆ ◆

I continue writing the letter...

It's a week since we've been sitting in the "cell for those condemned to death." Ber was home for a brief vacation, he came yesterday from Czhap by foot, and on the way to the brick factory he met his relatives who were already sitting in the cars [for deportation]. He managed to visit them twice with authorization, and today he already went back. If he can, he will contact you. Apparently, we don't have any chance...

They allowed us to take only our clothes and underwear with us, one garment worn on the body and the other in the bundle... We probably won't need them for a long time.

You can get information about our situation from some sources. The first: The *"ana"* [the maid] of Recha. The address: 60 Koshot Square. The second: Marguitte Karapatalia. You can go to them, they will help in any event.

There are some people, physicians, that are still free.

I'm on the verge of despair. I already gave up on life, and I'm full of pain and sorrow. You are already mature and will be able to manage. I have great pity on Aviva, and I only hope that she won't suffer. Why do we have to suffer from such despicable discrimination? Why is such a cruel event happening? I don't believe anymore in the existence of the Lord, because if all this could have happened — I must not believe in His existence, and therefore I'm not blessing you with the blessing of "May God safeguard you."

Perhaps this isn't our last letter...

◆ ◆ ◆

I sent you 100 Pango, I also gave Berko an extra 100 Pango for you. The father of Gross Moshe gave me 500 Pango. Berko took some of your clothes [for you] and some will stay here, he will explain everything to you. We also sent you two fine watches and a gold ring. Keep the watches for yourself, they are of great value and worth at least 1,000 Pango...

Rumors are that they're taking us to Debrecen [northeastern Hungary] or beyond the Danube [the western part of Hungary], so we'll write you from someplace — if we live until then.

Everything is printed from my book already (11 large sheets), and the remainder is ready for print. I sent the necessary amount to the printing press. I can't take upon myself to publish the book. Who will read it? Who can make a living from this? It involves a great bother. In any event it will be very important to add at the end of the book a paragraph about what is going on — Then, hurry (and try) to reach our ancient land, the land of our forefathers, as fast as possible and live there the life of a worker, the life of a laborer for the glory of our people and for the sake of our memory. Never sray far away from our national vision, be a wise fighter for our justice, but don't forget that England and America — two democracies — are the ones responsible for the lives of five or six million of our Jewish brothers. When everything calms down — demand a report from England —. Don't despair, don't feel saddened, because maybe we will yet be saved. And if we are destroyed, remember that in any case, we don't live forever and death awaits us any time, and therefore it is preferable that the end will come as fast as possible.

Try to manage as best as you can. Also Aunt Toldi will send you things when this is possible.

Kisses and love,
Your father

◆ ◆ ◆

Darling Yoshi,

Unfortunately, things won't be so good for me as they were until now. It seems to me that now your situation is the best one. It's possible that I'm now writing to you for the last time. My braids are shorn. The tenants from the Zinek house were taken out to the street.

A thousand kisses with love and sorrow
The sister who is deserving of you
Aviva

The letter was written to Yehoshua Szeremi from the city of Uzqorod/Ungvar in Hungray at the time of the deportation of the VI/I labor division. The letter was written over a few days and from different stations.

Letter 46

It is Saturday afternoon and I still don't know a thing. It is best to hope that I will surely return. You can depend on this with confidence. I feel strong and can well withstand this. Yesterday, on Friday, I received your package — it was great. Find out by Hashaobork whether - - - if not — send me a bowl to eat from, because I don't own a bowl to eat from and to take my food in. My dears, please remember - - - it shouldn't be forgotten, plenty of news - - - I know - - - Be concerned about me a lot —

The letter was sent from the deportation train that was leaving Westerbork, Holland.

Letter 47

July 1942

My Dear and Beloved Uncle Theo!

Even though I currently have plenty of work, I don't want this to keep me from writing to you for the last time before our trip. We just heard that Uncle Bolak is also coming with us. We just now received mail from Uncle Alfred; he was still lucky, but today — who knows what luck means? We are fine, as far as health goes and in general. Despite this, I hope that I can soon begin a new life in the Land of Israel. Things proceed in great indirect ways.

Your letter from September 6 arrived the day before yesterday and we are very happy that you are doing so well. Yes, it would be nice to stay in touch until the end of the war, but with God's help, this period too will not go on for too long a time. It's lucky that the three of us are still young and that we're not deterred from any work. Additionally, we will manage in any situation in life. After all, we've already proven this. This is a difficult school that I must learn in. The most beautiful years of my youth are going, but I hope that despite everything, it will be for my good one of these days. For thousands of years, Jews are accustomed to bearing a difficult fate and withstanding it. And nobody will see our generation show fear. Farewell, my dear Uncle Theo! Watch your health! With heartfelt wishes,

Yours always,
Ruth [Hadassah]

Mother is too busy, after all we have to be ready by tomorrow morning. That's why she wishes you all the best. If we have the chance, we'll write you directly.

Letter 48

Gorlice, May 17, 1940

My Dear Son,

     We received your postcard from December 25th and we were very happy to hear that you and Yehuda are fine. As I've already told you, everyone is in Gorlice together with Mother, your brother Avraham Arno, Grandfather and Grandmother and also the rest of the family. Everyone is fine, and you, our dear children, must surely not worry about us. Please send this postcard to your brother Yehuda, because it may very well be that the previous postcard that I sent didn't reach you. Please send us many letters, because this is our only remaining joy. We really hope that you're healthy and feeling well in our beautiful Land, and with God's help we can also immigrate to the Land, and the entire family will be together again. Many kisses and all the best to you and your brother Yehuda, from us all —

**From Mother and Arno, Grandmother and
Grandfather, the family,
And your father who loves you very much**

Letter 49

Doorn, April 20, 1943
All my beloved children!

Now it is Passover Eve and in two days Aunt Marie and I will go to the concentration camp. I am very calm and quiet and happy that the tension has passed and is behind us. I am sure and confident that we will see each other again and that Albert's telegram will come quickly. The copies of the Red Cross that I have will protect me, and I hope also Aunt Marie, from the most terrible of all. We have so many good and beloved friends. All the residents are like this, besides a few exceptions. My good friends Rick and Yo, with whom I've been corresponding for a long time, were and still are my angels. If I don't return, buy on my behalf a plot of land in their names. I will never be able to repay them for all they've done for me. I hope that I, even if I'll be in the Land of Israel, will come one more time to Doorn, and if I don't — you come here and relay our thanks to all who have been good to us. At the head of them all is the noble Van der Chos, a member of the Supreme Court. Mother lived by him for a year. We would play bridge with them every two weeks. In addition, they kept for us many things that came to Mother's address and are intended for you. She parted from us, from Aunt Marie and me, crying, as she kissed us on both cheeks. Look for the ladies Schodisvirs, on Aikenlan Street, they are good women. Mrs. Kamphois was very good to us and took in guests, we ate there many times. They went - - - Mrs. Osterzi, in the way of Prince Hendrik; Kinkvurxt, that old woman, who loves Jews warmly, who always worked for Jewish families. She also watched over [sic] many of our things. One woman was very lovely to us, Chaisbrechtsen, whose husband was a captain in the state police. A good, cultured person, who really empathized with our suffering. I really had feelings of friendship towards her. Most of the shopkeepers know us. I don't want to be sentimental, there's no use for this. If we don't see each other again, then my time has come, my age is 73. I would very much have liked to see Mano's son and little Misha and grasp them to my heart. Uncle is allowed to stay here because he intermarried. He has a good home and Mr. Van der Chos takes care of everything for him. I was by Mr. Cohen Terevart, who is also allowed to stay because he intermarried. He will try to befriend him and [I intend] to introduce the two of them. He is the grandson of Jup Israelis, a sweet, nice and modest person.

I want to go on, and if I stay healthy I will struggle for this. I hug all of you, Ina, Albert, Thea, Yost, Max, and last but not least — little Misha, from your mother and grandmother, who loves you very much.

[Bertha Cohen Goldschmidt]

Letter 50

June 20, 1941
My Beloved Son!

In my mind, I'm beginning to suspect that we will not see each other again. Therefore I would like to tell you some things, hoping that these words that I am writing will reach you sometime.

There is no need to say that I think of you all the time, but perhaps you sometimes think that I haven't made all the efforts to reach you, as you requested of me after Mother's death [she died on June 9, 1939, 10th of Tammuz 5699]. I feel an intense need to justify myself to you. It is true, I could have tried harder to get a certificate; but perhaps you know how unpleasant and complicated the matter is. I not only had to ask for favoritism from those in charge, but I really had to literally shove my elbows or even use underhand tricks.

As you know, until 1938 I didn't belong to any Zionist organization, and the reasons for that were not dishonorable. I fulfilled the usual duties of an "organized Zionist" most certainly more than most "organized" Zionists, but I hadn't yet reached the point that I was ready to devote my whole life towards this goal. In other words, to learn Hebrew diligently, to get to know the culture of our people, and that I myself should immigrate, when possible, to the Land of Israel, giving up what then seemed like great materialistic advantages. Mainly because I was not ready to assume responsibility for Mother and you.

In 1938, I already knew that it was not right to recommend to you another place of refuge, and I'm convinced that you are pleased with this decision. It is clear to me that you have a hard life before you, but if you get through the war safely, you can live a life free of giving any consideration to the hostile surroundings, something that we were forced to do. My hope is that you will live a natural and healthy life among our people, even if you greatly miss the conveniences of bourgeois life, as it's called.

I digressed slightly from the topic. Well, I do not regret that I didn't try enough to get the certificate, since I would surely have had to fight for it, and you understand this as well. On the contrary, I think that you would feel repulsion at any other conduct. But I did not utilize the other option to reach you. More than that, I was already registered with the last possible illegal immigration — and I cancelled the registration. I did not trust it; I truly wasn't afraid of the hardships, but I never believed that the transport would really reach its destination. Even though I know that a large segment of the people are in Mauritius, and some were killed in the explosion of the boiler [the tragedy of the "Patria" ship in Haifa Port] — despite all this I regret this decision. Perhaps we would still see each other. And if the Land, on which we pin our last hope, is indeed lost to us — I will gladly take part in this esteemed loss. And yet — who genuinely knows himself — perhaps the determining reason was only one of convenience? It is inconvenient to begin an entire new life and it is inconvenient to act against the cautions of good friends warning you against a dangerous step. But there is no point in these reflections; I just wanted to be sure that you don't judge me harshly.

It is easier to justify the step I took when leaving Vienna. I wasn't able to anticipate that the remainder of the school where I was principal [Chayut School in Vienna] would deteriorate because of the inability and laziness of the two people who took over. Anyhow the school closed down after three months, and had I remained, I would not have had a real field of action. Here I have only the satisfaction of my brother and sister being pleased with my presence, even though I cannot be for them and mainly for Aunt Othella what I would have liked to be and what they might have expected of me. I have no employment here, although I always keep myself busy somehow; but it does give me not the same feeling as being employed. Indeed I have more than enough spare time to learn Hebrew, but I find it very difficult. I am probably too old already [55 years-old]. It seems that in the Land, I would acquire the language quite fast, for the need to do completely humble work, preferably physical labor. I feel healthier than I did a few years ago. I'm not attracted to spiritual work like teaching, because I've always been aware that I could not accomplish this job in a perfect way. My life, which was established on wrong foundations to a large extent, is therefore behind me. All that I would want to do is to make a living from physical labor. But you shouldn't think that I am miserable or sad here. I do not think of the future often; I've made a rule to see this time as a transition period, and I plan to bear every external change in our condition with indifference. After all, you must know that I've always been fortunate with people, that people like me; this enforces my will to live, and to some extent, my self-confidence. Even though most of the time I do not agree with others about their estimate of my personality, their judgment is not entirely off. I enjoy working in the garden, [reading] letters from former students and friends, even a good book, but it's not like it once was. I frequently sit near Eva's [his niece] desk, and stare at the two pictures hung above, the picture of Mother from her youth (a pencil sketch of E. Escher), and your picture taken near the birch tree in Metzl [the village where Dr. Nohl was born; his son was about two years old then], and I think about the times that have gone by. Even more, I love to imagine your current life and would want to believe that a more pleasant and happy future is destined for you.

◆ ◆ ◆

- January 1942

My Dear Son!

I'm afraid that you are very concerned about us now. To our sorrow, there is basis to this concern. Until today nothing has happened to us. We must expect evacuation to reach us, too. The turn of the communities in Provincia has already come; first it seems, in Pilsen and Bodois. When our turn comes, we probably won't be sent all together. Anyhow, I cannot imagine Uncle Max being sent. According to news coming from Theresienstadat until now — and this seems to be the only option — the women are separated from the men, and this is nearly impossible for Uncle Max. But we haven't reached this point yet.

During the night, when I don't sleep, I think about you a lot. Indeed I am happy about the news I get via the Red Cross, but of course it is very little. I would like to know about your actual life. How many decisions did you have to make without being able to consult me? Who are your friends? How do you get along with your superiors and with your colleagues at work? What is your attitude to the Land? Do you belong to any organization? Did you make friends, maybe a girlfriend? How do you take the physical labor? And what would Mother have wanted to know if she were alive! She would have wanted to know if you take care of your outward appearance after work, it is good for you by Mrs. Zilbiger? [The son stayed by the Zilbiger family until being drafted in the British Army. Yosef Zilbiger was a friend of Dr. Nohl.] How do you spend your free time? Do you still have a chance to listen to music, and so on. Probably you never get to play the piano. Mainly Mother would miss your picture.

Until now Mother missed out on nothing, due to the

fact that she is no longer with us. She would have suffered without end. Do you remember how miserable she was when, for example, she would see a sad face on the tram? We once saw a movie that wasn't bad, I can't remember which, and in the journal of the week that followed, they showed refugee children from Spain when they boarded a ship on the way to London. Some of them had very sad faces. The whole evening Mother couldn't let go of this impression. After a few weeks she couldn't remember a thing from the movie itself, but kept on thinking over and over about the poor children. She would suffer so much now. From all areas comes only sad news, tidings of death and suffering. She would mourn so much with Aunt Anna. Poor Heinz is no longer alive. What a pity that he did not understand — or that I did not manage to tell him in a convincing enough way — that the Jewish youth, and Jews in general, should finally become aware that they should devote all of their energy to Jewish issues. What a great pity for him; he was an especially good and intelligent person. In August 1939, he had the chance to immigrate to England, but he did not make use of it because he wanted to receive compensation for his parents, from the bank where he worked, and this problem was not solved at the time.

But the tragedy reached many who were not at all to blame. So many were sent to Poland, Lodz and Theresienstadt, and it is so bad for them there. The cases of death are many. Sometimes it seems to me that we will never be happy, and on the other hand, I feel like I did in the World War, when I was ashamed more than once that I did not take part in the really difficult events.

So long as I remained I could still do something for the sake of the poor and miserable. It was not much, but each and every individual was very grateful. Here I have no field of action. But I wrote about this previously.

When I reflect about the distant future, mainly the future of our nation stands before my eyes. But I don't think of the many who still see themselves as belonging coincidentally to us, but foremost, of those who declare enthusiastically that they belong, of you in the Land, ready to offer sacrifices, and about the renaissance of Jewish culture. I am genuinely sorry that I hadn't found, long ago, the correct way; and I did have the chance for this. When I was young, in Prague, I visited the "Bar Kochva" organization, during its heyday, when Hugo Bergman, Victor Kelner, Robert Weltsch, Hugo and Leo Herman and Friedel's uncle, and Alfred Kraus were there. Apparently I didn't have the strength to devote myself entirely to the Zionist idea. Afterwards I lived, everywhere with my profession, a life that was evidently wasted to a great extent.

So, now there's no point in these reflections. The external course of one's life is influenced frequently by coincidence, and I must be thankful for this. The hand of coincidence brought me to Vienna where I met Mother and where you were born. After all there was enough happiness in this. Sometimes I suspect that you inherited from me a great load of inhibitions, that at times prevented me from feeling happiness, and so I would want to know whether the new life has changed you.

These letters are being kept meanwhile in my suitcase. If I have to leave, I will send them to Aunt Manshi [Maria Eizlet, a Christian from the Sudentland. She kept the letters and transferred them to loyal hands] who is a really good friend and will certainly safeguard them properly.

In two days it is your birthday. You are reaching adulthood [21]. I hope that you have a beautiful life ahead of you; perhaps despite it all I may live to be part of it.

My dear boy, be well.

◆ ◆ ◆

February 2, 1942
My Beloved Heini!

Some changes have again occurred last month. First of all, news came from you about the death of Yosef Zilbiger. Looking at it objectively, his fate should not be mourned. He came to you as a sick man; that is, his tragedy had started earlier. But he lived to have great happiness — to be in the Land for nearly two years, and he was able to be near his two sons. I don't know whether he was aware of his luck. I mourn him as a truly loyal friend and a dear person, and I am certain that he was your good friend, but one must not feel grief over his fate.

Probably the day isn't far when our turn for evacuation arrives. Now is the turn of the Kladno district with the communities of Raodnitz, Slany, Laun Rakonitz, Liboshovice, Prelice, Bierun. Among them again is a transport from Prague. Heda Pollack (the photographer of your many beautiful photographs) is in this transport, among others. Unfortunately, the transports are continuing from Vienna. Stefel Frishauf's mother and her sister, and to my sorrow also Chana Shidlof's parents, and probably my colleague Spitz are among the casualties. The matter is terrifying. One must search in the distant past of Jewish history to find similar examples. But then matters were straightforward [sic], even if perhaps, crueler.

Nobody knows the fate of the people in the camps, because no mail comes from there. The last postcard came from Richard Nohl dated December 4th. Since then the letters to him are returned, to Mrs. Yerushlem and to many others, with the comment: "Mail delivery has stopped on this street." Perhaps the reason for this is illness or a punishment. We are afraid of this more than anything: that we will be completely cut off from you and lose also the miserable connection via the Red Cross, a connection that despite everything gives us great joy. Besides this, I am not afraid, even though I know that it will be very hard, but I cannot expect a special fate. I only hope that I will find some work there, and then it will be easier to endure this. Nobody knows how long it will take and we must get more and more used to the idea that we will not survive. But one must rise over the fate of the individual and think of the fate of his nation, perhaps even about the fate of civilized mankind in general. With all this, I hope that you take root in the Land, find good friends, and later on, a fine girlfriend for your whole life, and that you should live with an awareness, more than I've done. Last week I read a book of Albert Schweitzer (you know his book *"Between the River and the Evergreen Forest"* [1925]), which made a deep impression. This is the first volume, very thin, of his cultural philosophy. He wrote the book out of an awareness that the entire Western civilization is in an awfully terrible decline which clearly found its expression in the World War. And what would Schweitzer say today? He sees the reason for this in the absence of any truly ethical world outlook. This world outlook can develop, in his opinion, if individuals — not organizations, etc. — will again start wondering about life's significance instead of cleaving to the materialistic. That way, with demanding thought, they will arrive at an awareness of their own, without allowing others to force upon them ready-made programs. Did he know how to give practical instructions — perhaps this is included in the second volume, which I don't have. After all, it is impossible to buy such books these days.

A distressing fact is that the expansion of formal education has also brought about great superficiality, and that the abundance of knowledge — and supposed knowl-

213

edge — have harmed the development of the personality. Now we, the Jews, can prove how small is the significance of a broad education, and how the importance of a strong character rises above it.

If we really don't see each other again, the wish of my heart is for you not to think of me in mourning and grief. Yes, mourn the hours that we did not spend with each other; perhaps also over those that I would devote, unnecessarily, to matters that had once seemed important to me, and indeed were without any value. I think of the many hours that I would devote to the Teachers' Union and those who benefit now (if there was any benefit at all) are only my Aryan colleagues. But here I must say that I was fortunate that I was popular, and you should be happy about this — as I am happy — that I found out over and over that I have really good friends all over the world. I cannot recall whether I wrote in these pages about how my former student, Turchiner, offered me in such warm words to send him a telegram in order to obtain a visa to Cuba. In any case, it wouldn't have helped, and I did not even want to go there; only one immigration destination is before my eyes. Likewise, I am happy that a former student, who now lives in Budapest (you know him, I think, from our trip to Kreuzenstein), Fejes, can now help a very good friend of Uncle Max, Max Epstein. Therefore, I cannot be ungrateful and I can establish that I had a beautiful life.

You shouldn't imagine me now as sad in any way externally. This is forbidden, if only for the others. Today people also look for my company; I probably help them feel better somehow. Sometimes it seems that the calm people felt in my company may have been detrimental, mainly in the last years: If they were less calm, they may have tried harder to run away from here, but I keep on telling myself that it is impossible that I had such great influence.

In this context, I recall that Mrs. Weil [a Christian who married Dr. Nohl's Jewish friend] would not calm down or be tranquil, but she thought only of how to get out. Now finally, she may be on the last boat, she has succeeded. At the end of December she traveled on a small steamboat from Bilbau to her friend in Buenos Aires. She wrote me a sad letter from the boat; she is very miserable because she will not receive any news now about her husband. Today she has probably arrived at her destination. The dispersion of families and the suffering are inestimable [her husband fled to Shanghai and died there without them meeting again].

Indeed, also the Germans and the Czechs suffer greatly. Do you remember the nephew of Aunt Razarelle, Tunral — were you at Uncle Carl's 50th birthday by them on Wambacher Street? I wrote to Mr. Fohl on Christmas and asked him if he knows about Carl and Razarelle. In response, I learned that their son, Tunral, fell in Russia. The youth was never likeable, but he was their only son, who caused them great worry. He was also an enthusiastic Nazi — but his parents' lives were destroyed upon his death. There are millions of cases like this throughout the world. This is a really terrifying tragedy that mankind is experiencing.

I've assumed for a long time that you will also have to be drafted, and I would understand this. How will the world go back on track? The truth is that we live in a time of profound barbarism, and indeed it is awful how somehow, we get used to it.

Fritz Essler was also drafted. He went to the air force, but is still in a course. Walter just stopped learning and volunteered for the air force. Mr. Opeltak is in Russia. Those that I mention here probably remain our good friends. People cannot grasp what is really happening with us, but they also don't understand what is happening to them. They still have delusions. Today I write down matters as they go

215

through my head.

I will give over all of these letters before we leave to Aunt M., and I am sure that she will safeguard them in order to give them to you in the future. She will be very sad when we are imprisoned. Of course it is impossible that the link of letters to us will continue, so I will give her also some pages from a notebook that Mother wrote after you had left, hoping that she would one day give you the entire notebook. When a search was conducted in our house, and another one was expected at any time, Mother lost interest in this and wanted to destroy the notebook. According to my request, she allowed me to take out the written pages and keep them. I first read them after her death. Besides me, Aunt M., Rudy and Gosti saw them. I didn't show them yet to Aunt Othella. I think that it would shock her too much.

It seems now that Mother's fate was good. Although I don't know what would have been her fate had she remained alive, but she would probably suffer inestimably.

My main concern is about the future — no, my main wishes are — that you should live a free life full of light. It won't necessarily be an easy life, this has no importance.

I hug you, our dear child.

Father

◆ ◆ ◆

June 15, 1942
My Dear Boy!

I frequently feel the need to talk to you, that is, to tell you more, because it is slowly, slowly becoming apparent that we won't see each other again. The expulsion of the Jews now to different places is so dispersed, that to gather them together anew will not be easy, even when the war ends. Only a small part will manage to reunite with their dear ones, and only a very few will be able to find the way to the Land of Israel. After all, we cannot imagine what awaits us. It will certainly be difficult. I still don't know what is easier. Will we (Uncle Carl and the Mahlers) stay together, or because of this, will it be more difficult? In any case, I show a strong will to go on, without fearing death. Good emotional preparation is to read Jewish history, or, for example, the trilogy of Shalom Asch. To my sorrow, we did not read these books in the past with the correct understanding. We would never consider the possibility that such things could happen to us, even if they were to be organized by state institutions — and they are organized in a most sophisticated way. If it would affect several thousands, I would not see the situation as being so hopeless, but in reality, the intention is for complete evacuation. Eight transports are leaving Vienna this month. Therefore it seems that we will leave in August. But today I won't discuss details. I just want to tell you that I am approaching it all without excitement, that I am ready to bear every shortage, in hope of seeing you again, while having a clear conscience. I hope that I will not lose my cool or self-dignity. If I regret something, it is the regret that I only recently understood the real situation of our people, and therefore I was active in the wrong place all the years. Or perhaps I should find comfort in the fact that thousands of Aryan students knew me, and therefore they will find it somewhat difficult to believe the official lies? This must be a childish delusion.

Sometimes I try to think beyond the fate of our people, about the development of the world after this war. I cannot reach any outcome here. It is hard to believe there will be a positive development. Yet, I do not easily call off such a belief, probably from an emotional tendency to invent reasons only after the events and to give meaning to existence.

And now over to you. I won't write a lot to tell you how much I think of you. I hope that you have started to think about building up your life. First of all, I think about the question of whether you are a soldier already; and only after that, about whether you're hungry. Are you still at your work, in what way do you live, how do you manage with people around you and what is your relationship with Eva and with Friedel [her husband]? Did you make good friends, perhaps you love a girl, and how do you cope with the difficult problems of life? Again and again I think of one sentence in the letter that you wrote after Mother's death: "Now it would be good for the two of us, if only you would come here soon." And you are really the only one towards whom I feel pangs of guilt. I find comfort in the thought that you are young, that in the new Land my viewpoints are not appropriate for the times. This is how we always find comfort in something when we cannot change a thing. In any case, we must not feel sorry about Mother's destiny now. Again and again I see her in her last hours and I hear her farewell from life: "I love all people." The diary pages, or more exactly, her letters to you, the ones that she wrote after you left Vienna, I will send together with this letter to Aunt M. I hope they get to you sometime.

Be well! I will still write before parting. I still have with me your composition from fourth grade, "My Father;" I carry it with me. I will send you this, too.

Your father

Uncle Carl and Aunt Olga were "drawn out," as it's called in Vienna, on June 8, that is they were brought to the gathering camp. Today they must have certainly been sent. Nobody knows where.

◆ ◆ ◆

July 7, 1942

My Dear Child!

Yesterday I wrote via the Red Cross. Of course, this is only a sign of life. Yesterday a letter (3.2) of the Red Cross, which greatly worries us came from Oswald Lobel. He doesn't write a word about Friedel. This is in addition to the fact that you also don't mention Eva and Friedel, not in one word (3.1). We reach the conclusion that he was drafted, if not worse than that. Does your comment about dealing with car engines imply something similar?

I assumed that it was obvious that you, as young people, would be in uniform. Now I'm really beginning to feel sorry that I'm not near you, mainly when I see that I will soon be completely unnecessary here. It's only a matter of weeks that we will be sent away from here, and then I will certainly be separated from Aunt Othella. According to the news, only some will be deported, and it will be a miracle if we, or I, are among those that are left. And how can we picture a meeting with you? To this we have to add the fear for you and your country. No one is wise enough to picture the future, and this is certainly very good for our current emotional state. We only feel the determined will of those around us to destroy us.

In order to bear such a life, a person must blunt his senses (and to a certain extent, everyone has become blunt) or to see oneself as a victim of war, and not attribute too much importance to his personal fate. Therefore, reading about our history helps. I enjoy reading now from Orbach's book "Desert and the Land of Destiny." One can draw from it the assurance that our people will not become extinct, no matter how many individuals will be physically destroyed; and even if a large segment of Jews are already lost to Judaism. How shameful it is that I did not have this aware-ness already 30 years ago — and I had the opportunity. But there is no point in this all. I always had too much criticism and too little enthusiasm. These are character traits and one cannot complain about it.

To summarize, our lives here were of no use and empty. I know that they will respond to me that I was very popular with my students, that I was perhaps a crutch for them, with many seeing me as a good friend — but all this does not matter now. I was just one in the large mass — and with it, I will be gone.

If you fall in battle over a better future, do not grieve your fate. It would be worse if you return as an invalid. But even then, I hope, you will be with people who are your friends making life easier for you. And this brings up the question, is life at all an asset; is it worth living? I still haven't reached the point of answering this question negatively. In any case, I am not requesting death, and I am firm in my belief to confront the great difficulties and shortage. But if I were condemned to die, I would want to be sure that this flood of lies and slander thrown upon us would collapse. I am sure about one thing — that I feel better under my skin than that of my enemy.

It is a coincidence that precisely now, when I stopped here, I read the chapter "Jeremiah" in Orbach's book. He reached a point in life when he curses his birth, but his mission causes him to come to peace with his destiny. It is not good to compare your life with those that are too great, not even from afar. One must behave more humbly. I would be pleased with myself if I did not suspect that I remained here out of some convenience, but nobody senses these doubts.

Today news came that my father's two brothers who are still alive (Uncle Ludwig, the father-in-law of Augen and Rudolph, the grandfather of Peter Kay-Katz), and their wives and also the widow of another uncle, the seventh out of nine, the mother of Ernest who once visited us on

Hatzendorf Street, were set up for a transport. That is, they are being torn from their children with whom they lived and will be transferred to the old-age home in Theresienstadt. Ludwig is 84, Rudolph and Othelia are 80. This is a very sad ending to the lives of people who have earned an honest living their whole lives. Everyone is exhausted and it cannot be assumed that they will live long. The plan is implemented without any consideration.

Today a very brief postcard also came from Ida Schwartz from Izbicia in the Lublin district. For months we heard almost nothing, and today she writes that she is healthy. Many of these people are sentenced to death.

I finish for today. In my thoughts, I am with you,

Your Father

◆ ◆ ◆

November 27, 1942

Well, yesterday the decision was made. On December 21st we are leaving. There is a certain possibility that we will stay in Theresienstadt. I hope to endure, and one should hope that this won't take much longer.

And again: My last thoughts are with you, if I bow down (I wanted to write "if I fall"). Do not forget your many good friends that you are to go to without hesitation if you need them.

It is hard for me to picture now the happiness of a meeting.

The letters of Dr. Emil Eliezer Nohl, of blessed memory, were written to his son Yeshayahu (Heini) between June 20, 1941 until November 27, 1942 in the city of Hradec Kralove, Czechoslovakia

Letter 51

[November 8, 1941]

My Dears,

I finally found the time to write you some lines. I hope, my dears, that you are well. We are deeply immersed in work. We must travel at the end of the week and you can imagine the work we have. We successfully moved dear Mother and Grandmother Flavel to the old age home here in the city. The two grandmothers will support each other, and we are happy about this. Gold sits near us, marking the articles. Yes, who would ever imagine such a thing in his right mind, but our heads are held upright, and we are happy that our two little ones are not here with us. Brand also wrote to us these days. I must write to Olga, that is, if I have the time. Fuld also doesn't work anymore. From this aspect, we finished everything. We would like to hope that we all remain healthy and then we will come back and see each other, with God's help.

—

♦ ♦ ♦

My Dears,

I want to part from you with wishes. Our time has now come. They will transfer us next week for resettlement in Poland; our two grandmothers are allowed to stay, thank God. Both Ilsa and I are strong and courageous, and we're not accepting our fate with a stooped head. Dear Victor, after all we know each other from the war in 1914–1915 and therefore we are strong and accustomed to many things. We just about liquidated our household, a big job. Besides this, there is not much to tell. All the best to you, be well and with God's help we will see each other soon.

With wishes and warm kisses,
From your Leopold

I send particularly warm wishes to your three dear sons and plenty of wishes for a better future.

Letter 52

November 1941

My Dear Max,

Today or tomorrow they will take me to the camp. May the Lord help me go through this, too. I suffered a lot, but survived because I believed in the kind Lord and because my great love for you, Mutz'ek [the nickname of her husband, Max], gave me strength. It's already been months since I heard anything from you both. Yassa and Katiusha know about everything. I've hidden some things, so if the kind Lord merits us with good fortune to return and see each other again, it won't all be lost. Katiusha was great. Everything is arranged according to the possibilities. Sasha and Eva are traveling with me, but I don't know how long we'll stay together. I sent you, through Yassa, 10,000 Italian liras; I hope you got them. Mutz'ek, I have dearly loved my mother and my dear boys, but I've never loved a person in the whole world as much as I've loved you. Therefore you also must be strong and patient, one day an end will come to this, too. Katiusha knows where everything is. I'm writing this just in case I'm not saved. But I have a feeling that we will return and see each other again.

You, Rudi, Freddy and Miltzek, I hug and love.

Your Regina

◆ ◆ ◆

Dear Rudi! In case we never see each other again, God forbid, you must stay with Father and take care of him. If you love me even a little, don't remarry Eva, because you will always be miserable. Maybe she's not to blame for this, but she has a bad nature. If it weren't for little Sasha, I would not support her. I worked like a dog for her and her child. She took a lot of advantage of me. Take care of yourself, and of Father's health.

Love and hugs,
Mother

Regina Kandet was deported from Belgrade in the month that she wrote this letter.

Letter 53

June 11, 1943

Dear Luzhin and Hassio and Your Wives,

I describe here the events of our lives during the four years of war, and enclose a photograph of me with Mother and Milo. I am now by Henia and Yozek; they support me because I don't have a penny or anything else except for four shirts and two pairs of underwear. This is my entire property after four years of wandering and running by foot in the forests, from Brody — 45–50 kilometers, through perilous ways. It is only due to my strength that I arrived here. The question is whether they'll manage to hide me and whether I won't be caught here. Only God knows the answer — until now I've had only miracles, He led me successfully and I live and exist when others have vanished long ago, tortured to death.

I promised Yozek and Henia Lokschwitz 20 *morags* (hectares) of land. Give it to them — because they're saving me. At the time of writing this letter, which they'll give you, and also at the time that I wrote the letter from Radziechow, after what was termed an "action," Mother is no longer alive. They took her in Radziechow together with Rozhia Fohorils and Clara Vassar, and I was miraculously saved. Local murderers killed Milo as well as Fritz Fohorils. Yozek will tell you everything. I also found out everything from his own mouth. When you will be here, I request that you transfer their bodies to the Jewish cemetery; and if God also designated that my fate is to be killed here or somewhere else — take my body to the Land. I ask this of you, my beloved children. You will have money for this when you liquidate the assets.

I'm writing this letter in pencil, because there's not enough ink in this place, and I'm writing on the knees. I get from Henia enough food; she gives me what she has. She is poor but she gives, and it's very nice of Yozek and her. I was never bad to them. Well, when you liquidate the assets, they should get from you during liquidation 20 *morags* of land. If the government will not permit the sale of land or so on — you must pay Yozek and Henia a handsome and generous payment, for what they have done for me. When I came here I was sick and half-dead, and now — only ten days have passed — I feel healthy and am able to write this letter. If no money comes in from the land — I don't know what your financial situation is now — in any event please compensate these good people for their kindness.

I wrote from here a letter to Motek to the address he had given you then. I received a letter from him in Brody already on May 14th. He is still alive, thank God, with Fanka and the children. He has always written me that Feivush is alive, but Feivush himself wrote us last year already to Radziechow and Studzianki. Why he doesn't write now — I don't know, maybe Motek knows why and doesn't write me. Motek was drafted as a doctor someplace in Lvov, and Fanka is there, and maybe Feivush.

I impatiently await a letter from Motek any day. I am very fearful for his life. They want to terminate us completely in Europe, but God is stronger, and I have complete faith in the Almighty, may He have mercy on us, because "the miracles of the Almighty repeat themselves day by day."

I write you because you or your wives stand a better chance of enduring. I don't know, maybe Luzhin went to war, indeed maybe Hessia or Tziporah or Shenka (her whole family was destroyed) will relate to my letter.

This is a person's end. I have completed 65 years of my life, and I don't know what's with Mother, Shenka, Lolek and Mirussia who were taken from Kolomyja, when the Soviets were there. They took Izio in Lvov on July 24, 1941. Where — I don't know. I got letters from Shenka and Lolek on September 28, 1942 from Kolomyja. They took Mother from Radziechow on October 28, 1942.

On my way here, I left a letter for you. Jan Marachischuk, in the forest of Sczesruvitza, had kept me for three days — to remain there. But I had to hide in the forest in the rain and cold — he was afraid to keep me in the house — that is why I went to Yozek. I walked another 10 kilometers as a blind man at night, I passed a patrol, and at dawn I came to Yozek. I couldn't find my way at night even though I'm familiar with the area. He should also be compensated, because had he not shown interest in me, they would have caught and shot me, and he would have shown you only my grave.

Perhaps God will help and Yozek will keep me — for the time being I've been here from May 31, 1943 — and I write today, on June 13 [sic]. If I manage to survive, it will be a great success and a miracle from Heaven.

I thank you, dear children, and forgive me if my behavior towards you as a father was not kind. Milo is in Heaven. He left a note for you by Henia; he could have gone to the Land but he dropped the issue on his own, and I didn't have money to send him. I kiss and hug you with my soul. Perhaps Luzhin has a child, he should be well, or Hassio — they should say Kaddish for their father and mother. Search for the corpses of the fallen. If you manage to take us to the Land of Israel, this will be a fulfillment of our dream.

Kisses to you,
Your father, Moshe Akar

◆ ◆ ◆

June 14, 1943
My Beloved Children!

As I wrote my letter from Radziechow — and now I'm continuing on June 14, 1943, when we are more knowledgeable. The people that were taken are certainly not alive anymore. Six months passed from the date of that letter, and all the tortures that we experienced then are nothing compared to the current tortures. They shot at people, women and children throughout the city, they [the Jews] were chased into the trucks; they drove them to the neighboring forests killing them there, took off their clothes and took everything. They destroyed and robbed property, houses and apartments, murdered the people, buried each other, and also slaughtered people with hatchets. Before that, the Judenrat slowly, slowly took away the authority from the Jews and destroyed them gradually — until they were all murdered. They say that those that were taken first are alive, but we don't know if this is true.

I add this in after I came here, to Henia and Yozek Lokschwitz in Uwin, and they've been keeping me already for 14 days and are hiding me out of pity. Every day there is a hunt in the area, and the question is whether I can get through this safely. For the time being, after all the adventures, I enjoy the Heavenly miracle that I remained alive. If I remain alive I will compensate the Lokschwitzes myself. If not — hear what they did to me and how they did this, where they buried me — and take me to the Land of Israel. What I wrote in the last letter is binding. I have with me a vial of "Veronal" [poison], but perhaps the date expired and I'm afraid that it may not work. That is why I await the murderers and perhaps God will save me. Until now, I put my belief and trust in God, and I avoid committing suicide also because of religious reasons.

I ask of you, dear Luzhin, revise my writings, make a

book of them and send it out to the world, so they should know.

These are - - - a handful of wild animals and stranglers of people. One must - - - each German and harm them every step of the way as much as possible. Take revenge against them for the tortures, in writing and orally.

Your father, Moshe Akar

◆ ◆ ◆

Instructions for division of the property, June 14, 1943

The property can be divided in the following way:

Debts that are insignificant, without a mortgage — if it is registered in the government office for land registration and if the registration is valid, there is an estimate and it is possible to liquidate them at very little expense. It is written twice about the debt to the health fund of Wolica, and the debt was already paid.

The debt to the health fund in Uwin is insignificant. About a fourth of the debts were paid. There is a debt for the plots of the flourmill and the distillery, and the plot on which a house stood in Radach but part of it was paid off and only the balance remains. In my opinion, it can be sold for profit.

The water rights with the turbine and the building plots in the village — do with them as the others will do. If specific requirements are needed — they must be met. Before the war they demanded 30 to 40 percent without - - - however I think that all this has no basis, because the people are gone and nothing is left. If Rozhia Fohorils' daughter is alive, give her 300 golden coins, 3–4 *morags* of land, take care of her. Her parents were murdered and she — a 16-year-old — went to work in Germany. She may be alive.

And now — the way to divide the lands:

Our fields are near the fields of the village of Wolica, and therefore it's possible later on to chop down trees facing the village's fields - - - and to sell the grazing lands. They will buy them willingly and pay for them. This is how the area from Wolica to Studzianki is cleared and later on give Yozek Lokschwitz the promised 20 *morags* - - - when the house and hut will stand, divide it into two big sections - - - there will remain about 30 *morags* - - - and to give each one - - — and about - - - *morags*. Well, one farm or until the field - - - if it will be possible - - - this is also there - - - on the Damhaduvka there are 24 *morags* of first-grade peat (two plots of 12 *morags* each) — it can be sold at a good price to people from Barilov and the area, half a morag to each one, because this is the best heating fuel in the entire area.

My dear children, get decent money, divide it honestly and live in peace and harmony, because in my opinion this lack of unity and lack of honesty between my brothers caused us such great suffering. We ourselves are guilty — long ago we could have liquidated everything and emigrated. God is witness that I am not to blame, and I am going to the grave with this, if I don't get through this cursed war.

I don't know what will be after the war. If they allow the sale of fields, under what regime will we be? These are important questions. Will they help, will they pay for the stock, the buildings they took, all of the harvest and the crops of that year, 17 cattle heads, 8 horses, equipment - - - if all this can be liquidated, may God be of help.

I write this to you when - - - Motek and Feivush - - - were taken - - - the children are alive - - - Motek and Feivush are helping them or Lolek - - - are old and will understand everything - - - but I think that - - - and wish

- - - good - - -

I kiss and hug you children - - -

With the wish "May God bless you and safeguard you.

May God illuminate His countenance for you and be gracious to you.

May God lift His countenance to you and establish peace for you."

Your father Moshe

Letter 54

Blessed the Lord, the day after Passover, the year 5704, in this millennium, here in Garani [sic], may our city be built, Amen.

My beloved, my sons and daughters, may God save you from all evil and bless you with all kinds of blessings and redemptions until the coming of our righteous redeemer, speedily in our times, Amen.

Difficult acts of heroism have been decreed upon us, and I do not know what each day brings and if I will merit to raise you to worship *the blessed and exalted* God, and to see you again. I have given all of the different articles to the neighbors. They are in Akira, to Saba Bella, and his brother Saba Andrash, clothes and *shleifering* [sic] — and to Saba Andrash I gave besides the above articles, gold jewelry, and eight hundred golden coins and besides this, fifty-nine coins from overseas. And I also buried a large chest with items on the southern side in the woodshed that had belonged to your uncle R' Wiemer, of blessed memory. And I also buried in our woodshed on the northern side, a small chest with the jewelry. If this letter reaches you, look in the places mentioned here. And I request that you go in an upright and kind way, with fear God your Lord, and follow His ways, and observe His laws and commandments that are written in the holy book of Torah, and in this merit you shall be privileged for the complete redemption speedily in our times, Amen.

Your father who blesses you and prays for you from a broken heart,

The small [one] Shalom Eliahu son of Leah
Son of my father, master, teacher and rabbi,
our teacher Rabbi Shmuel, of blessed memory.

Letter 55

July 11, 1944
A Will!!!

During the evacuation of the ghetto, with a pace between life and death, I leave behind some photographs of those dearest to me with the hope that somebody will find them while digging, and will search in the ground, and with the hope that this same person will kindly pass them on to one of my relatives or friends in America or in the Land of Israel, if any of them survive. My name is Frieda Niselevitch, born in Vaguva.

To my dear, distinguished father Nachum Tzvi Niselevitch, my sister Shoshana Stein, her husband Micha-Yehuda Stein and other relatives in Kelme that remained alive; to my dear niece, Esther Stein in Zagare. I hug affectionately my dear ones who will receive this will. If only they would know that I stayed alive until now, the only one from the family. I don't know anything about the others. I saw my dear mother the last time in prison. My brothers Simcha and Isaac Meir Niselevitch were in Ponevizh before the war.

I send blessings to my Jewish brothers who remain after the inquisition, if only they would be loyal sons to our holy homeland, the Land of Israel.

Frieda

The will was found where Ghetto Shavli, Lithuania had once stood.

Letter 56

These are the Jews that worked in Chelmno between Kolo and Dabie in the death camp:

1. Herskowitz Yosef from Kutno
2. Plotzker Moishe from Kutno
3. Plotzker Feivel from Kutno
4. Shlomovitz Shaya from Grabow near Lodz
5. Radkaivitz Noah-Wolf from Lodz
6. Chrach Chatzkel from Leczyca
7. Vachtel Simcha from Leczyca
8. Vachtel Yisrael-Chaim from Leczyca
9. Yastazhavski Banik from Leczyca
10. Nussboim Aharon from Sanniki
11. Strassburg Ozer from Lutomiersk
12. Shtayer Getzel from Turek

These are the last Jews that worked for the Gestapo in Chelmno located between Dabie and Kolo. These are the last days of our lives and therefore we are giving a sign, since maybe there are still relatives or acquaintances of these people. This way you'll know that all Jews deported from the Litzmenstadt [Lodz] were killed in a very cruel way; they were tortured and burned complete [alive ?]. If you are saved — you must take revenge.

◆ ◆ ◆

April 2, 1943

This note was written by people with 11 hours left to live. Whoever reads this note will have trouble believing it, but it's the truth. If it's not, the truth is that your brothers and sisters were killed in the same manner of death in this location. The place is called Kolo, 12 kilometers away from this town is the slaughterhouse for human beings, and we

worked in it like craftsmen. Among us were tailors, shoemakers, and shoerepairers, we were 17 craftsmen and these
are their names:

1. Pincus Green from Wloclawek
2. Yonas Lev from Brzezany
3. Shema Ika from Brzezany
4. Tzemach Shomirai from Sloclawek
5. Yassip Mayer from Kalisch
6. Vachtel Simcha from Leczyca
7. Vachtel Srulik from Leczyca
8. Banik Yastazhavski from Leczyca
9. Nussbaum Aharon from Sanniki
10. Ozer Strassburg from Lutomiersk
11. Mossik Plotzker from Kutno
12. Falk Plotzker from Kutno
13. Yosef Hershkovitz from Kutno
14. Chatzkel Zerach from Leczyca
15. Wolf Judkeiwitz from Lodz
16. Shaya Shlomovitz from Kalisch
17. Getzel from Torek

Thus, these are the names of the people that I present here.

These are a few of the hundreds and thousands that
have died here.

*These two wills were written by Jewish prisoners in the Chelmno death camp,
and found there after the war. They were transferred to Yad VaShem by the
"General Polish Committee for the Inquiry of Nazi Crimes in Poland."*

Letter 57

As I stand on the boundary between life and death, certain that I will not live any longer, I would like to part from my friends and from my works of art.

Ten years of work. I assembled, tore up and again worked on preparing exhibitions of my paintings, especially the exhibition "Portraits of a Jewish Child". I am currently saving, if this is possible, whatever can be saved, and whatever is appropriate to [the limitation of] space. I leave all of it here abandoned in the hand of fate, tens of oil paintings, portraits of Jewish writers, sketches and more.

I do not seek praise, I would only want some remembrance to remain of me and my little daughter, the talented young girl Margalit Lichtenstein - - - I donate my works of art to the Jewish Museum, which will be established in the future in order to rehabilitate the world of Jewish art prior to the war, until 1939, until the great tragedy of the ingathering of Polish Jewry. I cannot give details about our bitter fate, about the great tragedy of our people. I leave this for my colleagues, the Jewish writers. I request from people, from the public who will find my works of art, to realize that I had to cut around the forms of the paintings in order to adapt them to existing conditions.

I am now calm. I have to die, but I did what I was assigned to do. I am trying to preserve a memento of my works of art. Farewell, my friends and acquaintances, farewell to the Jewish people, do not allow such a destruction to repeat itself.

Gella Sakstein

Among the crates of the Ringelblum archives, found under the ruins of the Warsaw Ghetto, was a case with the artwork of Gella Sakstein: almost 300 pictures, aquarelles, paintings and sketches. There are also portraits of many Jewish writers, but the most emotional ones are her tens of paintings of children: Jewish children — their anguish and joys, their large hungry eyes; young children stooping over by the burden of life and the fear of riots; children full of worry and fear, already without a mother and father. Among the pictures is a self-portrait — probably her last picture. Her face is imbued with pain, steeped in anguish, and the shocking shouts of the ghetto being destroyed will be eternal. Here we presented parts of her will, written in the Warsaw Ghetto on August 1, 1942, during one of the actions.

Letter 58

Florence, November 29, 1943

My Dears,

I hope that you have received or will soon receive the suitcase and letter from Dr. Gazini. However, the various and numerous events occuring one after the other in recent days have rendered the news that I gave you in the letter no longer relevant.

We came here intending to stay only a few days, still hesitating whether we should continue on our way to you. But now we are forced to remain. We feel fine, don't be overly troubled about us and don't be concerned if you don't receive news from us. In contrast to this, we request of you to take the strictest precautions for your health.

I repeat what I've already written on previous occasions [details of activities to conceal articles belonging to the writer's sister, and arranging the matter of the inheritance of the sister's husband, who had died a month and a half before this letter was written].

Augenio is always in the same condition and so are Silvio and Umberto R. [relatives who were caught by the Germans]. I met Edgardo: a coward as usual, concerned with preparing a shelter under the stairs, near the pen, in Pinky's house, beyond the San Georgio Gate [the name "Edgardo" is a code word; as in other letters, followed by a description of the place where typical Jewish articles were concealed]. I hug you all with great love. May God protect you.

Germana [Ravena]

I feel fine and hug you with endless tenderness.

Marcella [Ravena]

◆ ◆ ◆

Florence, November 30, 1943
For My Brothers,

I write these lines from the Carmine Monastery, where we stayed when we came to Florence on the morning of the 26th. The Germans and the militia came at three o'clock that night and they conducted a search in the monastery. Mother and I, together with the other guests, were arrested (the ring with the diamond, a gift from Uncle Gigi, was taken from me) and now we await the crucial decision about our fate, which we predict will not make anyone happy.

Ask Mother Emma Louisa about our last days here. She, together with all the other nuns, was kind to us like an angel.

My dears, I want you to know that all of our thoughts are with you, and that in the last months I've fought with all my might to escape. When I thought that I had arrived at a safe harbor, fate mocked me so cruelly and everything collapsed. I hoped that I could reach Gabrielle with Mother.

If anything remains from all that we had, I would want half of my belongings to go to my sister Gabrielle, who has always done so much for me, and I request from her to prefer my dear Gracielina. The remainder will be divided between my Enrico and Valeria, who are very precious; I left for them a smaller part because I think that they need less than Gabrielle.

Be well, so very precious. I've always loved you very much. Make sure that there will be some memorial plaque for Mother and me at the cemetery in Ferrera, near the graves of our family.

I hug you with my entire being.

Germana Ravena
Carmine Monastery, November 30, 1943

If you want to make a donation to the Carmine Monastery, please look for Mother Emma Louisa and give it to her.

Germana

My papers will be inspected and destroyed by Gabrielle.

The notary and the lady have documents regarding Gabrielle.

◆ ◆ ◆

Verona, December 6, 1943

Mrs. Vitorina Guydetti
35 Lima St., Rome
May God bless you. I hug you.

[Germana]

Marcella,
My Dear,

We are here for five days and today we continue on our way. We are tranquil, therefore you too try to go on and accept our fate. We hope that we will meet again one day.

We had an unbelievable stroke of bad luck, and after we fought so much, we really don't deserve such a thing. I would like my dear sister to go and join Leona [a relative in Switzerland]; I think that she would have an opportunity for this. Also Orio or Nanda [Christian friends] may be able to accompany her, or Raph' [Raphel Kantoni, a Jewish friend and an anti-Fascist activist, who was on the same train, escaped and was saved].

We didn't have any ethical help from our uncles.

Everyone went about his own way; the youngest one joined his son.

I saw Edgardo. He built a shelter in Pinki's pen, under the stairs. I hope that he manages to be saved from the bombings.

I hug you, my dear, with my entire being; regard to Enrico and Valeria.

Germana

The last postcard was sent to a Christian relative and intended for the writer's sister. Germana and Marcella were deported to Auschwitz.

Letter 59

Belgium, September 8, 1943
My Dear Gilbert,

When you get this letter, I will no longer be [alive]. This is tragic, but true. I know that the day you read this letter, you will suffer horribly, but I will leave this place and my last thoughts are all with you. My heart bleeds when I think about what my parents have already suffered because of me, and how greatly they will suffer when they read this letter. You will find in this letter a final expression of my love to you and to my whole family. My death will be made easier knowing that they are in good health and shielded from poverty.

I don't want to prolong this torture, and you should know that my last wish is for my parents to outlive this nightmare and live a happy and easy life, as they deserve.

Goodbye to the whole family and to all my friends and girlfriends. I hug you all, Father and Mother, brothers and sisters, with all the strength still left in me, and with all my might [I believe] that my last wish will be honored.

Goodbye

Mauricio Rosenzweig

Letter 60

Poetia, April 30, 1942

To My Dears, My Mother, My Father, Gaston and Denis,

We know of this since this morning, but it is already final: we will be executed in about two hours, a punishment for the two attempted murders. I sit near my dear Maurice and four other friends. We are calm and tranquil. Yes, we are quiet and our greatest prayer, which we've repeated, Maurice and I, over and over to ourselves, is that our fate won't cause you too much pain, especially you, my dear Mother. We will no longer be on the face of this earth. In - - - it's not important, we are not even worried, but you — live, live for a wonderful future.

I would like to thank you, especially you dear Mother and Father, for all that you've given me since I was born. It wasn't in vain, because I have lived 20 happy years, free of any financial worry. Thanks also for all that you've done for me since my imprisonment. All this was never-ending proof of your love.

During the journey in the truck, we were able to see the route, the beautiful route of France, flooded in sunlight, cool, the same route that we happily crossed with our camping groups. Today I am pleased to have belonged to these groups.

Yes, the brief years of my youth were happy and I part from you with the thought, that great joy for Gaston and Denis is concealed within life. Young Gaston and Denis should look to the future, and soon they shouldn't dwell on their lost brother, they should have only one thought — to live!

To my dear brothers and sisters, I request of you to be brave, too, and envelope our grieving Mother with constant love in order to relieve her from the burden of grief. Father will be strong and bear his pain — he will overcome this.

I am not ending in sadness, because I'm confident of the future awaiting so many young people, my brothers and sisters, I think only of you.

Finally, I am strong, and face this last test bravely, and ask of you, too, my dear parents, to be brave. Your pictures are all before me and I look at your faces with joy, my dears, faces that I will never see again. My life was an honest, decent life and I am proud to die like this.

My dear Mother,
My dear Father,
My dear "elder" brother,
My dear, little sister,
Farewell, be brave!

Bernard

P.S. Thanks to Uncle Simon and Aunt Louise for all that they've done for me.

I'm sending you with this the pictures, the watch, the wallet, the ring, and hope that all the rest will reach you from Raviya.

Letter 61

Vienna, August 10, 1942
To My Daughter Anne-Marie Klauber
My dear Micheline,

I'm living here for four years, and I've survived it all because I've never lost hope of seeing you again. I've wanted, and still want with all my heart, to see you after the war ends. However, I'm fearful that I will be deported soon. This is extremely hard for me and I don't know whether I'll manage to survive the deportation. I'm willing to suffer anything, in exchange for the hope of seeing you again. If I cannot bear it any longer, I have the means to put an end to it all. It will be painless, my Micheline, there's no need to worry. I only wanted to be buried near your dear father. But I'm still avoiding such a decision, because the hope of seeing you is still extremely tempting.

During all these years, you were the sun of my life, and without you I wouldn't have been able to live. You were the best daughter I could have wished for, and you did for me whatever you could. In 1939, only a few days prevented me from being together with you [in England]. Your Aunt Lily shared my fate. She wanted to immigrate to Shanghai, to the United States or to Cuba. But God loves me, because you are in the good hands of such kind people. I thank them with all the fibers of my heart. Our grandmother is gone since June 1, she was deported and I don't have any new reports about her. This happened also to Aunt Mina, I hope that God has mercy on us.

My dear Micheline, I pray to God that one day you will find a fine husband to make you happy. I hope that you forget the German language, and if you have children, they too should never know this language. Your home is in England. Good people live there. Your adolescence was full of concerns. From today onwards, you will have to be happy and content!

Mrs. Hassel is an angel; she will tell you a lot.

I send you blessings, my dear, and I will love you until my last breath.

Yours,
Mother

I live with Lilly.

Elsa Klauber was deported to Minsk on October 5, 1942.

Letter 62

Hamburg, October 22, 1941
To my beloved and sweet little daughter [Ilsa]!

I am writing you on the eve of great events, I would like to part from you lest I die. Ada is kindly willing to pass this letter on to you. My sweet child, the most important thing is to be ready, and I am ready for everything. Lead me to life, lead me to death, Master; I respect Your commandments — this has always been my motto. Do not mourn; do not wear black clothes, because Father's wish was that you should not wear black over him. We are all mortals, but "you are dust, and to dust shall you return" was not said about the soul. And in a later Psalm of Life it says: "Footprints that perhaps another, Sailing o'er life's solemn main, A forlorn and shipwrecked brother, Seeing, shall take heart again"*. The good Lord knows — He must know — that I have always tried to leave my footprints on the sands of time, that in recent years I have never complained, that I have always tried to boost those around me and make their spirits happy. If there's anything that I regret - - -

Also Frantza, my new kind daughter, I imagine your pictures, I raise my hand and say first in Hebrew what one says to a son and daughter, and then: "May God bless you and safeguard you. May God illuminate His countenance for you and be gracious to you. May God lift His countenance to you and establish peace for you." And on the eve of Yom Kippur I bless you with the blessing from the orphanage's calendar, the handiwork of the teacher Uncle Yosef, with the blessings of a righteous one: "May it be the will of Our Father in Heaven to grant in your heart love and fear of Him. If only the fear of God will rest upon your faces all the days, so you will not sin. If only you will aspire to Torah and commandments. Look directly with your eyes, and your mouths shall say words of wisdom and your hearts shall only know the fear of God. Your hands should be busy with the Torah of God, your feet should hurry to do the will of Our Father in Heaven. If only He gives you sons and daughters, loyal to their duty, who will be busy all the days of their lives with the Torah of God and His commandments. May He provide you food in an honest way in calm and abundance from His open hand, and you should not need the gift of people, [even] a branch [a little] of food leaves time to worship God. May you be inscribed and sealed for a happy and long life among all those loyal to Israel. Amen."

Do you still remember, my dear child, how we would always laugh, especially Herbert, when our dentist told us: "Little Mrs. Von Son, immediately." She meant to say that the pain would immediately go away. And this is what I hope and aspire, that your pain over me, or your pain, my beloved children, will pass quickly and that you should deal with more important matters. Children should bury their parents, not parents their children — in this spirit I end with the words of Shakespeare:

"And whether we shall meet again I know not, Therefore, our everlasting farewell take: For ever, and for ever, farewell, my Ilsa, Manfred, Frantza. If we do meet again, for your lives we shall smile; If not, why, then this parting is sweet for the mouth".**

With great endless love.
Your
Regina

I must say in the words of Don Carlos, or perhaps it was the Marquise Possa, "Ho Queen, life was so beautiful." Despite everything. A short while ago I read the book "The Consolation of the People" by Aub. I did not notice that I had already read it once, and noticed this only when I saw the name "Rachel." Read the book, my good children, and it will give you strength as it gave me strength.

My dear Ada, a person must do for his family; this is why I am sending you this letter. Perhaps I will soon go to another place, and then I will send you my new address. Yesterday I already wrote you in detail. Warm wishes to you all, and sincere thanks for all that you have done and will do for me.

As always,
Yours
Regina

*[Comment of the editor [in Hebrew original]: The quote and line before it and reference thereafter to footprints on the sands of time are from Henry Wadsworth Longfellow's poem: "A Psalm of Life." Regina wrote the letter in German, but wrote the quote in English.]

** [Comment of the editor: This is a paraphrase of Julius Caesar by William Shakespeare, Act V, Scene A. Translated into Hebrew by Eli Tziper, Tel Aviv, 5745, page 39]

*** [Comment of the editor: according to the play of Friedrich Schiller "Don Carlos."]

Letter 63

Sunday, August 9, 1942
Dear Mother, My Father-in-law, My Mother-in-law, Max
and Philip,

Grabbing hold of a chair for a moment to write you
that it is possible to endure in Westerbork under the circumstances. We left on Friday night at 12:00 on the train
to the central station. We arrived at 3:00 at Hocheln. We
slept well in the train, the railway cars were nice and modern, comfortable places. Also Ess [Esther] carried on well.

Her medical records were not accepted, and neither
was my religious position. Now it is too late, but why not
us? I am happy that Ess is here and that the children are in
Amsterdam, because we will endure the situation here well.
Yesterday morning, I ran about in the Council of the Elders,
where I knew everyone, Koizer and Verkem and many others who promised me they would visit you, because I don't
know whether you'll receive this letter. I'm sorry about the
fact that Ess is temporarily separating from me, but I can
assume that I will speak with her tonight. The main thing
is that we know where we are, and a similar situation can
also come from Germany. In the afternoon I strolled with
Ess like an engaged couple, it's funny, isn't it? Yesterday
afternoon we ate some very tasty dish. We eat enough, I'm
satiated and feel invigorated, spiritually and physically, as
much as this is possible. Also Ess does not suffer from her
stomach or headaches. Other women in Amsterdam suffered from weakness spells, Ess did not. Therefore, please
don't worry. If we weren't here now, we would be going in
any event. What a pity that we are not allowed to write from
Germany. Therefore, there is no news — good news. And
if in some unexpected way bad news comes — don't believe
it. They are not killing us. I bear this with certainty; a per-

son can suffer greatly. Ess and I are enduring the situation with all of our might and all of our resources, thank God, and we hope to retain this. Yesterday afternoon we were in the synagogue, they read the entire portion and then there was the afternoon (*mincha*) service. I was called up to the Torah without payment because Leroy takes everything, until the last penny. I was fortunate that I had only two and a half guilder, and Ess had nothing. Later on there was a Torah class. Finally, I had a Sabbath until 6:00 o'clock — Shimon Machinkos and also Ben Machinkos behave like friends. We may be allowed to take with us a Torah scroll, it is for real, isn't it? It could have been a very good thing. I hope that Mother found everything, because what you sent is our only materialistic property. We have enough spiritual property; Ess and myself are tied to each other with an inseparable bond, and we are happy that the children are with you. Think of your health and of the children's health. Forget us, it seems to be the wisest thing to do. When we reunite again, you can again be reminded of us. We will not complain about ourselves. The difficult period is a tax we must pay for such happy years that we've spent together. We the young ones could tolerate it better. Yakov Reiness from R. Hart Street is here. He is my friend and we support each other. Also Eli Veggen and his son who suffered from nerves yesterday, maybe it will go well for him. I don't suffer from nerves, on the contrary, I encourage others. Also Zawab from Pacht Street (a brother-in-law of Barres) and Zagrius the shoemaker are here. The son of Rector de Yung, the brother of Rabbi Cohen de Lara, Bernhard Dodes, Eli Ascher — tell their families that they are fine. I slept well last night. I find that my life in the camp is an adventure. If I continue to accept life in the camp like this, and if I can cut myself off from my past, I don't worry. Max should learn Hebrew well, it may be useful for him under all conditions.

If the studies in school do not continue — seek private lessons for him. Teach Philip a little to pray, if it is possible.

[Esther and David Lamm]

Letter 64

Bonn, June 12, 1942

My Most Darling Children,

We are about to leave to the unknown, and since we don't know what will happen to us on this unknown way, we want to write you some lines.

We owe a lot to Miss Hella Benta, of 45 Koblenz St, so much so that it's doubtful whether you can compensate her. If we don't meet, also the Ordingen family that lives in the same place and knew you well. I don't have the strength to concentrate, and that's why it's brief. Be blessed, all of you, and receive the heartfelt kisses from your father who loves you so much,

Father

Dear Darling Children,

I see you vividly before my eyes, but many times we hope that the war would soon end and then we would hurry over to you. The idea is so wonderful that it has me standing tall, but to our misfortune, we can't flee our fate. Here, in the freezing Aulenburg/Evilenburg ??[Monastery], we feel quite well, despite the horrible food. To our sorrow, we haven't been allowed out lately, but the fact that we're surrounded by a large park has given us a sense of calm. For the time being, Father isn't yet fit for work, and we hoped we wouldn't have to leave, that we could stay here until the war ends in order to hurry over to you, but fate wants otherwise.

Miss Hella (Marichen) Benta — she and Dr. N. were wonderful to us. All the others abandoned us, but she was a pillar of strength and support for us, in her own brave and humble way. She is the one that helped us over and over, with dignity and courage that are hard to describe. Every

Sunday a package would come for us, and she would visit us with a family, Ordingen (taken from - - -), a friend and Lutheran who was so devoted to us; what courage she had to keep up the relationship with us! May God bless them for this great deed, of love and kindness. And you, my darling children, you cannot thank them enough. This is my greatest request, because it's impossible to describe this in words. Brothers and sisters would not be able to act like this. Such kindness and dignity. We would call her, this good person, "Himella," this one who risked all despite the great danger; also the Ordingen family and their most lovely daughter, my heart fills with gratitude to them. My darlings, she will transfer to you all of our things. Yes, I've dreamt that I could hand it all to you myself - - - be courageous, my most darling children. May God bless you, these are my last words!

My darling Ruthie, you are my eldest. You have gone through experiences with us at home — you have such a kind and warm heart, my beautiful and darling Ruthie. You always radiated such strength, and then I told myself: I will ask Ruthie. I didn't have to worry about her because she thought about everyone and took care of them.

Utichen, you went through a lot in America, I had to work a lot, my poor Utichen. My heart is full - - when I think of you all, but now, when Nurissa is able to work again, I'm not afraid for your future.

My darling Nurissa, your beloved mother and Janter have written me many times out of concern and love. They even sent me lately, with a gentleman that traveled to Germany, a sausage that was very tasty and - - - my God, we were so happy, dear Kurtzi. Utichen take care of our - - -.

My dear Lilichen, my Lilichen, I see you standing on the stage, I was always so proud of my Lilichen. I can't write more now, because we're getting a notice that we must leave with the first transport. I'm losing my head — Sigmund

255

Meyer could definitely have left us here another three months (Wanham, Oscar, Ada, Willy — they have better luck, they can still stay). Kellerchen in Berlin, she can also stay, she went through so much with the plane sirens lately. At this moment, I'm not able to think.

Lilichen, Runichen and Bobichen! My God, my sweet child, how I would love to hug and kiss you, my heart bleeds. My Auierlla, the youngest of all! What can I write you? My darling, be brave. Live a life of health, happiness, we have lived our lives, don't have pity on us. Always think of how happy I would be to know that you're happy. I have a last request, darling children, always stay together, whatever happens, love each other with all your heart — and then you will live in my spirit. Auierlla has always given me the last penny. It was so lovely on Hoenzulern Street, when we waited in the summer for Auti-Kurtzi, and Lilichen and Yinchen surprised us. Heinchen was always so good and she helped, not with words, but with deeds - - -

Darling Auierlla, I hope that you will soon find a person that you love, my child, to have a home of your own, a little child of your own and then you will be happy. Don't be choosy; you only have to love him. My God, if only I could see him, look in his eyes and whisper — grant happiness to my Auierlla!

Now we must simply be courageous. My dear children, my deep thanks for all of your love. Each one of you has made me so happy with his love - - - this is how I part from you. With tears and kisses, I hug you. The good Lord, protect everyone and bestow on them happiness. Don't mourn now the fate of the Jew. This isn't fate — this is the manifestation of violence, and we bear it with such magnitude. *Now the Buchnes have come, from here upwards, the transports go into nowhere.*

Urtchen, Hildchen, darling son, Auchen, I wanted to

write you a lot more but I can't anymore. Meyer the engineer couldn't hold us back here, as he had told me.

The miserable people — no, my darling, it cannot be described!

A thousand times thank you. Thanks for your great love. Gretchen, be a great man. Auchen, if only I could look at you just now. May God bless you all - - - warm kisses.

Ruth, Lilly, Aui, Nurssa, Yinchen, Bobichen - - - in three months it is forbidden for any Jew to be in Germany.

For: Ruth, Lilly, Ev

Letter 65

My dears, I sit down heartbroken to write you some words. Perhaps this is the last letter to you.

My dears, I don't know whether you will ever receive this letter, but if you do receive it — at least you will know how your beloved were killed. Dear Andzha, I will begin with our late mother. Our late mother passed away naturally, thank God, in 1942. According to the Hebrew date, it was six days in the month of Tammuz. Remember to have a memorial service for our dear mother. Our father was killed three months later by the murderers. From the entire family, unfortunately nobody survived. There is no sign of Zhurik. Now I face a new danger.

Andzha, be strong and keep on going with all your might, there is no chance that we will survive. And remember only one thing, to take revenge — if you can. We have no advice. There is no other rescue, because there is nowhere else to escape. We are bound in on all sides. I won't write you more, because I don't want to cause you sorrow. Dear Vebtcha, your dear mother and Hella with her husband and son — they are still here, thank God. My dears, if we still remain here for some time we will write again and a lot.

Your sister,
Natke

◆ ◆ ◆

Dabrowa, July 23, 1943
My Dear Sister and Brother-in-law,

I write this letter with the hope that it will reach you some day. Regarding Itcha — I don't know where he is. He was in a camp, and I haven't heard a thing about him. I managed to leave Shaindeleh with Mr. Turkin. I met Mr.

Turkin a few months ago. Well, you should know that he and his wife are very respectable people. You can't find such dignified people like them. They took Shaindeleh under their care. And so Andzha and Vebtcha, you should know that when you get word from Mr. Turkin, you should take care of my girl. Be good parents to her. My dears, I'm writing this letter during the last days. I'm staying with Velvel and with Nechale. We await death any moment, and we know which death awaits us. My dears, I am already three and a half years without Itcha. I supported myself and my child from my work. I worked in a shop for ten hours a day. When I came home I worked privately and made a living for four [sic] years, and our end is bitter and sad. But thank God that I had met Mr. Turkin. He is an angel. I have no words to describe him and his wife. And so nobody will survive from the entire family except my daughter Shaindeleh. I hope that she survives. I am sure that Mr. Turkin and his wife will protect my girl. My dears, I am unable to compensate Mr. Turkin for his deeds, I leave this to you. Andzha, I ask that you understand and believe Mr. Turkin and compensate him, my daughter will survive for you. I know, I am sure, that in my eyes I am already called before the angel of death. I don't believe that miracles can yet happen and we'll remain alive. No, no — such a thing can't happen. But my dears, you should know that I and Velvel and Nechale were the last victims. Aaron with Shaindeleh and their child are still alive. Also Mosheleh's wife and their child are still alive.

My dears, I write this letter in blood instead of ink. I am confused. My heart feels light only when I think of Shaindeleh being saved and of my leaving her in good hands, with dignified people. No longer can I help myself. Dear Andzha and my brother-in-law, be healthy parents to your children and to my Shaindeleh. I feel at this moment how your hearts are in shock as you receive this letter. It is not our fault. We fall innocently. Gone. It can't be otherwise.

My dears, inform our uncles in New York about everything. I had plenty to write. There wasn't enough paper, but to my sorrow I wasn't able, I am going around like a sleepwalker. My dears, it is very bad to die with a clear head when you see death in front of your eyes. I hug and kiss you, my dears, and also your children.

Your unforgettable sister Taibe'leh,

My dears, it pains me and tears my heart to pieces to have to write you this letter.

In 1945 the Jewish Committee of the survivors in Dabrowa received this letter from Mr. Turkin, in whose house Shaindeleh was saved. He gave over Taibe'leh's letter.

Letter 66

My Darling Child, My Poor Child Pierre,

I am about to die tomorrow. Take comfort in the fact that your father is about to die only because he is a Jew.

I am about to die on the first day of Chanukah. This is strange.

Forgive me that not everything with us and between us was as it should have been. Now you don't have one close person to you on the face of this earth.

I am transferring to you through - - - my gold watch and 500 francs. My bag with various manuscripts, is still in apartment P. And in Hotel M there is a suitcase with a package of books. Try to transfer the manuscripts for editing. I've lived my entire life for the sake of Russian literature. It was the most precious thing to me. Don't forget your poor mother; don't believe anyone who tells you uncomplimentary things about your mother and myself. God alone can be the judge. Be courageous, be honest, be a Jew. The love for our Judaism is always just. God will be with you as much as you are with Him.

I am about to die tomorrow morning. I still have much to do, I have sinned plenty, but I have always atoned for my sins. Genuine and honest atonement was my singular strength. My last thoughts are with the Lord, with my writings and with you, my darling child, my poor son.

Don't forget your father, it is such a pity that I cannot see you, even just one more time… But I will always be with you.

Send my regards to R. His memory and Mother's memory will always be with me until the end.

Pierre, little Pierre, why is it all ending like this?

I can't find more words. Am I afraid? Hardly. Perhaps only of the pain — but to live… to live… I would like to live for a long time.

May God protect us, and my people, my poor people!

I kiss you, my poor child, stay faithful to me. [I hope] that all that has happened to me on my way will be a guiding light for you. Pray for me and fight like a Jew.

I finish and return to God.

I kiss you, Pierre, Pierre, my Pierre,

Your Father

Letter 67

March 3, 1943

My Dear Daughter,

I'm writing you some words in a railroad car with 30 Jews in it. We are now passing Lourdes. It's obvious that we don't know where we're going. Forgive me, my dear daughter, for perhaps upsetting you by asking you to send me proof that you, Simon and Jacquo are French. That's what they instructed us to do. Imagine, my child, that before the trip they gave back to us - - -. It was all done so fast so we wouldn't be able to move. Don't be so upset about this; everyone is traveling. Thousands of Jews — from the camps and not from the camps.

Tell this to Simon. I'm sure that we're traveling to work. But where to? If we're traveling to Germany, we'll work in Drancy. I'm traveling courageously and in a very good mood. Of course not everyone feels this way, and so it is with the Jews, one says this and the other one says that. All of these people didn't yet experience the trials that we faced. It doesn't bother me, and secondly, I'm going with hopes in my heart, and it will be like this until I find your mother, my Sarah. This hope warms my heart because I must see your dear mother.

And I request from you, my dear children, it is unpleasant to remain now without your father, but you and Simon are - - - and especially you, my dear daughter, I know your nature and know that it is similar to Mother's nature. I think that you've seen how much the suffering and pain have affected your mother, and my opinion is that you also have my character traits, and in this way — a little from Mother and a little from me. You will be a perfect person. You see that I have courage? And if I really am in Germany, I will know that there is nothing to worry about you.

I'm writing better now because the train stopped in Lourdes, and when we travel — the train rocks.

If only I can, I will continue writing to you. If I meet Jews at the station, I will ask that others write in my name, because at some stations the - - - await us. They give us something to eat. They were already here today at Poe.

My dear Brett, I met in Gurs a merchant from Palikau Street, the owner of the laundry. He is not traveling yet because he is a Romanian. I gave him 1,500 francs and asked him to send it to you. The money will get to you — if not through him, then through "Uza." I left for myself only a few francs. That they shouldn't steal the money from me. I was in Gurs for two days and at the transit point I saw Mania Aurweiss. She is alone. I also saw Mrs. Lazar and the lady whose husband was with me in the train. They were with me in Goussain Ville. She has - - - like that woman whose mother has white hair on her head. I also saw - - -.

I will finish the letter. Write to the same address, Belac Jacques Belstein, who will send you whatever he received and also the things that I left. Write him to send you the blankets. Write him that you and the children don't have what to wear, and he should mention there that I took the blankets with me. I attach here the bread coupons.

I give you many kisses, and take care of the children. If you buy something for my sweet Jacquo, don't forget to tell him that it was sent from Mother and Father from Lyon. I hope that you understand everything that I write and that you should grow up and be a successful girl, as I've always expected.

Read this letter also to Simon, it is also intended for him.

The train is standing now in the station and I am finishing the letter. Regards and kisses to Nathan, to his wife and children, to the Green family and to all our friends and acquaintances. Regards to the worker at your workplace and to your boss.

Your Father,
Hoping to see you soon.

◆ ◆ ◆

Dear Brett. It is already the fourth day. I am now in the railroad car. We are surely traveling to Germany. I am also certain that we are going to work. We are about 700 people. 23 railroad cars. In each car there are two Gendarmes. This is a commercial railroad car, but it is neat with benches and a heater. Of course German railroad cars. Of course without compartments. They put a pail in it. Imagine the impression this makes. Not everyone can use it. You have to be strong in every situation.

I hope, my child, that you receive all the letters. If you can, keep them for a memento. Dear Brett, I attach here two lottery tickets. I don't have a newspaper. I believe that I will be able to write a letter to Aunt Paula. I hope, my child, that you will know how to behave as a free person, even though you are meanwhile without your parents. Don't forget that you must survive, and don't forget to be a Jew and also a human being. Tell these things also to Simon. Remain free people and observe everything with open eyes. Don't be influenced by the first glance. Know that you cannot open up a person to look inside, at his concealed thoughts, even if he has a serious face, or if he laughs or even if he is pleasant. I don't mean one specific thing only, but everything that lives around you and everything that you see. False thoughts and also honest thoughts are often blurred, and you should observe how a person behaves in your presence. You don't see the falsehoods or the honesty of a person in one day. You understand that my intentions are for your benefit. Always remember these ideas. My dear child, I think that this letter will be my last letter because we are nearing Paris. If I can — I will write again. My dear Bretshi, take care of your health, don't drink cold drinks when you sweat - - - and then I will be able to once again see healthy children. Tell Simon everything that I write you. Tell him to study and be a good student, because he is gifted. I finish my letter, many kisses. I am going with confidence that you will grow up and be a good, healthy and smart girl.

Your Father,
Hoping to see you soon

◆ ◆ ◆

Dear Nathan, I am writing you some words, but I think that there is no need to write you a lot because you understand what I mean. I request that you pay attention and say a word for the children, if it's necessary. I am traveling with courage and in a good state of mind, as I have had until now. I can't write because the train is shaking too hard. Lots of kisses and regards to all my friends.

Aaron Lieukant wrote the letter to his children Bertha and Simon in a train deporting Jews to Auschwitz.

Letter 68

May 14, 1944
My Dear Natalie, My Dear Esthie!

I write this letter to the both of you, because I don't want to, and I cannot describe our suffering and pain twice. Today I wrote you for the last time from the village where I was born, Tacovo, where my grandparents are buried. I don't want to make you cry; the fate that hit everyone has reached us here too. Tomorrow, that is on Monday, May 15, we are going on a journey on cars in the direction of Mosonmagyarovar, a distance of 60 kilometers.

We must all leave here, except for those who work in Margit-puszta, that is Bolli remains and so does Dr. Wolf, and all the rest must go. Poor Bolli, who will wash his clothes? Who will give him extra food? Where are you now? At home? Where is the place that we're going to? May the good Lord have pity on us, at last!

My dear Natalie! If dear Esthie isn't going to work anymore and the hostel closes down — speak to Mrs. Buchran, maybe she will take her in with her. If not, take her in with you; Aunt Molner will not oppose this, after all she is a kind woman. And add something for payment for her, put your dear one under your wings, after all you are older.

Poor grandmother and the other elderly and sick! You saved yourself the emotional tortures, because you're not at home. According to the attached note, I deserve another 2.40 kilos of bread from Weitz the baker. Take it from him. With all the sorrow, we must thank the good Lord that we can take food with us and underwear and even furniture. Every family gets 2 cars reserved by the local establishment, but we must pay. I hope that you got the package.

So long as we don't write the address, don't write.

Don't cry, but pray to the merciful God and tell Him, my God, after all, our father loves us, so You should too, Our Father in Heaven, love Your children! We can't do anything except pray. Dear Mother just cries and cries and I can hardly console her. It's good that I came, thank God, and I am near her.

May God be with you, my dear girls!!! We hug and kiss you with infinite kisses,

Your parents and Bolli — he is at home until he travels

Loving you very, very much

Warm regards to Aunt Molner, write to Bolli!

His address: To Markovitch Antel, for Paul Zhigmund.

Letter 69

Merciful People.

Save the child, May God repay you, don't hand over the child to the murderers!

Everything will be paid for, he has two pieces of property in Lukow, everything will be paid for.

Have mercy on the miserable child!

This is the request of a mother unable to do otherwise.

The distressed mother, H.P.

This is a note that a Jewish mother left with her son. She probably threw him off when she was taken to be murdered, hoping that he would be saved.

Letter 70

Dear Rubin, I leave calmly. I kiss you, your mother Chana.

♦ ♦ ♦

My dear daughter Yadzha, I am calmly going towards death. Don't lose hope!
I kiss you, your mother Moshkovitch.

♦ ♦ ♦

I am going calmly, Yozhek Yung.

♦ ♦ ♦

Zasha Vinder is parting from her husband Kalman. I am going calmly, Zasha Vinder.

♦ ♦ ♦

I am already tired of running away all the time from death. I am going calmly. How will my children live? What will become of them? Ch.S.

These inscriptions were found on the wall of the Hasag factory in Czestochowa.

Letter 71

Thursday, May 14, 1942

My Very Dear Spouse and My Dear Children.

I am writing you these lines to tell you that everything ends well. You don't have to think about me anymore. I am not suffering. It is over: Today at 10:00 o'clock I will reach eternal rest.

My thoughts are with the children, and this gives me courage. This is very important for me: One must die and therefore I am going to die. [My wife,] your mission is to raise the children as you are obligated to do, be courageous; this is my sole comfort.

My dear children, be good to your mother, from now on, all you have is each other. Don't make her suffer; your role is to be men in order to ease her suffering. Remember these words of mine always. Make her life less gloomy than it was until now.

Albert, you must take care of your younger brothers and your little sister, your role is to understand and behave properly. And you, my dear Odette, your role is to help your mother so she won't be sad always. I hug you for the last time with very deep sentiments.

Your father

And you, my dear wife, I request that you forgive me for any sorrow that I have caused you, and do not cry anymore.

Courage! Courage! Farewell!

Max Kawer was executed in the Cherche-Midi camp after he refused to turn in his underground comrades.

Letter 72

Rivesaltes, September 1, 1942
Heddi, My Dear and Kind Child,

It is hard for me to write to you today, but there is no choice, it has to be done. Your last letter from June 20 came to me while I was still in Gurs. Since moving from there on July 3, I haven't heard from you, and I hope that everything is all right with you. Concerning health — by me it's also like that. For all of us and especially for me, the last weeks were full of tension. Dear Father was deported on August 12, from the La Milles camp, and to my sorrow I don't know to where. The last news that I got from him was from August 9, and my hope is that we will yet meet somewhere on the way, because on the same date another transport left from this point to an unknown destination. I stayed here because dear Father was a slave laborer as of late. But currently another transport is about to leave, and this time I'm also going. My sole hope is that I will meet Father there, and I want to bear our fate, as hard as it is, with honor and courage. My dear and kind child, I am doing all that I can in order to stay in touch with you, but it seems that a long time will pass until we hear from each other again. I ask of you to write this also to Manfred and Max. I don't have the strength to write another letter to our dear uncles. I send them warm regards, I will never forget what they did for us, the poor ones. Also to you, my dear and kind child, I would like to thank from the depths of my heart for all that you've done for us lately. Always continue to be kind and honest, stand upright and never lose courage. Don't forget your dear parents. We continue to hope that the day will come when we will see each other again, even if this takes a long time. Please say hello also to Aunt Anna Velbea.

My dear and kind child, I bless you and kiss you with

my entire heart, I will never forget you and will love you
forever,

Mother

◆ ◆ ◆

Mantauban, September 4, 1942
My Dear Heddi,

I am going East, with wishes to see you again from
Mantauban, your loving mother.

Gabbi Epstein was deported to Auschwitz on September 11, 1942.

273

Letter 73

September 3, 1941

My Dear, My Husband, Most Beloved of All,

I write this letter to you two months after you've gone. Much has happened to me during this time, and now I must part from you! It's impossible for me to describe to you the hell of our lives. I will try, in only a few words, to tell you the main stages.

It started immediately after you left, on the very same day. On Friday morning, the city was already occupied — yet battles continued for six days. It seemed that no stone would remain intact over another. We managed to go through all this with the baby, under terrible hardships and harsh tortures in the cellars and in the church.

We knew that life wouldn't be sweet, but we had hope that they would let us live, and the worst case would be death from starvation. Kind people were found who brought us a slice of bread until it would all settle down a little. We started selling things in order to get food. We were so satisfied; it was as if we cast the lottery of life. This is how we lived until August 4th.

In the morning of that day, the terrifying drama began, as if from Dante's dramas. No, this isn't correct. Dante wasn't capable of imagining such terrifying spectacles as these. Between two rows of soldiers, armed with clubs, we were led to the forest; we stood there on a plot, surrounded by machine guns, and we silently waited for death.

1,900 people found their death there. The rest returned home. On this plot we left our father. We didn't grieve his death a lot. Healthy logic dictated that we survived to live a life worse than death.

But the will to live was so strong, that we were happy even with such a life. We didn't believe that we would be forced to go through something similar again. This period of life continued for four weeks and it had its "surprises" like: handing over silver and gold, payment of a ransom of 100,000 rubles, while waiting for them to organize the ghetto for us.

On August 31 rumors circulated that tomorrow the drama would repeat itself, the one we had already experienced. I didn't believe it, and yet the drama was repeated. This time we handed over Rossi, who was our "father" after our father's death. She had a strong will and physical strength for everything: she sold her articles, got food, managed the entire house and in addition she went daily to forced labor, from six in the morning until six at night. She ended her life yesterday, and today nobody deludes himself that the dessert was taken.

Today the rumor circulated that it would already be tomorrow. Since lately all rumors have come true, I'm parting from you already today. I've described to you only the dry facts. But my feelings, sometimes insane, I will not succeed to describe! And mainly when I look at my son. My dear, if only you would know what a beautiful and wonderful child he is. The heart explodes when I think that tomorrow I myself will carry him to eternal rest, and he laughs and shouts "Ay"..., God does not want me to be privileged to hear him say "Mother." He saved my life twice because they sent back mothers with their little children, and now I wanted to save him but there is no chance.

I wanted to convert to Christianity (many would like to do this). The Christian clergy went to ask permission for this, but they don't have any hope of getting such permission — therefore I must part from life. Mother is holding up pretty bravely; she is just grieved and pained that she can't save the child, and that she won't see you again.

I and Mother kiss you all strongly, and we request

275

that after your return — don't stay behind here, on our parents' land. Run away from the memories, from the place of our suffering, as if you're running from the plague. Weep over our fate, and try putting your lives in order.

And you my dear, whatever happens, put your life in order, because life has its own rules. Don't forget me and don't forget your firstborn son, whom you would have been proud of, if God had not given us such a punishment.

We kiss you one extra time and part from you,

Bluma, Mother and our son.

Master of the Universe! I've lived another entire month and again I deluded myself with hope, but it's in vain. Tomorrow is Yom Kippur, and it will really be the Day of Judgment for me and your wonderful son Yoske.

I so much don't want to die!

The boy is so wonderful,

And to die like this!

Bluma Stirnberg left the letter with a Polish neighbor called Piotrokovska.

276

Letter 74

Rivesaltes, March 14, 1941
Dear Children,

    You must be surprised to read once more that we're no longer in Gurs. From March 11 we've been in Rivesaltes. Grandmother and Uncle Emanuel are still there. Dear Manfred and Heinz — do you go to school yet? It must be lovely by you, be happy that you're there. I hope that you've gotten used to it. Dear Manfred — you're older, watch over Heinz and try to make sure that he learns something. Listen to the teachers and be good children, kisses from your father.

    […]

    Mother is in a different island [block]. I've already visited her. She wrote you. Did you get her letter? Answer soon. Manfred, don't lose the stamps.

◆ ◆ ◆

Rivesaltes, April 20, 1941
Dear Manfred and Heinz,

    I begin the day with writing a letter. I hope that you are healthy, and thank God, this is also our condition. We were very happy about your letter, and especially that you're content. Be happy you're there. This week a package will be sent to you, Mother knitted a vest for Heinz and she lengthened Manfred's vest. The other things you should divide nicely between you and don't fight over this. We didn't get anything from the United States. Manfred, save on the stamps. What's new with you? Write soon.

    All the best from your father. Heinz should also write.

My Dear Children!

We received your letter which we were so looking forward to. We were very happy with it, especially that you're healthy and pleased with the place. The men are in the same island with us, that is Island B, just that they're in different barracks. Which tooth of Heinz did they pull out? Was it a baby tooth? […] Did you also have a Seder? I would have sent you the things that I bought for you 3-4 weeks ago in the village of Rivesaltes: shoe polish, a lock and a toothbrush. I wanted to finish knitting Heinz's vest and make yours longer, Manfred, before sending off the package. I would have finished long ago, but I worked the whole week in the kitchen cleaning vegetables. In exchange for work in the kitchen we get extra soup, Father works on the roads. Uncle Emanuel wrote, and so did Uncle Mauritz write two letters. Aunt Alma didn't answer my letter, you didn't have to write her!

Are the trees blossoming by you? There are no trees here.

Manfred, do you still need the coat? It is very expensive to send large packages. You didn't answer my questions from the previous letter. There's no more news here. The men live in the island where the women live, and they can visit their wives from 9 am until 8 pm, but Father works daily from 8 am until 5 pm. It seems that you have good food, do you have meat every day? Write soon. Regards to Leo and Hugo Schiller. Mr. Rosenberg has a relative in Aspeh. His name is Frei, go visit him.

Kisses from your mother

◆ ◆ ◆

Rivesaltes, April 22, 1941
Dear Children,

We were very happy with your letter. We learned from it that you're healthy and this is our condition, too. Manfred and Heinz — we write you once a week, and this should be enough. What can be written already? Manfred, when you write you should write across the page's length and not it's width, and at the most two pages. You will get the package this week. Manfred, why are you upset when […]? We will write you every week, count on it.

All the best and kisses from your father

My Dear Children,

We received your letter, and we understand that you're satisfied. We're fine also as far as health goes. My adage says: "Even longstanding suffering will end well." Tomorrow I will send the package: two pairs of pants, toothpaste, a toothbrush, of course the two vests and a few things to nibble. Heinz dear, I was so sorry to hear about your toothache, I've also had toothaches in the last days, and so I know what it's like. We have vegetable soup each day. Usually carrot soup. Sometimes I do laundry for others, but I don't have a clientele like I had in Gurs. Give Leo and Hugo some of the candies. Are Ernest and Richard Willheimer in the room with Heinz? Manfred, send me the address of Dr. Frank from Limogoues. He is a relative of Richard and Ernest and he released their grandmother. He is supposed to know where to find Henrietta Zandler of Hopenheim. Did you visit Mr. Frei yet in Aspeh?

Seder night took place in the barrack that is used as a synagogue. A week ago it was warm and now it is again cold. This week it was possible to buy in the canteen only nougat. You must have suffered from your diarrhea. With God's help, it passed. Can't you get shoe polish in Aspeh? And toothpaste? Who actually mends your socks? Do you have wool for mending? I'm enclosing some wool. Regards to Hugo and Leo.

All the best to you and kisses from your mother.

◆ ◆ ◆

June 4, 1941
My Dear Children,

We got your letter, and were especially happy to see that you're well and content there. Do you have school again? You, Manfred, wrote only a little this time. You would have received my letter long ago — but it was sent back because it was too big. What did you do on the Festival [of Shavu'ot]? Did you have a prayer service? Here, on Sunday the prayer service took place outside because of the pleasant weather, on Monday it was in a barrack because it rained. On Sunday I worked as usual in the kitchen, peeling carrots and preparing the vegetables for the soup. What do you get to eat? Do you know if the Limogues children traveled to America? You're not registered, are you? You didn't write whether the vests were in the package. Does it fit Heinz? Don't lose them. I spoke with Theo. He wrote to you a few weeks ago. You didn't get his letter? Take good care of the new hat; use it only on the Sabbath and on Sundays. I am happy to see that you put on weight; I have a modern figure! Spring has passed and gone by, how time goes by — what will be with us? I miss the forest. Do you remember our hikes, for two to four hours to Neidenstein? And then, when we saw the beautiful castle we recited the poem "Be blessed shining sun..." and when we went to Steinport?

Perhaps it is better like this? Is it nice by you in Aspeh? That's all for today.

All the best and kisses from the bottom of the heart,
your mother.

My Dear Children,

We read your letters with joy because we see that you're healthy, and we are well as well. We are especially very happy that you're content. Be good children. Manfred, you ask about your English book — it's not with us, after all you yourself saw how it was. From [...] we haven't heard yet, I'll write him another time. We got a letter from Uncle Emanuel and from Grandmother; they feel fine. Please write soon.

All the best and kisses from your father.

◆ ◆ ◆

Brest, August 16, 1941

Dear Manfred and Heinz, I assume that you heard from Mother, and I hope that you are healthy, as I am.

Dear Manfred and Heinz — don't worry about me, it's enough that I worry about you.

My dear children, I have just one small request, and it's not a big one: Manfred, watch over Heinz so nothing happens to him; after all, you are the big brother. You should learn well in school and behave nicely. This is my request, my dear children, fulfill my request so I won't have to worry about you endlessly.

Write to Mother and send her regards from me. Write soon.

All the best and kisses from your father
Regards to Benny, Horst and Allenstein.

◆ ◆ ◆

Rivesaltes, November 8, 1941
My Dear Children,

Yesterday we received your letter, and thank God you're healthy. Take care of yourselves in this extreme cold and wear warm clothes. You still have the warm socks, and does Heinz's vest still fit? I assume that the dark blue suit with red is already too small for him. Why does Heinz write all the time that he has to stay indoors, is it because he doesn't have shoes? After all, I gave him three pairs of high shoes and a pair of rubber shoes. Where did they all disappear? It's a pity that I don't have wool — I would knit socks for you. If only we could have taken from home the vests and the woolen socks. Do you get warm clothes? Should I send you the blue winter coat? We bought a lock for Heinz.

Manfred, I don't know what advice to give you regarding Heinz. Find out whether you're allowed to take your brother [to the United States. Only Manfred got a visa]. It seems to me that the two of you should stay together, rather than one here and one there. I heard from the OSE [Oeuvre de Secours aux Enfants — an organization that helped children] that soon somebody will come to Aspeh about the issue of traveling to America. Mrs. Salomon is here at the moment and says that she will soon go to Aspeh. I want to send you something, but freezing winds are blowing outside and it's impossible to get to the post office, which is far away in another island. In addition, I had a swollen cheek and they had to pull out an infected tooth, something's always happening... I have to watch myself, because I get diarrhea easily. A letter came from Aunt Elsa, dated August 15. She says that she got one from us in August, and we actually wrote her several letters?! Theo left and works in some restaurant, Kurt Altstater left also. I don't know if he went to an institution or some other place. Father still works in the military camp with the vehicle for the toilets. He gets some additional bread and soup. Uncle Emanuel sent your vaccination records from Gurs. Should I send them to you? Just don't lose them. Do you have heaters and are they being used? By us there is no heating and the barrack is big, there is room in it for 90–100 people. Did you get the stamps that I sent you the last time? Manfred, on second thought, perhaps you can take Heinz with you, I think it's better for you to be together.

From now on you must write a number near the name. The number is: 5273

Be well, kisses from your mother.

◆ ◆ ◆

Rivesaltes, August 10, 1942
My Dear Children,

I would like to write you some lines, quickly before the trip. Since we're traveling and we're allowed to take only one piece of hand luggage, I sent you the case of clothes yesterday evening. If you go to America take with you what's necessary. With God's help, maybe we will also end up there. Regards to Aunt Elsa when you write her. I don't know whether we can write you — perhaps via the Red Cross. Be good children.

Your mother, who loves you.

My Dear Children,

Just some lines before the trip — I don't know where we're headed, we don't feel sorry at all about leaving you behind, you are more sheltered. Maybe you'll hear about everything.

**Stay healthy. All the best
and kisses from your mother [from your father]**

Dear Manfred and Heinz, be good to each other — these are my concerns.

Carl and Matilda Mayer and their sons were deported from Germany to France and moved to confinement camps. The boys were rescued by a Jewish organization that worked among the prisoners in the camps. The parents were deported to the Rivesaltes camp. From there they were sent to the Drancy camp. They were deported to Auschwitz on August 14, 1942.

Letter 75

My Dear Aliza and Shlomo Wald!

Today 6.6.42, I, Binyamin, and my father Moshe Wald live as sole witnesses from the entire family. It is already nine months since our relatives went to Treblinka, my mother and my brother Yakov from Szydlowiec and the others from Tomaszow since then.

Five months ago Chava and Estera, the mother of Shlomo, were by us. They were with us in Szydlowiec for two months and they went to work to Pionki, and fate has my father and me travel from city to city, from village to village. There are kind people who hide us, but the public [Polish] is very bitter, and is happy with the fate of our people. Our lives are very bitter, but we wish to live after the war in order to take revenge against the Germans and also most of the Poles, for fate of our people. And now we don't have a place to stay by people, and we have to walk to the forest and live there by the sword.

It is possible that we'll live to see you, and if not, so peace unto you.

But remember, the revenge against our enemies is allowed to be very great and the people of Israel, if it wants to live and if it doesn't want what happened to us to happen a second time. And what happened to the nation in Poland I cannot write, it was plenty and worse than death. It's entitled to be like other nations, "a nation apart," with land, with an army and with thoughts only for the homeland, I am in favor [in the name of] the people who were killed to request of my brother to work without stop for his Homeland, because Eretz Yisrael was our hope until the last minute, and at the last minute, we saw how bad were our ways. There is much more to write, but our heart and soul are sick, and it is not enough for us to write because we are individuals of the many.

I send a blessing to my land and to my brothers in Israel and to all my relatives.

One of the last ones Binyamin Wald

Today our names [the name which appears on the false certificates] are Stanislaw and Thedaush Skalski.

We send our 2 pictures for a memento.

◆ ◆ ◆

To the prominent and kind one who finds these two attached letters,

I request a favor to send the two letters to the address, to the only ones of our family who live in Palestine, to Shlomo Wald who lives in Haifa or in the Bet Yehoshua colony in Palestine or to Aliza Birnstock who also lives there.

If the address is not enough I request to send the letter to some institution in Palestine.

It is very important for us to pass on the news to our family, since this is the only sign of our lives.

We are now in a very special and crucial situation, our tomorrow — and even the most imminent moment — are not certain.

Again, we request of you to do us a service, perhaps the last one, by sending these two letters with pictures to the address mentioned above.

Thanking you in advance.

M. Wald and his son

We lived before the war in Lodz, 21 Polodniva St.

Letter 76

Iyar 5703, June 2, 1943

Dear Friends,

The writer of these lines has already written a letter a few weeks ago, but in my opinion, now is not the time to think, but the time to shock the world, the entire humanity and particularly our brothers, the children of Israel. I came a month ago from Poland to Pressburg [Bratislava]. I ran away from the inferno, in order to shock the world into neither resting nor remaining silent. Rather it should do something and take action for the sake of the survivors remaining out of several million Jews in Poland. According to my assessment and estimate two hundred thousand Jews survive. They are mostly in confinement camps. They suffer the pains of death, they are tortured, slaughtered, burnt, hung, hungry and thirsty and strangled. Day by day their number decreases. There are still those that are concealed, hidden in secret hiding places in the thickets, in the forest shrubbery, and are supported by democratic Polish farmers who feed and support them with lean bread and scant water. In my opinion, if our brothers, the children of Israel, do not come quickly, as soon as possible to help these brothers, then the sentence is already decreed for them to die from these tortures which are harsher than death. I have left Poland not only to save my body — I have lost all my family members, they all died sanctifying God's name — my son, my father, my brothers and my sisters. I have left to inform and publicize to the humanistic world all that I saw with my eyes and all that I heard with my ears, to arouse the hearts, the hearts of all those who are not sealed and fossilized from hearing and knowing about the entire brutal tragedy that has happened to our people, and I have two intentions:

1. And this is the main one, to come and rush assistance to those that can be gotten out from the lion's teeth in Poland, while there's still a chance.
2. Our brothers, wherever they are, should know that when the war is over and the bloodshed comes to an end, they should avenge the blood of our brothers spilled like water on the ground. I myself heard hundreds of times from the martyrs whom I saw — I was forced to do this — as their souls departed in holiness and purity and their last words were: Our brothers, remember, take revenge, avenge our blood. I saw with my own eyes how men, women, children were buried alive and covered in dust, and they shouted for help and revenge, but *Heaven is my witness* that they could not be saved from these leeches. It was impossible to take revenge on the spot, because the lives of all Jews in that city were endangered. Indeed we, my brothers, are the ones assigned a sacred duty, and this duty is — revenge. However heading our duty is to rescue by smuggling across the border, the hundreds and maybe thousands of Jews who can still be saved while their soul still stirs within them.

In my previous letter I've already described to you the killing locations of Belzice, Melikinia, Treblinkka near Bialistok. Locations where millions of Jews were murdered and killed, choked to death by gas. In my opinion, you must publicize this in the newpapers of the United States and Israel, so the world should thus know where these murdering locations are. Lately, the Germans write of the Katyn [Forest], a place that according to the German press is supposedly where Polish military people were killed. And I myself could have shown tens of locations in the thickets and in the fields where the Germans murdered tens of thousands of Jews in each and every place, burying them in their clothes and shoes. I took note of all of these places, and these tragic incidents, so that if I remain alive when the war ends, I can at least publicize it in the press and condemn the evil ones before the entire world. I have figures, dates, details; I myself was eyewitness to this. I will tell you one incident which happened a few weeks ago in a confinement camp, and this should be enough for you to grasp the whole situation and the conditions there. This is what happened: Two young girls, one was twenty and the other was eighteen, two pretty and pleasant girls. They worked all day under guard and supervision, outside of the confinement camp, and towards evening they went back to the confinement camp after twelve hours of grueling work. When they entered they were inspected and a half a loaf of bread was found on them that they had brought from their place of work. In the confinement camp one gets only eight *deca* of black bread a day, and it's forbidden to make a living from the outside. They brought these girls to the head of the camp, a German, a foe and enemy. He, this murderer, sentenced these souls to be hung. And in order to further torture the Jews in the camp, he ordered all of the Jews in the camp to gather round, to the place where the sentence would be carried out, and ordered the Jews themselves to construct and set up the gallows — this was his custom. These girls fell at the feet of the murderer, the head of the camp, and begged him, pleaded before him, perhaps he would have mercy and forgive them for "their crime", but he was adamant. All the Jews started to cry and plead before him, but the murderer threatened them, that if they don't hang these girls he will condemn two hundred people to death. And the Jews with broken, shattered hearts were forced to build the gallows and lift these girls up on it, in front of all the camp's Jews. And something happened and the ropes tore and the girls fell to the ground while they were still alive, and then they approached the ruler once more to perhaps pardon them, and then the ruler himself took out his gun and shot them, and the Jews had to bury them. Stories like these are daily occurrences. They shoot, they hang, they burn without any reason, without any sin. The people that still survive work until their strength is gone, and when their strength fades away, and they can't work anymore, that's when they come and kill them. These are the Jews who survived and are tortured and suffer — they have only one question: Why, why are our brothers silent and why don't they shock the world, and they don't come to help rescue by smuggling over the Polish border. There are still some important leaders from the Zionist organization, public figures, pioneer youth, who can still be saved by smuggling over the border. It all depends on money, expenses for the route, payments to the smugglers. And you must help, to rush the help and not to be late, time is tight. My concrete suggestion is that you send funds to the rescue committee here and enable them to bring many Jews and this should be as soon as possible.

Forgive me for the form of this letter, my nerves are tense, my hands shake, a consequence of my experiences in Poland.

Yours, Eliezer Unger

Letter 77

The gates are opened. Here are our murderers. Dressed in black. On their contaminated hands they wear white gloves. They shove us from the synagogue in pairs. Dear sisters and brothers, it is so hard to part from a beautiful life. You who remain alive — never forget our little and innocent street of the Jews. Sisters and brothers, take revenge against our murderers.

Esther Shroll

◆ ◆ ◆

Reuven Atlas, you should know that your wife Gina and your son Imus were murdered. Our son cried bitterly. He didn't want to die. Go to war and take revenge for the soul of your wife and your one and only son. They are taking us to die, and we are innocent.

Gina Atlas

These were inscriptions on the walls of the synagogue in Kovel, Volhynia. Esther Shroll and Gina Atlas were murdered on September 15, 1942.

Letter 78

Hello to My Friends!

I write you once more. We passed Kovna and Vilna. So much destruction, blood and tears. In Minsk, in the train station, I met some boys from my city. I heard a story from a 19-year-old boy and his voice was like that of an old man. He told me that the Nazis murdered my family on June 3, 1942. My one and only son was carried by my wife's brother. My older brother, Tzvi, hid with his baby daughter in the attic. The crying of the baby gave them in. The Germans shot them on the spot, killing them.

For three days the slaughter of the Jews in the city continued. They threw people in the pits while they were still alive. They prodded them with clubs, like dogs. They shot on the way at whoever couldn't come.

No! No! It is impossible to forget this.

Many young people died as heroes. Only those that lived in the forests as partisans and those hid in all types of hideouts survived.

One thing I know now: These savage Nazis and their collaborators must be killed. The hatred burning within has strengthened me, giving me courage and strength.

They told me that a young man from our city turned to those near him while bullets were splitting his body: "Jews, be strong and courageous! Avenge our blood ....".

I don't know a thing about my sister, and also not about my brother Yehoshua, who was drafted in May 1941.

They killed my mother, my brother, my wife and my son.

Why do I write to you, after all you are strangers!? - - - It is hard for me. I must share it all with someone. I don't have one person who is close to me, understand me.

Doesn't Yakov write you? I write him often.

Good bye

◆ ◆ ◆

January 24, 1945

I am waiting for a letter from you. Write about how you are and how things are with Yakov. Why are there no letters? I write you all the time. So little time! We are advancing day and night. The Red Army is doing its mighty duty — victory over the Germans. Everyone is resting now between battles, instead of sleeping — I write to you. Who knows when I will write you again.

We are striking at the enemy.

Peretz

◆ ◆ ◆

Hello to My Friends,

Regards from the front.

I have some free time and I write to friends.

We are advancing, pursuing the Germans, the land of the enemy is ablaze; we are taking revenge! We are winning! Proudly we march forward. Lacking sleep and in an uplifted mood.

I feel good now — I'm participating in the destruction of the enemy.

Peretz

Excerpts from the letters of Peretz Levine, sent from the front during World War II. Peretz fell as a soldier of the Red Army on February 8, 1945, in Eastern Prussia.

Letter 79

My Small Will

I, Yitzchak Aron, the son of Moshe and Tzirel, was born and raised in the town of Miur, in the district of Vilna (I was born in 1914). I was saved from the brutal slaughter on June 2 (Tuesday) 1942, when the Hitlerian brutes took out all of the town's Jews, 926 people, and with the help of the local police they slaughtered 800 Jews, women and children in a bestial way (only 70–80 people were saved). Every day I wrote down my experiences of the slaughter, that is from June 2, 1942. I wrote every day (indeed briefly, because of a paper shortage), everywhere and under all conditions that I was in. I wrote when I was hiding in crates, in wheat, in the stable, in the forest and in the great mud. And so, I wrote for three months and five days, that is until September 7, 1942, until I completed the notebook. I decided to leave the torn and dirty notebook, like my life, with a Christian acquaintance, son of - - - I have complete trust in him that he will hide the notebook. My goal was to perpetuate the experiences and the immense inhumane misfortunes that we, a handful of Jews, about 30–40 people, have gone through since that awful day of the slaughter. But I did not manage to do this. First of all, because I don't have writing skills, and secondly — when I would take a pencil to write, the dreadful wound in my heart would immediately open up wide. My eyes would fill up with blood and I couldn't write any more… The wound is not small and it will never heal as long as my eyes are open. The Hitlerian murderers spilled so much Jewish blood, they murdered the town's Jews. I lost on that Tuesday my father Moshe the Kohen (everyone knew him), my mother Tzirel, my married sister Frieda with her little angel, five-month-old Shneur'leh, my brother-in-law Moshe Frumin, my younger sister Essinka, 19-years-old, my elderly uncle Menachem Mendel Aron, my good friends Isik Engel and his wife Chaya and their son Kalvina, my friend Leah Aron and her daughter and son Faige and Arka, my young friend Aletzik Lifshitz, in short, I lost everyone and everything. I was left with my sister Gita and a few other Jews and we're not - - -

They want to terminate us in all ways, so nobody should remain alive. They, the murderers, don't even grant us the broken lives that we have today.

I requested of the man with whom I deposited the deposit not to show or give the notebook to anyone while I'm still alive. After my death he must give it to my sister Gita and if she also isn't alive, he should give it to a Jew that he meets, a survivor of the brutal slaughters and persecutions.

My wish is that, if I cannot look forward to some comfort of revenge against the Hitlerian murderers and the local police while I'm alive, at least my own notebook, with its 14 tattered pages, will serve as a picture of the enormous tragedy happening to the miserable innocent Jews in our region on the part of the violent criminals. May my notebook, written in blood and amid the most difficult moments of my life, and the lives of the miserable Jewish refugees, serve as proof and evidence to the world of the bloodbath of the murderer Hitler, his name should be wiped out, and his gang of criminals — the Jewish blood of innocents. This notebook should at least serve somehow to help take revenge against the German murderers for our parents, brothers, sisters, children, for our blood spilled with no wrongdoing on our part.

Letter 80

July 23, 1942
My Good Friend Jacob Skala,

I write this letter during grave moments of despair. I have a great request from you: To comply with all that is written here. I will not write a lot. I will do it briefly.

I wrote a book about the dreadful slaughters in the town of Huszt. In my opinion, the book should be printed in as many copies as possible — that the world should know! The price of the book will be one Polish zloti, as per its value before the war.

From the revenues, they should build a monument in memory of the murdered from Huszt. They are located at a distance of five kilometers from the town, in the "Simnover Brezins" Forest. The monument should be built according to the latest technique. The balance should be given to Mr. Kapar. The Kapar family consists of three people: the husband Theofil, his wife Brigida and their daughter Gabrinia.

This will be a very comprehensive operation. The following people will help you in America: Aaron Pasis and his family in Brooklyn (they will refer you to Abraham Mazern in New York), and David Cohen in Brooklyn. Regarding additional addresses you should turn to Moses Friedman in Buenos Aires, Argentina. You will get much assistance from the engineer Yosef Weinshel of Haifa Port in the Land of Israel. The work should be comprehensive. In every country there should be a person who will make sure that the book is printed. The revenues are intended for the goal that I mentioned above. The balance will be handed over to the Kapar family.

I hand over to Mr. Kapar the management of the work of building the monuments, and also the rights for the book's translation and the revenues from it. All other additional jobs that ensue should be done with his participation.

This request should be fulfilled whether I'm alive or not.

Except for Mr. Kapar, don't authorize in my name the receipt of additional addresses.

The address of Jacob Skala: *"Forwards"* Editor, New York.

The address of Yitzchak Finklestein: Magdiel, the Land of Israel.

The photograph is attached to the document to show how the Kapar family hid us in their house for a long time.

1. [Signature]: Kapar Theofil, born 1899.
2. [Signature]: Kaparova Brigida, born 1910
3. [Signature]: Kapar Gabrielle, Born 1929

I authorize all of the signatures of the Kapar family.

[Signature] Peretz Goldstein

July 24, 1942

Letter 81

Konin, August 9, 1943
My Dears!

I will relate to you in a few words what's been happening to us until today. I arrived at the Konin labor camp on March 8, 1942, me and my father-in-law, who is dear to us all. 868 Jews were brought here.

I guess that it was fortunate that I was elected to be the Elder of the Jews. Only due to this was I able to watch over the life of dear Father, as long as I was alive. On April 17 all of our family were deported from Gabin. Among them were our dear mother, Marishia and our beloved daughter Freitza. The meaning of deportation, I clearly understand — they are not alive anymore.

What meaning had our lives then — you could just imagine. I had only one ambition left: To protect the life of our dear father so that we can see him again, but destiny wanted otherwise.

It is already the second day since the Gestapo took our papers. We know that the death sentence was decreed for the remaining 60 people.

There is a gentile who wants to take me in, despite the fact that by doing so he will suffer the same fate, but I decided not to part from my dear father, you can learn about this from Max Pokrivka in Poznan, Garberska St.

Do not imagine that this is because of light-mindedness or cowardice on our part. We are not like this. We have seen more than enough and we do not have what to live for. I am enclosing also photographs of dear Marishia and of our beloved child, born on February 22, 1940. He was killed with Marishia and with our dear mother.

I and some friends are planning to act like Samson*, if only we succeed to have the opportunity.

No news has come from Mark, Leon, from my parents and from the families for a complete year. Meaning that they too were annihalated.

You can learn about details of our life from Max Steinhaker of Hamburg, who lived in Altona, and maybe also from Vaclav Visniakovski of Gabin or Yossele Kantorovski of Nieslusz, in the Konin district.

I write this letter in the last moments of our lives. We have one request and that is revenge. No matter how much revenge you take — it will not be sufficient. I and dear Father kiss you: Fania, Adash, Dora, Samek, Yehoram, Genia, Sonia and Amira.

Be strong and courageous

Feivish

*The prophet Samson was captured by the Philistines and when led to their celebration, brought down the pillars of the building killing more in his death than during his lifetime (Judges 16:30)

Letter 82

Sophie Heiman
Noe Camp, August 22, 1942
Dear Martin and Dear Children!

When you receive this letter, I will no longer be in the Noe Camp. Lately, so many transports have left all of the camps that we, who remained in the camps, have to cope with the possibility that one day we will be sent further on. We don't know anything for sure, but the general assumption is that most of us are liable to be sent. You, dear Martin, know where, to the place where the Berliners are, and you can tell this to the girls. As long as I am able to — I will continue to write to you, but please don't worry needlessly if you do not get any more news, because they say that no mail goes out from there, and there is no point in sending a telegram. We must just hope that you, like me, stay well and in one piece, and when the war ends, we will see each other again. Give this letter also to dear Gerdel and Eli. Do not lose the courage and trust in God, to Whom I always cling. God has watched over us until now and He will be with us also in the future. After all, I am not alone and am part of a large company. Stay healthy and safe and get ahead in life.

But if something happens to me and the spirit of my life runs out, this is also the wise will of God, which would have caught up to me wherever I would have been, because some day it comes to everyone. I take with me the soothing news making me happy that all my three precious girls have become independent and can now manage without me. To you, Martin, again thanks from the bottom of my heart for all of the love and good that you did for us, things that I will never forget. You, my dear children, continue to correspond with your dear uncle, and when the day comes, we will return, with God's help and find each other through this.

Therefore, hold your heads upright, and do not despair, but always hope for the best.

All of you, stay healthy for me.

All the best to you and be blessed, again from the bottom of my heart,

Yours always,
Mother Sophie

Letter 83

Angeles, near the sea (Mediterranean)
June 8, 1941
My Dears,

After five months of wandering, your postcard came at last to the right hands. Since you, my dears, got our last letter, so much has changed by us. I have to and want to report to you but I will do it briefly. Sima and Shaya [the oldest sister and the brother-in-law of Helen] were at home. Oscar, his wife and daughter are in Antwerp since October, and continue to manage the factory [for raincoats]. The situation there doesn't seem bad, as he [Oscar] claims in the letter that he sent to Peltzer in Portugal. Leon, after a brief stay in Portugal, traveled with his wife and child to America. We passed on to you news about them regularly, but to our regret with no success. Adolph stayed with his family in the same village [in France, Vichy]; with all the tragedy, it's lucky they got permission to stay there. They will certainly become farmers there [they finally escaped to Switzerland].

My dears, the families of Sima and Adolph have multiplied, thank God. Sima gave birth to Hersheleh, may he live [Sima's entire family was killed in Auschwitz], and Adolph has Yitzchak, may he live. May God Blessed be He, give them, the entire family, *maza*l and happiness for the big event.

Meanwhile we don't feel anything - - - we, the three girls, are already switching to the fourth camp since November. Mina and Evaleh (Chavaleh) went home in good luck with the Belgian transport six months ago. Since Oscar is at home [in Antwerp, to which he returned from the village in France], Adolph hasn't received any mail from him. He is doing everything to make contact with him. We are in contact with Adolph through letters. Every so often he sends us food items which we need more than he can offer us. He also sent us your last postcard. It is already three months that we are near the Mediterranean Sea, and if he can get us out of here, this will be fortunate. I sent you a registered letter four weeks ago, and I hope that you will get it. Dear parents, how are you? Are you healthy? Do you have a livelihood? Do you still live in the same apartment?

Sabina, Bertha [Helen's younger sisters], did you get married yet and are you happily married? Are you healthy? Make sure to take care of our parents and not to worry about us too much. You cannot imagine what an emotional state we're in.

How is David, Betzalel and Eva [more brothers of Helen] and their families — are they all healthy? Do they all have a livelihood?

My dears, you must try to help us. Maybe dear Father has someone in America or another place, with whom you can make contact to get us out? Also Adolph needs such a way to get out. Do whatever is possible to enable us to have this chance.

We are, thank God, in a condition of good health. What we're going through is beyond our strength. My dears, don't be upset with us, think, discuss — only calmly — how to help us. I am ending with this urgent request, with the hope that all your attempts will merit maximum success. May God have us meet again on joyous occasions.

All of you be well and in good spirit, and inform us as soon as possible about whatever you can do.

To all of you from the heart, wishes and kisses,

Yours, in the hope of quick help and a joyous meeting,

Your hopeful girls,
Helen and the two Feiglech

Helen wrote to her parents Henia and Yisrael Rappoport in her name and the name of her sister Feigaleh and her cousin Tzipporah (Feigaleh). The family was from Antwerp. The parents and other brothers mentioned in the letter were already living in the Land of Israel. Helen and her sister were sent to Theresienstadt on June 1942 and from there to Auschwitz. Their cousin was saved.

Letter 84

Budapest, March 29, 1944
My Beloved Children!

I pray the following prayer day by day: The great Lord, residing above the sun, above the stars, You Who is in every place and also with our beloved grandchildren, with our beloved children, with my beloved wife, and with myself. Hear our prayer, grant us kindness and unite us in life, in health, in freedom, in love, in happiness and contentment. Disrupt the evil intention of our enemies every time and every place.

My beloved, May God bless you,

Your father who loves you,
Address: Henry Adler
[…]
Michigan

Letter 85

September 6, 1942

I must overcome the difficulties and write you about my situation, as follows. The Jews of Estrik were deported yesterday, and we're going today, men, women and children. Thus also Estrik went to a nearby village, near Linesk. That is where Shmuel Leib works all the time. They say that 3,000 people, fit for work will remain there, and the rest will go to the slaughter. From the entire area of Tanik 15,000 people are being deported. Now you understand my situation and the situation of all the Jews here. It seems to me to be worse now than the destruction of Jerusalem. Therefore, beloved children, as we see, it appears that I'm writing you now a farewell letter and parting from you and this world, because people in my condition don't have anything to look forward to. But it says in the Torah: "Even if a sharp sword is placed on a person's neck, he should not despair from requesting mercy" [Brachot, 10]. God the Blessed One can still help me and the entire people of Israel. Only you, children, can request this of God, if you get this letter while you still have time to request. As we see with our actual eyes it has been decreed from Heaven, and if this is the verdict — each Jew must accept it with love and go with the awareness that he is being sacrificed on the altar which will atone for his sin and for the entire people of Israel. If this is the will of the Creator, it cannot be otherwise. But you, children, don't think that I've completely given up; so long as my eyes are still open, I hope for the redemption of the Creator of the Universe. But you, children, if God saves you and by the Creator's will you remain alive — do not forget Him and remember that you had a father in this world. And you, Moshe, give a note to a righteous person [to praty] that something should remain of the Rosin children, and if Shlomo stays alive — tell him, he will know on his own what to do. I'm writing you the address of our Yisrael: "A. Weiss, Tel Aviv, Ben Yehuda 161, Land of Israel" and if with God's help you stay alive, tell him immediately and write him that he should mention them [?] in the holy places and by our venerated, master rabbi and teacher [ADMOR] of Leipzig, may he blessed with long life, and he should mention me in the letter to our venerated, master rabbi and teacher from Tchernowitz, may he blessed with long life.

You, children, cling to the faith, and trust in God the Blessed One will surely be of help. Just who will live to see the good? I hope to God that you, young children, will live to see also the good. I request of you not to forget me and the Creator, and remain faithful to Judaism until the end.

Beloved Feidsha! I now understand your situation, but what can be done that you were born in such a sinful generation such as this one? Since the time you were born and until this day, you haven't really started to live, but if God the Blessed One helps you and you stay alive — you can still enjoy life's experiences. If only God the Blessed One protects you from every obstacle. Seek for God the Blessed One, after all you haven't sinned, and He will help you.

Therefore, beloved children! I don't have much to write here. Stay healthy and strong and do not forget God the Blessed One until the last moment, and do not forget me, too. But maybe God will help and we will still see other, with the Lord of the Universe everything is possible. Don't lose your temper from so much sorrow, because it is from Heaven, and I only request that God the Blessed One save you, children, from every obstacle and that you stay alive. You can write to Shmuel Leib in Zaslava. I think he will stay there to work.

Be well and strong. I bless and kiss you. Keep this letter and remember that you once had a father in this world. I wish for you to be inscribed and sealed in the Book of Life, and have a blessed and good New Year, from your father

Yosef [Hagar]

Letter 86

August 24, 1943

My Dear Wife,

I am about to travel with complete confidence. I hope to come back soon because the struggle is reaching the end. We should only remain strong spiritually, I for your sake and for the children, and you for my sake and for the children.

The kindness of the Lord wanted it like this; I accept His will with equanimous faith. I think about how much kindness He has granted us, I think about you and the children, about my parents and your parents, about the love I was privileged to have from brothers and sisters - - - about our wide circle of genuine friends - - -. If you consider all this, you must be grateful to the One who has shown us so many kindnesses, and He will certainly continue to insure us the kindness. Don't forget this. I trust in "for your salvation do I long, O God!"

Your husband

◆ ◆ ◆

Dear Children,

You feel awfully terrible that I have to travel but I know that you understand that is the will of the Creator and therefore it is forbidden for us to complain. Be strong and anticipate that it will all pass by and work out. Try to do your best in everything. Be kind to Mother, Grandmother and to our friends. May God bless you. "May God bless you and safeguard you."

Your father

◆ ◆ ◆

Dear Mother,

I have learnt from you to accept the will of God and that is why I am traveling with equanimity. You should also think like this, so that we will see each other in health. I know how much you worry about my wife and the children.

Until I return, I and the others, a kiss from one who loves you.

Eli

The writer was sent on August 10, 1943 to Westerbork and from there he was sent to Sobibor two weeks later. His wife and children were saved.

Letter 87

With the help of God,

Kamionka, Rosh Chodesh (new month) of Iyar 5700

God! — my child! — created the world, heaven and earth, all that exists in the world. God created man at the end, already at twilight, to show how inferior, how small man is; or how big and important man is, by creating him at the end, when everything was ready. And in God's likeness, in God's image, he was created. And sometimes along comes the inferior and cursed man, and destroys the lives of the important creatures of God. My daughter! You are little, new to the world, and certainly it is not because of your sin that the wrath of God broke out at the world, but you are part of the destiny of the world and you suffer, too. Yes, you cried immediately as you entered the world. Other children cry immediately (perhaps) for the sake of crying, you really cried, because in your time it certainly would have been better not to be created than to be created.

My child! You don't know, but maybe you sense it, that your father's lips haven't touched you yet, and perhaps you don't need it yet. I know, I feel you and need to absorb your soft breath into me. My child! When you cry and your mother doesn't know why, if only you would cry for me and your pure pearls of tears would certainly awaken the compassion of God.

My child! Other children, of other fathers from other times, when there was still good and evil in the world, and there was a choice to choose between good and evil, would pray for one thing: for good. Today, when only the second thing exists in the world, "Hear our voice", God and "renew our days as of old"! And then: "Bless us with justice and compassion and peace and all good things!"

My child! Don't be surprised, because this is the

Creator's will. This is not our first sorrow and if only it would be our last sorrow. If only the heavy clouds would go far away and the sun would shine again, the sun would shine on us forever. "And all of the common people would see that God is the Lord!" These are some short words from your father who longs for you from far away. Stay healthy, and if only the Father of all fathers watches over you.

A.D.

The letter was written when the father was under the Soviet regime. He wrote it to his daughter who was under the Nazi regime. He never got to see her. His daughter was killed in the ghetto and his wife in Auschwitz. His friend Ch. Volnerman kept the letter.

Letter 88

Budapest, May 1944

My Honorable Lady!

I hereby confirm that I received your postcard. At last I was able to send the package to your relatives. But then all contact [with them] ended, because afterwards they were put on railroad cars, and only God knows where they will be taken. I do not know whether they received the package that you had sent them. We will place our trust in God in Heaven.

May God bless you,

Sincerely,
Mrs. Prager

The letter was sent to Rena Guttman.

Letter 89

My Dear,

We received your last letter in the presence of two tall police and Gestapo officers and four regular policemen who surprised us at 9 a.m. with the news that we're leaving on the transport in 30 minutes. Father resisted; he did not want to leave and then they threatened that they would take him just like that. Finally, after I signed that I relinquish all my property, he calmed down and joined us. Meanwhile, the time passed and they expelled us from the house with the help of rifle butts. Of course we packed all the wrong things, but at the end it made no difference.

We live on the floor. We have no table, chair or bench. We lie in bed wrapped entirely in fur and a coat. Your fur, dear Ida, saves me, it warms me up day and night. The beautiful pillow that Erna had sewn for me anew on velvet is my resting pillow. Miss Erna Rosenthal, from where you previously lived in Konstance, was my neighbor in the straw sack. We play "Purim" and "Gypsy Family," Erna does fortune-telling with cards and tells people their future.

Because of my age, I was transferred now to the barrack where there are older people who were brought from old-age homes in Manheim and Gailingen, blind, lame, deaf and with physical and mental disabilities. [They make sounds] at night of a cackle of some thousand geese, from the deepest bass until the highest soprano. This, when I go to rest "in bed" — that is on the straw "spread out" on the absent board.

I had luck again. The young woman who took care of me in another barrack also came here with her old mother. On my left is Mrs. Steinem from Konstance, she has a golden sense of humor; she helps us to overcome everything with humor from ages ago. Also Miss Shen of Freiburg,

313

from a family well known in the whole world.

"The menu:" In the morning, at 9:30, ersatz black coffee; for noon and evening: one portion made of — peas (so hard that it can make a hole in the head). Sufficient bread. We help ourselves to concentrated milk, which I had ordered while in Zurich.

The barrack city is so tremendous that it is impossible to see it all with the eye. This is the camp where the Red Spaniards stayed at the time. Every square section is locked with barbed wire fences and under the supervision of soldiers. The hygiene is unbelievable, but we, the Jews, have clean blood and we will overcome everything. Father is across the train tracks with the men. Many from Emmendingen are with him and take care of him. Yesterday he visited me, since I cannot get out through the door because of the mud. The sunrises and sunsets could have been wonderful, if it were possible to enjoy them, but to my sorrow we are very high in the Pyrenees and there is a storm around us, it rains day and night.

Last week we had such a rough storm that we thought there was a downpour of stones on the roof. We are all full of hope and are courageous! We don't see sad faces here, so they won't be happy with our humiliation. Yehuda keeps on going! Don't worry, God does not abandon His own! Julius, Katherine and Toni — are healthy. Toni, the aide with all of her extensive knowledge about everything, comes to me, too. Our dear Anna, the sister of Mrs. Yalepsbrook, comes each and every day and brings me something. God sends us a good messenger in every situation!

I expect and hope that you are all well. Lots of regards to all the precious ones there and lots of kisses.

Yours,
Mother

◆ ◆ ◆

I gladly join [the mother's letter] and can confirm that the condition of health of our parents is good. Indeed it is a very sad existence, but faith in God is within us all. I hope that you live as you would like, and bless you,

Yours,

Anna

The letter was written by Rosa Wei, 84-years-old, fom the Grs a

Letter 90

May 15, 1943

Dear Shmuel!

I received your letter this moment. I'm leaving everything (it looks terrible) and am answering you immediately. First of all: I wrote you already twice and I didn't even read one line. I didn't get anything, even though I hoped for some news like this from you, and not because of the money. I have to write quickly, because the young man is returning immediately. I didn't get the 100 zloty that they sent two weeks ago. I feel bad for you more than I do for myself, because it's so hard for you. To speak about myself? The situation is very severe. How do we cope with it? For the sake of the children, for the sake of revenge, oh, to get away from this distress! I hope! I live! Do you still believe in God? Also Margot goes to D. Didn't you get my last letter, where I wrote that I could be a typist? Did you get that letter? Well, Margot is going and Leah lives by me. Alas! Three times alas! I am doubly miserable. Such a despicable person barely exists in a double version. You sort of know her, but only sort of. She became awful. And then I'll have another one! Never mind! You can't help here. I'm trying now to sell coffee with Bolienic, today is the first time! We were on a street where we had to hide the whole time. I take a lot of risks, I don't have a choice. No one can help me, but I can't give up because of this. Either we succeed or we don't. You didn't request Yolek's address, I'm sending it now: Vibrehovpakiget #7. But your letter, I answered. Please continue to write. Today I saw the Weinbergers in prison. Unfortunately, his mother and sister-in-law with the child are there. Stay healthy and whole.

A thousand warm wishes,

Maya

Letter 91

November 20, 1941

My Beloved Trio,

I didn't hear from you in a very, very long time. Didn't you get my letter? Do you know that our dear parents don't live there anymore? To my sorrow, I didn't get any mail from them, otherwise I would have written already. How are things by you? Why do you make me wait such a long time for mail? If only you knew with how much longing we anticipate a letter! Chanaleh, you also don't have time to write me a few lines? I also didn't get mail from dear Heinz. I got a letter after a very long time from dear Erna, she is in trouble and suffers from a similar trouble to Heinz. Manfred and Regina work, thank God. With God's help, for a very long time. Is there a God at all? I'm beginning to doubt this. Our dear Terry was sick for 14 days, eight of those days she had high fever. Now, thank God, she has somewhat recuperated.

Also Santa was sick for over eight days. And today she is fine, more or less. It's not worth discussing me. I would like to hide in some corner and close my eyes forever. I still have within me a bit of hope to see my one and only child again and you, my dears. Despite this, I will pray every day to my dear parents to try for us and to spread their protective hands over us, Amen. Therefore, it is my wish to go in the next few days to the Association for Assistance regarding our dear parents. If only you wouldn't rely just on the Association for Assistance and desert it, I would be happy, if only I could give you better news. Chanaleh, tell our beloved relatives that the Gross family and also Yani and Heinz send warm regards. How is my beloved Yosseleh? Send him regards and kiss him a thousand times. He should pray and pray for our health and that we should meet soon, in health, Amen.

Our beloved Aunt Frieda reached her children safely, there was great joy and Adolph has already written us. Therefore, the Wolf family also sends you warm regards. Enough for today, I have no more patience. You should all be well, and if only a miracle would happen and we would all meet each other in health, Amen. This is my most urgent request. I bless and kiss you from my heart.

Yours,
The inconsolable Rosa

Santa, Regina, Manfred and the families, write soon. Why doesn't Max write?

◆ ◆ ◆

And you, my beloved Chanaleh, how are you, and my dear Yosseleh? I didn't hear from you in a long time. I myself am extremely depressed with my nerves, and I will hardly be able to recuperate and write. My heart doesn't always want to, as I would like to. Also with my stomach something's wrong: sometimes it seems that I have tumors because it's not absorbing, every little upset does some damage, and I have plenty of this. Chanaleh, do you remember that you once spoke to me on the telephone? You told me then about a bad dream, and I laughed at you. This time I had the same dream and it became reality. Heinz and his family are relatively fine. He will certainly be traveling soon to Mor. He writes very little. Did you ever write to Gronerdess? Can't they help? Oy, I would so much want to be with you. My heart says that you will be a good mother to my child. I only made sure that he would have good profession, so that later on he can stand on his own two feet, Amen. And now farewell, my one and only Chanaleh, my beloved, be well and strong. May God safeguard you and protect you, and give you - - - quickly, Amen. We send you regards from our heart and kiss you - - -

Your sad Rosa and - - -

And now to you, my child, my one and only, most beloved. How are you, my good soul? Are you healthy? Do you work at your studies? Your beloved mother misses you so much. Pray, my child! Pray every day, morning, noon and night, for your Mamaleh, aunts, uncles, and nephews. Pray, my child, so we can meet again in health, Amen, Amen! While my eyes are still open, I bless you, my beloved child! May God bless you and protect you along all your paths, Amen! And that you should have luck in all of your ways, Amen! Never forget your Mamaleh, be good and obey your educators. Obey Henny and heed them, because they all want the best for you, like your Mamaleh. Ah, how much I would have wanted to be with you. For now, farewell to you. Be well and strong, a thousand hugs from Mamaleh who loves you forever, Aunt Santa, Regina, Katha, Uncle Manfred, Heinz, Walter, Siggi and the families, all of the acquaintances send regards and join me in my wishes. Be well.

This is Rosa Timberg's letter.

Letter 92

November 15, 1943

We are writing you with the blood of tens of thousands of martyred Jews. We are experiencing now in Poland the end of our dreadful tragedy. The Hitlerian barbarians are now butchering the remaining Jewish population, due to their defeat at the front.

They started in the region of Lublin, which is not far from the front. In this region the Germans concentrated together some camps, with approximately 40,000 Jews, most of them from Warsaw and the Lublin region. The largest camps are: Trawiniki (10 thousand) and Poniatova (15 thousand). We were in constant contact with these camps, we helped in whatever ways we could, we supplied money and arms.

On Wednesday November 3 at 6 a.m., the men in the Trawiniki camp were commanded to dig entrenchments against air attacks. Two hours later they surrounded them and shot them with machineguns. Later the Germans brought 50 trucks full of women and children to the camp; they stripped them naked and shot them, too. After this slaughter they brought to the camp 3,000 Italian Jews, who also await the same fate.

A similar slaughter took place on Friday in the camps in Lublin. There they killed several thousand Jews. At the same time, a selection process immersed in blood took place at the Poniatova camp. They killed most of the men and almost all of the women and children.

During the first days of November, the Germans began to terminate the Jewish camps in our region, which is near the front — in Eastern Galicia. In one camp in Lvov, on Yanovska Street, which had had some 7,000 people, they selected 2,000 people and killed them in the most brutal way.

We have grounds to believe that during the next few days all of the remaining camps will be destroyed, and likewise the small number of ghettos. We are desperately attempting to save the most important people of our social and cultural activities, but this is very difficult and costly. We are convinced that in a short time, from the Jewish community of Poland, which has numbered three and a half million Jews, only a small group will survive, several tens of thousands of Jews, who are hiding away from the camps and ghettoes, in the Aryan neighborhoods or forests. After the past month, we estimated the number of Jews in Poland to be approximately 250,000 to 300,000. In another few weeks, 50,000 will remain alive and no more.

In the last moments before their death, the survivors of Polish Jewry cried out to the world requesting help.

We know that you are with us in heart and spirit, that you experience with us this most terrible tragedy in the annals of time, and we also know that you are helpless. But the authorities that could have helped us should know what we think of them. The blood of three million Jews of Poland will take revenge not only against the Hitlerian beasts, but also against the indifferent authorities, that did not do one thing — except for pretty words — to save a people condemned to destruction by the Hitlerian murderers. Not one of us, the last ones to die, will forget this or forgive it. May this last voice reach out from the abyss to the ears of the entire world.

We want the Jewish people and the entire world to know that like heroes, our youth defended the life and the honor of our people. Following the heroic epic of the Warsaw Ghetto, we experienced in the last months a wonderful chapter in the history of the Jews of Bialistok.

It took place at the end of August. August 17th was the beginning of the termination of the only large ghetto in Eastern Poland with about 40,000 people. For the first three days seven transports were sent to the Treblinka death camp. In addition to this, a train packed with little children left Bialistok. It was obvious that before their murder, their blood would be sucked as revenge for the wounded German soldiers. On the fourth day, armed battles began with weapons taken. Difficult battles raged on a number of the streets. The Germans used tanks and artillery here, exactly as in Warsaw. They recruited about 1,000 Gendarmes and SS men, and also Ukrainian troops. The Jews mostly used hand grenades, incendiary bombs and rifles. They fought with exceptional resolve, and they also earned the deep respect of the entire municipal population. In these battles several hundred Germans and Ukrainians were killed and wounded. In order to destroy the Jews' spirit of resistance, the Germans set afire the ghetto from all sides, just as in Warsaw. The difficult battles continued for eight days, but the resistance continued for a longer time, close to a month, until the middle of September. The heroic battles of Bialistok will be recorded in history, like the defense of the Warsaw Ghetto.

During the last months, the Jews marked two battle operations with tremendous symbolic significance. The two death camps, in Treblinka (near Melkinia) and Sobibor (near Chelem) were destroyed. In these camps, the remaining Jews condemned to death organized fighting units, and at the designated time they started fighting. In a heroic surge of battle, they attacked the Germans and the Ukrainians, took their weapons away and in most cases, killed them. Later on, they burned down the gas chambers and the "crematorium for people who are alive" and later on they fled to the surrounding forests.

The Jews fought and resisted with armed resistance not only in Warsaw, Bialistok, Treblinka and Sobibor but also in other cities: In Czestochowa, Bendin, Vilna, Tarna and smaller cities. Participating in the battles in these cities were fighters from all sectors and Jewish parties: the Pioneer Youth [No'ar HeChalutz], HaShomer HaTzair, Poalei Zion, and the Bund. The battle of death for the sake of the Jewish people's honor united them. We helped to organize this battle with the assistance of our Jewish Fighting Organization and we supported it in all ways.

In addition to the battle operations, we are focusing our efforts on helping the Jews who are still in the camps or hiding in the Aryan areas. We are trying with all of our forces to rescue people from the camps, and we have succeeded in rescuing some public and scientific figures. We stay in contact with the camps through our emissaries; through whom we provide financial help in the camps, documents and more. We are spending significant sums supporting Jews who are hiding in the Aryan areas, arranging documents for them, housing (this is one of the most difficult tasks) and more. We support a relatively large number of people who belong to the public-cultural sector. We, a small group of activists who remained alive, took upon ourselves the role to provide public help for the remnant of the hurting Jewish population — despite the danger and constant difficulties. We are determined to perform this mission until the end, despite all the difficulties.

We direct our operations as the National Jewish Committee, to which the following parties and organizations belong: General Zionists, Left Poalei Zion, Right Poalei Zion, HeChalutz, HaShomer HaTzair, Dror, Akiva and Gordonia. Heading the National Jewish Committee is a presidium made up of three people. The National Jewish Committee is in contact with the Bund with which it coordinates its activities. The National Jewish Committee and the Bund have authorized a Coordination Committee; the Committee is not a political body. Its role is to coordinate the defense and support operations. It is the most supreme authority of the Jewish population that has remained alive.

We bear the majority of tasks of the Coordination Committee. The Coordination Committee works together with the Council for the Assistance of Jews of the Polish government. The secretary of the Council is a representative of the National Jewish Committee. In addition to this, the National Jewish Committee is constantly in contact with the National Minorities Division of the illegal Polish government (which operates in Polish areas) and also with the Division for Jewish Affairs of the leadership of armed forces in Poland. The National Jewish Committee has close and warm connections with representatives of the Polish underground movement.

The National Jewish Committee has collected material and documents, which will bear witness in the future to the terrible suffering of our martyrs. We received lately worrisome information from the Bergen [Belsen] camp, not far from Hanover, where there are Jews from other countries. About 4,000 Jews were there. This camp was supposed to be under the supervision of the International Red Cross. There are rumors that this camp was terminated just like all the camps in the Lublin region. We are appealing to the Red Cross and to the Swiss delegation in Berlin. There are also worrisome rumors from the Vittel camp (Alsace). Let us know what happened in these six camps.

I sincerely thank the [Jewish] Agency, the directorship, the Jewish Rescue Board and to all of the organizations of our brothers from all sectors. In the Krakow region there are about 15,000 Jews in the camps. Their fate is sealed.

The Jewish Resistance Organization in Poland salutes all the Jewish soldiers, who are fighting on all fronts in the world against Hitlerism and Fascism, for the sake of liberation.

The National Jewish Committee
(-) Berman, (-) Kaftor, (-) Zukerman

Letter 93

Confidential!
Zerubavel, Tel Aviv [sic]

We are fighting with weapons for the life and the honor of the survivors of the Jewish people. We are short funds to purchase weapons, to rescue the children and the national activists. We await immediate help. Battle blessings to the Jewish workers in the Land of Israel in the whole world.

(-) Anthony, (-) Adolph, (-) Emmanuel
Left Poalei Zion

A telegram from Poland that was received by the Home Office in London on April 27, 1943.

◆ ◆ ◆

Confidential!

The General Council of the Polish Republic
The Bureau of Vice-Counsel Tz. Andzhivski
Jerusalem

No. 112/43
Jerusalem, April 28, 1943
To the Jewish Agency in Jerusalem

I hereby notify you that the Home Office in London has transferred to my bureau a telegram that was sent by the National Jewish Committee in Warsaw to the Zionist Executive of London-Jerusalem. The Committee calls out in this telegram to cry out to the entire world for the sake of the Jews, who after a shocking slaughter, anticipate total annihilation. The Committee requests in its call also to rescue, via exchange, those that remained alive, and to send the Committee without delay the amount of one-hundred thousand dollars to extend immediate help.

(-) Tz. Andzhivski
Vice Counsel of the Polish Republic

Letter 94

September 24, 1942

I am sending you this postcard to tell you that I will travel tomorrow morning eastward to an unknown country. I am traveling with courage and in good health, but it is beginning to be cold and winter will be harsh. We are forbidden to receive packages of food and clothes, and we are also forbidden to receive letters, tell this immediately to Mr. Jan.

I trust you.

Roger's father also traveled.

My dears, be brave and do not worry, I might find family there. I leave you with heartfelt kisses. I am traveling with courage and in good health,

Your daughter and sister,
Esther

Letter 95

To my very dear ones!

We are all caught up in a frenzy of letter writing before our death. If anyone of us has acquaintances abroad — he writes and believes that our murderers eventually will be punished. This letter, these words and the images that they describe will be unfathomable for you. They won't enter your consciousness. And it doesn't amaze me at all, because after all, I who have a full awareness of these things, am also incapable of believing such cruelty.

I don't know whether I'm capable of relating even one-hundredth of what has happened to us during these two years. I will try to partially explain to you with poor skills the meaning of the well-known "Ausraten:" On July 1, 1941 the Germans entered Lvov, where I was together with Mother and Father. I will not describe to you detailed memories of those days, because despite their horror, they were somewhat wiped out of my memory. I will only mention the most salient memories: The Ukrainian pogrom in which thousands of people fell in torturous deaths [...] On September 1, we came to Brzezany, where my Igo is. We were full of hope that perhaps in the town it would be possible to bear this hell. Our joy did not last long. On Yom Kippur, all men between the ages of 18 to 60 were called to be counted. They numbered 700. They were imprisoned. Among them were Igo and his brother. The reason for their arrest was not known [...] When I went after three days at 7 a.m. to get a document for Igo from a doctor acquaintance (at that time I still believed in nonsense like medical committees, etc.) I saw before my eyes a sight that curdled my blood [...] From the prison they took people in trucks incidentally giving murderous blows, just for the sin of their being Jews. There were four such trucks and in each one there were about eight Gestapo men and fifty Jews. I stood and waited, because I wanted to see Igo one more time. After 30 minutes, the trucks returned and took new cargo. And this happened four times. I couldn't see Igo in the crowds, but I saw the despair of the other people. My aunt, I will never be able to express in words what was conveyed by the eyes of these people who sensed their imminent death.

The next day the farmers came and related that everybody was shot. None of us believed this. After all, the authorities had promised that they took them just for work. For half a year I deluded myself that perhaps my Igo would yet return. But the trucks that returned and loaded up a few times proved that I must believe the farmers [...]

Now we are also at death's door, which is worse than the others, because we are waiting for it to come. When it became unbearable, I decided to go without the "band" to Midowa, in the company of the gentleman with whom I leave this letter. They caught me and gave me in to the Ukrainian military which arrested me once more. I sat for three days and three nights sunk in gloomy thoughts until miraculously I was released. A few days later Mother's leg broke, and again the deportations began. It began in Warsaw, where there were 500,000 Jews, and 60,000 remained; out of 80,000 in Lvov, 16,000 remained, in Tarnopol and other small cities. And on September 21 (it was a pleasant day) the "action" came to us. We were sitting in the storehouse in back of a tree, in a shelter 120 meters long, 50 meters wide, and a height of 1.30, for 3 days and two nights and death appeared twice before my eyes. When they entered, it would have been over if they had lifted up one plank... The landlord rescued our lives; a man whom we didn't believe would do such a thing, by saying that the storehouse didn't belong to Jews. On October 15, we were ordered to move to the neighborhood. We felt like a fox feels when he falls into a trap. For a month and a half we were under constant fear of an action, we would get up at 5 a.m. and every car made would make our heart skip a beat again. On December 5, once again on Chanukah day, they wake us up with a shout: Action. We went down to the shelter, but at 6 p.m. they discovered us. We were sure they would drive us to the plot and from there further away, but we suddenly heard the words: "We'll make a deal" (in German). We started to collect silver and gold and whatever we didn't hand over ourselves they took with force. For two hours they kept us tense with the fear of death [...] Then one of them took me above and tested the courage of my spirit by pointing his gun to my head. He ordered me to count to three. I had no choice — and I counted; For this I received the title: courageous girl. I forgot to write you that they named these actions — deportation to Polsia. They would travel in freight cars [...] After a few days they arrived in Belzice [...] There they would terminate them with an electric current, in order to make soap and chemical fertilizer from the bodies*. You surely don't believe my words. You surely think that my head's not on right; but no, it's entirely true [...]

And now we are also on death's door, which is worse than the others, because we are waiting for it with total awareness. And there is no escape, no flight, no compassion. How great is the will to live — to go beyond this nightmarish time and continue to live, to laugh towards the sun, the whole world and to live, to live.

I am 23 years old and my heart carries a painful wound for a year and a half, and despite this I want to live in order to avenge Igo's death and tortures. But it is impossible. And therefore I write to you — that at least you should avenge our terrible death. So many people have poison, and yet they still allow themselves to be led like sheep to the

*[Editorial comment: Historical research does not support this rumor.]

slaughter, because they still believe in some miracle that will save them from their foes. We don't have poison, because it is very hard to obtain it today, and therefore we have no other choice, but to take part in our funeral, to remove our clothes, to stand with the face to the side of the grave and wait for the bullet in the neck. I will surely go alone, because Mother cannot walk, they will surely deal with her at home. And for Father another camp awaits him. It will certainly happen on the Passover festival — and we assume that this will already be the termination action. You see, at the time that you'll be pouring wine on the occasion of the festival, by us, the red blood of human beings will be poured [...]

I write on and on, but still haven't been able to relate even a fraction of what has happened to us during this whole time. After all I cannot count all the heart spasms before each impending action; I cannot describe also the awful fear when the Germans entered our storehouse, or when they breached our shelter. I cannot describe to you the images in the shelter, when they mocked our men for not protecting their wives and children [...] and I particularly cannot describe the dread of the horror of death. And despite this, we still live, we haven't gone insane yet, we don't cry and don't shout. We are alive, as if all that is going on around us doesn't affect us. Until the last moment of our lives, we laugh and sing. And only sometimes, when reality becomes too lucid, we forget the laughter [...]

My letter is long by now, and I can part from you. Believe me that I would want to see your faces when you get this letter [...] I could write much on about this subject, but I don't have the patience. I still hope that you can form a clear picture based on these words of what we've experienced until the day that we die. And with all this, I'm sure that you cannot understand and perceive this life of ours, that all this will wash over you, like a nightmare, and how I

would not want this to happen... I would like you to publicize at the crucial moment these letters (there will be many),
so that the revenge will not be less than our tortures [...]

Be well, all of you, enjoy yourselves and don't poison
your life with nonsense. Now I could have looked at life dif-
ferently, but I remembered this too late. Now I know, that
all is vain. And the spring is so beautiful. How awful our
death will be.

I kiss you all strongly, all of you together.

Yours,
Chulda

◆ ◆ ◆

April 12
My Dear and Beloved,

I won't be able to write like Chulda, I don't have
enough strength for this, me with my poisoned nerves
(I continue to use the powders). For a few days, I sense
death within me, hovering over me. I sense it in the blood,
mouth, teeth, on the chest. From all sides death beckons
me. And people seek and beckon at life so much. Chulda,
the youngster, could have saved her life; a man wanted to
take her in and hide her. I scolded, I cried, nothing helped
— she refused to go. She did not have enough strength to
leave us and save herself. Her nerves and strengths weren't
enough. Dear children! Words cannot describe what we're
going through. Are you able to understand our situation,
that when Chulda was imprisoned in jail, the Gestapo came
to kill all of those imprisoned. A miracle happened and
Chulda was released. We don't look forward to a miracle
anymore. Four-five million are gone and we will also be
gone with them. I would want this letter to reach you [...]
We are dying like homeless dogs, like a hunted beast. I get

the chills in all my bones when I think of this. I try to control my nerves as much as possible, but I'm awfully scared of this moment. If only the three or two of us would fall together.

Be well. I write these words for you to know in what conditions we lived and how we died. Life is terrible, but death is seven times more terrible. Indeed my life is unimportant to me, in any event I am not able to live more […]

Your sister, aunt, sister-in-law
Rosalka

Today we waited for the termination operation or the one before the termination. It's not known why the plan was changed. One more day. I always thought that I knew how to describe in clear plastic words what I would feel and see. All of those words are not even a minimal reflection of what we're going through […] You won't believe all of this. The head is in chaos when thinking of it.

Today the letter will be passed on to these people. I part from you once more and kiss you long and hard. I thought that despite everything I would yet see you. It happened otherwise.

Yours,
Rosalka

◆ ◆ ◆

My Beloved and Dear Ones,

Chulda and Rosalka wrote about everything that we went through. What am I saying? If we had to describe all that we went through in this war, particularly from 22.6.1941, numerous volumes would not be enough and these wouldn't include everything. Can you imagine life with barbarians for 22 months, when not one day went by without tragedy? Whoever didn't live through this would not understand it. If you ever read about what happened here — don't think of it as some hallucination of an author, but as the one-hundredth or one-thousandth part of what happened here, because nobody is capable of understanding the soul of a Jew. The Aryan author will give you only dry facts. Is it possible to understand that a person marches in the crowds towards his funeral, and before nearing they tell him to get undressed, because the murderers are loathe to [waste] the clothes. This is definitely unbelievable! And despite this, that's how it is.

Only Yosef and his son have survived from my whole family, but they won't live long, because soon there will be a "purification" operation of Eastern Poland from Jews — and an "operation" means that they kidnap people, lead them to the cemeteries and shoot them.

Under these conditions, we've spent 22 months, we hid and concealed ourselves in different bunkers, but finally we must surrender [. . .]

We are leaving this letter with decent people who we knew here, who have done a lot for us without any benefit for themselves. They can tell you when we were murdered and where we are buried.

We could have concealed Chulda, but she didn't want to leave us and unfortunately she must die with us; a wrong deed on her part, because she can't help us and after all she can save herself.

Be healthy and at peace.

I kiss all of you warmly.

Manak

◆ ◆ ◆

Zagan, July 16, 1946
Dear Honorable Doctor, R.Sh. [Reuven Shugar], in the
Land of Israel,

I am hereby sending you the letters, written by your family, which I received before their death with the request to hand them over to you: I was delayed doing this because I came to the areas of western Poland only a month ago, and only from here can the letters be dispatched safely [...] It appears from the date on these pages that they were written right before your family's death, during the mass slaughter by the Hitlerian murderers on the land of Poland. You can say that they died a heroic death, because on the day of the mass termination of Jews [...] 1,760 people fell at the hands of the hangmen, among them children a few days old; but Emanuel, in his wish to avenge the death of those dear to him, shot the police that wanted to take them out of the bunker; and with the last remaining bullets he ended his family's lives and his own life — because he did not want to be led by the murderers to the execution spot and undergo all the tortures prior to their death.

I note that I had a warm friendship with Manak [Emanuel] already before 1939; and during the war, when he lived near my house in Brzezany, we formed an even deeper friendship.

It is impossible to describe the mourning that befell my house after their death — but also the hell that the three of them went through during the occupation until their death is beyond description. May their memory be blessed!

[...]

If my sir would like to know additional details about this tragic death of his family, I would be pleased to be of service.

I end here with feelings of respect,

S. Tcherbinski

Letter 96

July 7, 1944
My Most Beloved and Precious Little Girl,

When I gave birth to you, my beloved, I never imagined that six and a half years later I would have to write you a letter on this subject. I saw you for the last time on your 6th birthday, on December 13, 1943. I had the false hope that I would see you again before we left, but now I know that this won't happen. I don't want to endanger you. We are traveling on Monday and today is Friday evening. Your father, Paula, and I together with another 51 "friends in trouble," are about to travel to an unknown destination. I don't know, my dear child, whether I will see you again. I take with me your beloved image, as you were in our home, the voice of your cute, childish chattering, the smell of your pure body, the rhythm of your breath, your smile and your cry. I take with me the awful, dreadful fear, which the heart of your mother could not soothe for even a moment. I am taking with me for my way your image from December 13, 1943, with your grown-up before its time look, the taste of your kisses that are sweeter than honey, and the hug of your little arms, my chick. This is the baggage that I'm taking with me for the road, perhaps Providence will grant us the privilege to go through this nightmare safely and send you back, my treasure, to our arms. If this indeed happens, I will explain to you many things that you don't understand yet, and I can assume that you will never understand if you are educated in different surroundings and in an atmosphere of freedom. My little child, I would like you to read this letter when, with God's help, you will grow up and be mature enough and able to be critical of our deeds towards you. I yearn with all my might, my beloved child, that you shouldn't condemn us, you should cherish our memory and the memory of this much-hated nation which are your roots. My chick, I want you not to be ashamed and not to deny your origins. I would like you to know that your father was an unparalleled man, one of a few in the entire world, and you could have been proud of him. His entire life he lived doing good for mankind and good deeds, if only God blesses his path wherever he goes and protects him and makes him privileged to receive you back to his heart. My treasure, you are your father's entire world, his one and only ambition, the one and only compensation for the suffering and tortures, therefore I would want you to remember him favorably if destiny doesn't light our way.

Remember favorably your most distinguished grand-fathers and grandmothers, your uncles and aunts and the entire family. Retain all of our memories, and please, don't blame us. And regarding me, your mother, forgive me, for-give me my dear child that I gave birth to you, I would have wanted to bring you into a world in your own community and that you should live your own life, but if things ended up otherwise, it's not our fault. Therefore, I implore, my precious chick, my one and only child, please don't blame us. Try to be kind like your father and your father's fathers, and love those that replace your parents, and their families, who will certainly tell you about us. We would like you to appreciate how they sacrifice of themselves so much for your sake, and that you should be a source of pride for them, so that they won't have any reason to regret the burden that they willingly took upon themselves. Another thing I would like you to know is that your mother maintained a proud carriage, despite all of the humiliations that we suffered from our enemies, and if she is sentenced to die, she will die without condemning, without crying, but she will put a scornful smile on her face while facing her executioners.

I grasp you close to my heart, kiss you with passion

and bless you with all the might of the heart and the love of a mother.

Your mother

◆ ◆ ◆

What can I write to my one and only, most precious girl in the world? One would have to pry open my heart and look in it because no pen is capable of describing what it holds at this moment. I believe with complete faith, despite everything, that we will all overcome and return our hearts to each other.

Your father

Sarah and Yechiel Gerlitz of Bendin (Poland) left their only daughter, Dita, six years old with a Polish friend named Florchek; they had a feeling that they would never see their daughter. They left her a letter which she was supposed to open when she grew up. The couple was saved and together with Dita they immigrated to Israel.

Letter 97

The Ten Days of Repentance, 5705
September 1944
My Dear and Beloved Parents!

It is very difficult for me to write you this letter. When you get it, I will be on the way to an unknown destination. Indeed, this isn't the first time that I part from you, but the circumstances give extra meaning to this parting — the end of a stage in our lives. When I now try to thank you again for all the love, the kindness and consideration, for the education and all the good and beauty that I've experienced because of you, I try to put in words that which lies deep within me, something so obvious and known to you , too, but my attempt will anyhow be a weak one. May God grant that this should be just a brief separation and that the five of us should meet soon in health with the rest of our beloved.

It is clear to me that the moment I go on the train I will be making the final step towards my materialistic proletarianization, and with this I will complete the process that started with the journey from Westerbork. But it will be just a physical proletarianization; I will always remain who I was spiritually. And you can be sure that I will get out of this distress, despite the fact that I have no control over some situations. With my thoughts I am able to seal myself off from the world so completely that I resemble a rolled-up hedgehog trying to protect itself from hostile surroundings. In addition to this, I also make do with very little, and although I like to dress nicely, I can also survive with clothes that are not so good, because my deepest ambition is to "live in peace," that is, I will always try to strictly preserve my spiritual independence. With all that's happened to me until now, for better or for worse, I've always been able to learn. And I also hope that from this new experience, towards which I'm traveling, I can learn lessons to be used later when I move from a passive struggle to an active struggle for the sake of our Jewish people. I believe that this is the role and purpose that God designated for me: to help as much as I can that this tragedy which now befalls the Jewish people, specifically, and the nations of the world, in general, will not repeat itself. How I will go about doing this — this is still hidden in the bosom of the future. At this time, our mission is to endure with an iron strength and ward off any hardship, and internalize every good matter. To wait and to hope that the gates of freedom will open.

Faith and hope — courage and goodwill

These will help us all get through this period in order to approach our duties later.

And now I would like to request from you, my beloved parents, not to lose hope in any way whatsoever, and also not to wallow in tears and lamentation. Not only won't you be able to change the situation this way, you're only making things hard for me. Be strong, and don't talk to each other about how things could have been, but -

Believe in our reunification

Hope for the future,

Be brave in overcoming the obstacles

And strengthen the will to live for our sake, your sons.

Be strong and courageous [in Hebrew and German]
The future is ours [in Hebrew and German]

With thanks!
Leopold

Letter 98

March 14, 1943
Dear Ghenia!!

I thank you from the bottom of my heart for your visit to the prison. I wanted to see you very much. I thought all the time what we would discuss, but when I saw you I was so confused and couldn't utter a word...

Did you ever think, Ghenia, that I would ever return to the place where I was born and raised, the place where my lovely years of childhood passed by, where I lived happily — that I would return there as a dangerous prisoner?! Oh, Genia, how hard it is to anticipate death and to count the final hours, tormented and in tears. If only the thick stone walls of the prison could speak, they would tell you about me and my bitter crying, and how I pull out my hairs and torture myself to death. I've already tried to commit suicide a few times; I despise life but I don't have the courage to end it. Therefore, my dear, I am sentenced to wait and wait patiently for death, until my pursuers come and take me, young thing, to the death pits in the green Oshanti Forest, from where one never comes back.

My dear Ghenia, I am not scared of death, because you know how they say: *"All troubles sleep peacefully in the grave."* And after all, I've had so many troubles, life wasn't pleasant and interesting at all. I, in my world, have seen only suffering and sorrow.

Imagine, Ghenia, what I went through when I saw before my eyes how they shot and killed my sister Esther'l and many, many others. The whole night I heard the moans bursting forth from the fresh graves, the groans of children before death, because after all, nearly everyone was thrown into pits while still alive... Oh, what an awful and terrible night that was! Yes, on that night I heard also the weeping of the trees surrounding the pits... It was on the night of August 8, 1941.

After the tragedy, and after I managed to stay alive, beginning August 11, the illegal episode of my life began with all the troubles that go together with such a miserable existence. Although the people in the houses where I found shelter took care of me, loved me, I couldn't find emotional peace. Imagine, Ghenia, outside it's spring, blooming, and I have to be enclosed in a hiding place and keep my eyes shut. The whole day I imagined them chasing me and shooting me. I don't think anymore about the past because it's impossible to bring it back, and regarding the obscure future I cannot dream of it; I don't want to delude myself, because I know well enough what to expect. I would want to be the last victim of this tragedy that befell our people. You should know, Ghenia, those who think that victory can be achieved by tramping on corpses and washing their hands in the blood of innocent human beings are mistaken. Evil people, capable of doing these base actions, must be hung on pillories in order to condemn them publicly.

Ghenia, it is hard for me to bear the stares of the people around me. Everyone thinks that I'm scared to die and therefore they tell me that they'll take me to Kovna... I know that it is also hard for you to tell me the truth, and condolences — I don't need. I am helpless. I will die with a clean conscience because I didn't do evil to a soul, I didn't hurt or cause pain to anyone on the face of this earth. Yes, with a clean conscience I will die...

I believe, Ghenia, that you will not forget me quickly. On days when the sun will again shine, the fields will turn green, the forest will whisper its mysterious secrets and the birds will again chirp and sing the anthem of freedom — remember me, Ghenia, frequently, and the days we would spend together. My wish for you is that your life's path will

343

be full of sun and light, that you shouldn't know from suffering, torments and humiliation, pain and tears...

Many thanks to you, Ghenia, for the clothing. They're not necessary for me in prison. From the faces of the awful, almost bestial people surrounding me, I know that my days are numbered. Tell your mother thanks for the food. All of the prisoners here love me and help me as much as possible. They give me cigarettes to ease my suffering. Therefore, I smoke a lot. I didn't think that the hours of anticipation would be so difficult... The end of my life will finally arrive... It may be tomorrow or in two days and then my "eternal redemption" will arrive and everything will be silent forever...

Ghenia, if after the dreadful war ends you find my sister Chaika, who may have stayed alive, tell her about the tragedy of our family and about me. Father and my brothers are buried in a common grave, my mother and Estherka in a forest, about 6–7 kilometers from Jurbarkas. Perhaps there is some indication of the grave?!...

I am going to die without fear...

Send regards to your family, stay well and happy.

I kiss you,

Mika

Mika Liubin hid in the homes of Lithuanian for a year and a half until she was caught, probably because of informing, and she was imprisoned in the Jurbarkas prison. At the end of the war Ghenia found Chaika and gave her the letter.

Letter 99

Bialistok, the prison, July 1943

My dear!

I write you today for the last time. How strange life is. So much time has gone by since our Yozek is not with us any longer. They took him away from me. He died like a true hero. He calmed me down, he kissed me on my mouth.

He worked hard in public buildings and at night he would read diligently and solve problems in mathematics. He was handsome like a dream.

The day they took him, I slit my throat. The Germans took me to the hospital and treated me until I recuperated. Despite this, I'm going today to my Yozek.

My dear, I want you not to forget who our executioners are. Think of this in the name of Katanko. Even if I see him again one day, remember everything that happened to him. I taught Yozek to die with dignity. From you, on the other hand, I request with my whole heart: you must continue to live! I bless you. I kiss you.

Yours,

Zlata

Zlata Brizitz was a member of the underground. Her husband joined the Red Army. After she was saved from the suicide attempt, she was tortured by her captures in order to extract information from her, but she refused to talk, and for this was about to be executed.

Letter 100

Dear Stephanie, forgive me, remember my love. There was no other way. My life was absolutely beautiful with your love and the love and friendship of those surrounding me with concern. I thank each and every one who stood at my side during those days of emotional anguish. I hope to die conciliated with the world and in hope of kindness and love. Be strong. Perhaps justice and humanism will build up a new life. Support one another. I am becoming sleepy and my pulse is slowing down. I am happy and falling asleep. My life has been completed and was beautiful. I have no bitterness.

Anna Trauman wrote to her friend Stephanie Plisair in Heidelberg before committing suicide. Anna was about to be deported on August 22, 1942. Due to her frail physique, which was the reason why she wasn't deported to Gurs in 1940, it was obvious to her that she wouldn't survive the transport. Therefore she chose to part from life at her own will, with the means provided by her friend, Dr. Marie Klauss.

Letter 101

Hello to you, Bergenski!

I would like to write you a few words before my departure. This is not a farewell — we already parted in the Land. But I feel a need to tell you a few things as a good and close friend.

I realize that there can be situations when you will be uncertain about our fate, or you will be completely certain about difficult situations; and I realize that then you will ask yourself questions — and I would like to answer you in advance. Not in the name of the others, in my name only. Although I know that everyone feels the same.

I am going with joy, with a free will and a clear awareness of the difficulties. I see my going as both a privilege and a duty. And the knowledge that you are behind us will help everywhere and in every situation.

I also have a request of you, which may be needless for me to say, but I must. We are accustomed to our friends' activities becoming known in public; we all experience together the successes and the difficulties. But you should know that in order to satisfy the friends who want to know about our destiny, we could pay very dearly. Every word of appreciation and publicity — you realize what this means.

I don't want to waste words. But before the journey I must still thank you for all the help that I got from you, and for the friendly attitude in which you extended this.

And about the other matters, we will discuss them when I return. Until then warm wishes of farewell.

From Hagar

This is the letter of Hannah Senesh to Yehuda Bergenski — a member of the United Kibbutz movement who dealt with her mission; Hagar — her name during the mission.

◆ ◆ ◆

Beloved Mother,

I can tell you only this: a million thanks, and I request your forgiveness if possible. You alone will understand why more words are not needed here.

**With endless love,
Your daughter**

One—two—three…
Eight feet long,
Two strides across, the rest is dark…
Life hangs over me like a question mark.

One—two—three…
Maybe another week,
Or next month may still find make here,
But death, I feel, is very near.

I could have been
 twenty-three next July;
I gambled on what mattered most,
The dice were cast. I lost.*

* Translation found in A. Ben David, Around the Shabbat Table, Jason Aronson, Inc. Northvale, New Jersey, Jerusalem, 2000. Originally from: Hannah Senesh, Hannah Senesh: Her Life and Diary, Hakibbutz Hameuachad Publishing House, Ltd, 1966..

Hannah Senesh's mother found the note and the poem in her daughter's clothing.

Letter 102

To the Honorable
Mr. President of the Polish Republic
Vladislav Ratchkavitch
Prime Minister
General Vladislav

Honorable President
Honorable Prime Minister

I allow myself to appeal to you gentlemen with these last words of mine, and through you to the Polish government and the Polish public, to the governments and the public of the Allied nations, to the conscience of the world:

According to the latest news coming from Poland, it is established beyond doubt that the Germans are currently murdering the remaining Polish Jews with unbridled brutality. The last act of the tragedy is taking place behind the walls of the ghettoes, an act with no historical precedence. The responsibility for the crime of the murder of Jewish nationals in Poland is first and foremost on the perpetrators themselves. But responsibility indirectly falls also on the entire mankind, the Allied nations and their governments, that have not taken any concrete action until this day in order to halt this crime. By passively observing the murder of millions of the defenseless, tortured — children, women and men — they became partners in sharing the responsibility. I must establish, that even though the Polish government has contributed to a great extent to the stirring of world public opinion, it has not done enough. It did not do anything beyond the ordinary as would have been appropriate for the dimension of the tragedy happening in Poland.

Out of approximately 3.5 million Polish Jews and approximately 700,000 Jews deported to Poland from other countries, according to official data of the "Bund" which was transferred by the government representative, only some 300,000 survived as of April of this year. And the murder continues.

I cannot live and be silent at a time when the remnants of Polish Jews, whom I represent, are being murdered.

My friends in the Warsaw Ghetto have fallen with weapons in their hands in the last heroic battle. I was not privileged to fall like them, together with them, but I belong with them, to the grave of the masses.

I seek to express with my death my deepest objection to the inaction, in which the world is observing and allowing the destruction of the Jewish people.

I know that there is not much value to human life, particularly today. But since I was not successful in achieving this during my life, perhaps my death will contribute to shaking off the passivity of those who can and must act, so that already now, perhaps at the last minute, the handful of Polish Jews who are still alive can be saved from inevitable destruction.

My life belongs to the Polish Jewish people, and therefore I give them my life. I yearn that the surviving remnant of the millions of Polish Jews will be privileged with the masses of Poland to be liberated, that they will be permitted to breathe freedom in Poland in a world of social justice, as a compensation for the inhumane sufferings and tortures. And I believer that such a Poland will be established and such a world will indeed come about. I am certain that the President and the Prime Minister will refer my words to all those to whom they are intended, and that the Polish government will immediately take action in the diplomatic and propaganda arena, in order to save the living remnant of Polish Jews from destruction.

I part from you with wishes,
From everyone and from all that was precious to me
And whom I loved,
Sh[muel] Zigelboim

Letter 103

Warsaw Ghetto, April 23, 1943

It's impossible to describe in words what we have gone through. What has happened is beyond our boldest dreams. The Germans fled the ghetto twice. One of our companies held out for 40 minutes, and the other — for over six hours. The mine planted in the area of the brush manufacturers exploded. Some of our companies attacked the Germans who fled. Our losses in manpower are very few. This too is an achievement. Y. [Yechiel] fell. He fell as a heroic soldier from machine gun fire. I feel that great things are happening, and what we dared to do is of great and tremendous worth...

Beginning today we are changing over to the partisan method. Tonight three combat units are going out to the field, and they have two aims: to scout and to obtain weapons. Short weapons are of no worth to us. We rarely use these weapons. We urgently need: grenades, rifles, machine guns and explosives.

I cannot describe to you the conditions under which the Jews in the ghetto currently live. Only a few will endure. The rest will perish sooner or later. Their fate is decreed. In nearly all the hiding places, where thousands are hiding, it is impossible to light a candle because of a lack of air.

We heard through our transmitter a wonderful broadcast of the "*Schweit*" broadcasting station about our warfare. The fact that they mention us beyond the ghetto walls encourages us in our struggle. Farewell, my dears! Perhaps we will meet again! The dream of my life has become a reality. Self-defense in the ghetto has turned into a fact. Armed Jewish resistance and revenge have become a fact. I have witnessed the wonderful courage filled fighting of the Jewish fighters.

M[ordechai] Anielewicz

The letter was written to Yitzchak Zukerman.

Letter 104

Grabowiec, June 5, 1942

Dear Yitzchak,

Good fortune has brought us to Grabowiec. We sent a telegram to Tzila seeking help. We are supposed to stay here for 7 days; for now, this is all we know [...] We have no means to exist. We left all of our baggage in Werbkowice [a training kibbutz] because we were forced to go on our way by foot; I had no way of getting a car [...]

Do what you can. We are under great danger.

Ita Levine

The sender's address: Hannah Sharvit (trainee of the movement from the Grabowiec branch)

Sent to: Y. Zukerman, Warsaw, Dz'elna 34/8.

◆ ◆ ◆

Chanoch — Hello!

We cannot erase from our memory your leaving without parting from us. But it's not important. Imagine that it is our fate to be alone during these difficult times. You must certainly know that we've already reached Grobowiec [the town's name] or Grabowiec [the graveyard]. Here we've stood facing death. There's an order to leave the city within 7 days. We live in the shadow of fearful anticipation of serious tragedies! Or else it will be a continuation of the journey of wandering, to a labor or death camp. In the city, the feeling is like that before a sacrificial binding (*akeida*).

Two weeks ago there was a 'holiday' enjoyed by some 30 people. On that day of deportation, Shaul (Dubna) was by us, and since then we've lost all contact with him. We are in critical condition here.

♦ ♦ ♦

Grabowiec, June 5, 1942

We don't have a penny. No bread and no oil. If it's decreed that we continue like this, we are lost. Chanoch (Henik), we've sent you a telegram and we've even sent a letter requesting help. Make all efforts to get us out of here, by means of travel permits, even if it's only to Warsaw. Or someone should come to us [...] Fischel is still weak, but he is recuperating. In contrast to this, we've left Chaim Shidla in the hospital and he is sick with the same disease that Fischel had. Besides this, we carry on, somehow, due to drinking. A famine prevails; we do not want our lives to be rescued [sic]. Our family is with us doing whatever it can. We left the storehouses and bedding in Werbkowice, and we have only what's on our bodies. Klabek had already intervened a few times with the authorities with the intention of getting us out of here, but to my sorrow, it was all to no avail. Henik, is there a possibility that someone will come? I kiss and hug you strongly.

Goodbye — Yatzak

♦ ♦ ♦

Hrubieszow, March 1, 1942

My dear!
This is my last letter from Hrubieszow. The die was cast and it was sentenced that all of the Jews must leave the city. This decree also applied to Jews in nearby villages and workplaces in the area, previously concentrated in Hrubieszow.
They say that only 800 Jews will remain in the city (a list was compiled with names marked in red pencil). We do

not know how the deportation will be implemented. Rumor has it that they will transfer us to Bialistok. It is very possible that we can expect the same fate that befell the Jews of Lublin, Vilna and others.

The kibbutz in Werbkowice was also forced to abandon the place, despite our involvement and Shaul's visit with them. We wanted them to come to Hrubieszow, because we thought that it would easier to go from here to another place. But they were forced to move to Grabowiec.

That is to say: They now expect the same fate as us and as all the Jews in the area. Peretz Fiernik is in the hospital and so is Chaim Shidla. He is sick with typhus and is staying in Hrubieszow.

I don't know what fate has in store for them. Shaul does not write because he is working [in forced labor]. They thought that work is the key to rescue, but it turned out that with work, too, there is no security. If they keep us alive, we will look for a contact. You, on your part, should also look for the kibbutz in Werbkowice. Do your best.

Sincerely,
[Mottel Bernstein]

Letter 105

Monday, 6:20 [March 1943]

I recently received a letter. I agree to a talk. Now. It will probably be hard for me later on. After all, in order to talk, one must have inner peace and some breath of life — and only a little more twinkle in the eye — and some degree of curiosity about the people near him, about the surroundings, about the changes taking place. But for now — let it be.

I would amuse myself now with such a chain. Only to myself. Deep in reflection. Instead of this — a talk.

The right hand writes, the left hand supports the head; I whistle as I write. Polish folk songs. I used to love them so much. So simple, indirect, gloomy. Whenever I start humming to myself — they always surface. It seems I am "exceptional", unique in the family. Why it is like this — God knows, I know. And you must also know: Wanda [Tema Schneiderman, the signaler of Dror and the Jewish Resistance Organization. She was sent in 1943 by Tannenboim from Bialistok to Warsaw; she was caught and sent to her death in Treblinka] loved them so much. She would always sing them. She would laugh.

But this — this is too much. Stop, Lirika. It is not proper for someone like you, etc., etc.

I have stopped whistling already. Enough (your very own eyes can see — our issues are similar: you find amusement in the chain, and I in the sequence of tones — there are so many memories, the beauty, the longing, the sense of celebration…)

I have 17 minutes left. At seven they are coming. So I will tell you how yesterday went by.

The same blue sky. Sun. Less mud already. The

357

breeze is so airy, spring-like — nu, it's like this, nu, it's like what? nu — it's like braids caressing the face — so close to the heart. In the afternoon I went to the garden. They're already installing the windows. They're planting radish, lettuce. They're milking the cows. They're bringing fertilizer.

Spring? — A gray detestable autumn.

Everything is so desolate.

To hell with it! So much does man view this world through his eyes only.

Always at the same time — a call to the distance, to the world. A call of adventure.

To where? To Warsaw? To Vilna? To Krakow? To Bendin? It's all the same!

To sit here — is even worse.

Yet, I am after all the prophet of death. I have already "convinced" everyone. Beware for your life — lest you are entrapped also.

Nu, how? How is our conversation? The influence — not so much. War, abnormal times, etc.

By the way, I would advice Schweider to keep his writing to a minimum. And only family letters, exclusively. And what's with Irna — the devil knows.

And one more thing: if you thought of visiting us — not now, only in the event of absolute necessity — bring flowers. Agreed?

After all, man sits himself down in a different way near the table. The bulbs of your willow-branch, their lives are coming to an end.

I really liked your room. I only forgot one thing — and after all I knew this by heart — where does the closet stand and on which side is the mirror? But of what worth is a new room, one that does not involve memories, whose interior was not stamped with a smile, a song, a "mess"?

That's how it is. And I would have preferred to live

in an enormous room, glazed entirely in glass. Without any furniture. A couch, with walls of made of glass. The roof is made of glass. And the path goes to the Lord of the Universes. (Darkness should overtake him, I can't bear him — I am fed up with Him ad nauseam were 12 sick people. A light flu. The tendency now is to recover. New sick people are not being added.

Wissotzka says she will stay with you. If it concerns me — please do it. I only worry about the formal arrangements. And should one dare without these arrangements? We will still think over the matter.

I have told Helina everything.

Have the mailmen ceased to exist? Perhaps there are others — mailmen, rail workers, the telegraph — as long as they take someone with them. It is definitely necessary to search.

Regarding Philip, almost everything is fine. There will still be a third transport.

They're coming. Enough. One more thing: Why do you recount in the letters our distinguished names? I don't intend "You shall not take My Name in vain," but — this is unnecessary.

You will certainly understand.

How do you manage to decipher my letters? You've already learned? Do you guess?

Be well, Bronia, stand upright! The turtledove has not yet gone by, and the smile of such a Bronca will actually still be of great, great value. And maybe even in this reincarnation (it's such a shame that we're not Indians — barefoot, hot, bananas, rice).

Enough. Here comes the second one. I must stop.

During all this chatter: I've remembered — a small home of your own, definitely a home entirely of your own. If I ever visit you — I will bring flowers.

And again — talk, talk.

[Mordechai Tannenboim-Tamaroff]

◆ ◆ ◆

Saturday, 11:15 in the evening [May 1943]
My Darling,

My sense of gratitude for your letter is so great; it is so good, it speaks dignity, beautiful. Yesterday I expected the "mail" — not a thing. Twice I returned home, I looked for our mailman — in vain.

Also today — I expect, expect — not a thing. Therefore I went to him — I found him asleep. I requested to conduct a search in his coat — and indeed it was found. And he goes on sleeping. I began to read (later, in the street), at first I became so sad, so miserable was I — I was afraid, that I might have hurt you in some way — but later on it became clearer, and the sunlight increased. I felt better.

And you must be thanked also for the first page and also for the last page. It is all so close to my heart, so much a part of us. Majestic, beautiful.

Allow me, to squeeze your hand, allow me, allow me — see how you feel about this — I am simply asking to write, allow me to kiss your hand. After all this is an acceptable way to express gratitude.

I must write you now about my flowers. So many, so many!

Pay attention!

A wonderful branch of the acer maple. Resembling a triangle. Standing upright — as if it grew straight out of the ground.

This is one.

A daffodil, a reed (but a beauty, from the garden — each leaf — is like a sword). An assortment of field flowers resembling the lily. In the center — golden irises, a meter high. Yesterday they were still bulbs — during the night they blossomed in their full glory. They resemble memorial candles, like candles that are lit against a dark green background. These are number two.

On the floor, before the small table, an enormous bouquet of the acacia plant. All together — it seems like an ancient prayer house, like a corner of a cemetery covered with wild plants, or perhaps like a domestic altar. On the big table — irises of lofty stature, closed within themselves. Overnight all of their bulbs blossomed. So elevated, watching from above; a stance that speaks dignity, boasting royalty. Pleasant, pleasant.

If you were here, you would also praise it.

If it ever crosses your mind that I don't know anything, that I will not manage in anyway , and so on, please remember that I know well the art of flower arranging.

Nice?

And now I must take leave of you — the light disturbs the girls.

Tomorrow we will continue our chat.

Well, good night to you, Bronia.

If you would like — I will give these flowers to you. But the branch of the acer maple — this one leave for me.

OK?

Have a pleasant sleep, a restful sleep!

M.

◆ ◆ ◆

Monday, June 7, 1943 The time is 5:00 PM
Bronia,

In only two or three hours I will get your letter. In two hours I will read it — I will gulp it down at once. And then I will go back and read it slowly, slowly, I will dispute with you, I will smile, I admit. How good it is, Bronia, that you are with me!

Tz[ippora] is already working in the garden. All day nobody is at home. (How good this is!) I sit for entire hours, lying down, going out — supposedly on "important matters" — to town, back again. And nothing.

Usually nobody comes to me. And if somebody comes — so it's the sun, and silence, and I'm alone — he would position me like an empty vessel. Of course the girls. I don't know why, but that's how it seems to me. And after all it is legitimate to stay away from me like the plague. Yesterday a lady asked me — the one who brought the jasmine flowers — whether I worry about myself at all, is my day completely full and so forth "theoretical" questions. So tactless! She should go... It's lucky that the whole gang got together. But we'll leave such nonsense.

Thunders outside. Oh, another one. Let it be.

I have roses. I picked them in the garden. Tiny, wild roses. ("He's still wild, uncurbed– stinging".) I have so many flowers! How beautiful!

Do you know why I deal so much with flowers, why I write about them so much?

It is the law of contrasts. Despite the fact that conditions are like this, etc., etc. — I love them so much.

For the future generations — for psychological assessment.

I don't have a sausage [weapon] yet. The assumption is that it will be tomorrow. If I get it — I will notify you.

Oh, what a shower of rain. What a stream! If you had gone outside — it would "cover you with his kisses". (Do you remember?) Wait a moment, please, I will take the flowers outside.

It will be sufficient; it will be enough for them. Do

you know, Bronia, you gave yourself in. When you smile and you won't want to say why you laugh — I will know anyhow. And I've known beforehand, but I wasn't completely certain. Do you remember, I've always said: "Tell me, it seems I know — I will tell you whether I've guessed". Well, I guessed.

Pretty "girl"... You are so immeasurably smart ... Nu, if I say it — it will not be much of a great compliment, but you are much smarter than all types of the "elderly". An extraordinarily sensitive womanly sense. Or — nu, nothing, remind me — I will state (for a long time this was not stated, right?)

Here, the rain has stopped, and the sky is clearing up. A good sign. A sign that heralds of a long and pleasant letter, very long. Forty five minutes at least. And now — farewell! Enough of my small-talk. "If only he were younger, better looking, oh, and in general... so boring."

What can I do?

Only one time does the goddess of fortune grant her smile to a person, and the years rush by so quicky. And a person ages. And old age — as is known — has no delight.

Here, I will lie down on my couch.

Farewell, Miss Bronia!

◆ ◆ ◆

Tuesday [June 8, 1943]
My Child,

(Select for yourself a name — I wanted to write — no, nothing, I'm ashamed to say — but I truly don't know your real name.) Ah, indeed there was a letter. The same handwriting, the paper was the same paper, the same failing letters (one doesn't get a flogging for telling the truth) — but so very brief, like this, nu, I myself don't know. And how wise you are: Every other sentence quotes the Scriptures, relates

363

about some water maidens, and I bow my head and blush from shame and ignorance and... "Not at ease"...

Returning to me. Today again I picked wild roses. But different ones, not like yesterday's — open, straight, resembling narcissuses, but of course pink. They have a wonderful scent. I would send you — it's impossible by mail. They asked me for some flowers, I told them that I had promised them to "someone else". It sounds altogether serious.

Now — at 11:00 a.m. — you are still working. And I will sit down "to work" — I must review some songs, prepare the material for copying. I therefore apologize to you very politely.

Be well!

M.

P.S. Regarding "the anxiety", "the prevalent attitudes" and so forth, the tone of your letter shows, I think, that your mood is not bad. Indeed — this is for the time being. But nothing serious.

My Darling,

Yesterday at home: plenty of foliage, flowers — white tablecloths, "rare" [food] dishes — splendor. What a shame that you were not here. Imagine, this guy with a similar name to mine — the smaller one — vanished together with his sickly townsman — they picked up their feet going to their hometown or something like that. It was wild. Piggishness of the worst kind. And other news — but I must hurry to the post office — will there be mail today? — I myself will not know.

Be well, my darling.

Six months ago, on January 9, at six p.m. I parted from Wanda.

Thursday, the time is 2:30 p.m. [June 10, 1943]

At the last minute I didn't bring the letter to the post office. I didn't feel like it. By the way, according to what was agreed upon — you were supposed to come only on Thursday.

I don't feel like sending you all this prattle, but I have written — and it's yours already.

The heat is so terrible. And the head is so confused. Fear — under cover of pleasant words — is rearing its head. In the heart — poison; on the lips — honey. On Sunday they will receive a shampoo of the head.

My girl! Indeed, do you truly and sincerely think that I memorized your letters as in those days... The "improvisations" of Mitzkivitz? I read 2–3 times and remember every typical expression, every note and nuance.

And a request: Please buy for me peony and dahlia flowers — but dark ones, the color of blood. Fresh flowers — which I can keep for a long time. OK? After all, it would not be too hard for you, and for me, it would give me so much happiness.

Buy, buy — a lot.

And for this, that yesterday you were hurt — I am very, very sorry.

That's how the weather was. So much confusion, it was enough for ten.

Be well, Bronia.

Be strong and have courage.

M.

◆ ◆ ◆

Tuesday, 10:20 a.m. [July 6, 1943]

Bronia,

And again I write to you. It seems to me, as if I haven't seen you for ages and ages. And if you were to come now — after a break of two days — my joy would be no less than then, two weeks ago.

For such a long time I haven't see you!

And for my writing, please don't be angry. You have indeed said, that you would not write anymore, but I am, after all, allowed to write. I write because I must. After all it is impossible to prohibit the thought, the conversation of a person; it is possible not to listen to it, but speaking is allowed. And I believe, that you will indeed listen and that — maybe — you will even respond.

Sincere thanks for the flowers! They are so wonderful! I gave him the small bundle, and the rest — that is: all of them — I took for myself. Now it looks like this: In the large vase — are yours; in the center — in a small jar — are the yellow ones, and on the side - in the red vase — are all the poppy flowers.

And during the night the red rose opened up in all its glory, and the poppies now resemble umbrellas — with sprawling petals, that straightened out.

When I don't have flowers — I'm so sad, it's so strange — because of Wanda.

But for now it is good. Like always Wanda stands among the flowers and to me it seemed — how silly — that things are better for her.

Tomorrow we must leave the apartment. Where to — I still don't know. I always claimed that I would like to leave here, yet now, when they came to tell us — all of a sudden I feel gloom. Why?

Is it because I became attached to the place, because of habit? Or perhaps it is the shadows of Wanda, Lonka,

Frania, Marassik, Bella? Already five, and yet the chaff remains, to hell! And he walks about the face of the world of the Lord. Brrr!…!

The biggest problem will be the flowers. They will probably suffer during the transfer. And the devil knows what the new room will look like: will it have sunlight or will it be dark, will it be clean or will it be a kingdom of bed-bugs? (Pardon!) There you are, something to worry about.

Quiet, tranquility and boredom.

And "there is nothing new under the sun": "joys" go by, minor worries, small stings and so forth. And a pleasant event, one that's anticipated, will be your letter (if you write).

Write Bronia, write! I measure time and count the days according to your letters. Write. I will thank you very, very much.

◆ ◆ ◆

Wednesday, 11 a.m.
My Beloved,

And again — despite the agreement, more accurately: the one-sided agreement — I write. Yesterday, today. Probably tomorrow. Pay attention: If you send the letter back on the spot, if you do not accept it — I will not write any more. Or — I don't know. Maybe I will still write.

Yesterday was called a "good" day. Profuse "diplomatic" victories. So, the "attack" of the elderly [the Poalei Zion party] against us failed completely. H. B[arash] is full of admiration, good will, etc. Andzhei [the Jewish Communists] — you should know — summoned for talks. Helina's [HaShomer HaTzair] family got her reward [the writer used the expression from the Tractate Yevamot, page 105] from all the acquaintances, and only I (meaning we) was authorized to…, etc. etc. This means only the finest honey. And I received a sausage. And also today I will receive one. And I — at the time that that gang sat and held such a wise and sophisticated discussion — I heard the entire time "the seagull"… that same "seagull" that pursues me without stop. If only it would fly above the Volga! This "seagull" circles over me without stop. To hell and the flowers are so wonderful. And the weather — after you went — it improved. You can see for yourself.

I already have the suitcases to transfer the articles. Those same famous suitcases, that were supposed to wander, etc., etc.; where to — I still don't know.

The most important thing — the worn out family leaves, if one can say this, were already moved. The rest is waiting. The greatest burden — the altar, the flowers. But somehow things will work out.

And I yearn so much to get a letter from you. What's with you? Did you travel? Are you waiting? — I myself will not know. Be well, Bronia, and May God be with you.

I went to live at… home. The place where the rivers flow, that is where they will go.

Farewell!
M.

The are letters of Mordechai Tannenboim-Tamaroff, commander of the revolt in the Bialistok Ghetto, to Bronia Vinitzky-Kalibenski, who was a signaler of the Jewish Resistance Organization on the Aryan side of Bialistok. Mordechai Tannenboim-Tamaroff fell in 1943.

Letter 106

Dear Friends,

What we are really missing is a manual for those who are caught. It's obvious that we cannot reveal anything, but it would be much better if we were able to prepare for each accused person a story which would be true under any conditions, that is many names and addresses that the police could actually visit. But of course they won't find anything in these places, only people who would tell them our story...

My situation is bad. The police have a file with all my details. And I have to tell them what's written there, or disprove it one hundred percent. In the event that I remain silent, they will accept the file. But this is impossible and it means that I'll get a bullet. There is also a communist file. They decorated my illegal name with such nice deeds (sabotage, conspiracy with the resistance, a murder of a policeman!) that I could not go through this in silence.

But what can I do?

I remained standing without stop from Thursday, at 2:00 until 11:00 Saturday morning, my hands e chained behind my back, a daily portion of food with four slices of bread and a bottle of tea. Investigations were conducted in a dark cell in the cellar. A place with enough room just for standing. They beat me, tied me for a while stooped over, yanked all my clothes over my head and that's how I was investigated. After every answer I could expect a kick or the lash of a whip.

This morning they officially notified me that they will take me before a military court. [They asked me] would I want to write a parting letter from my wife? When I started to do this, they again interrupted me for investigation. Now I have a little break, but I can await the same thing again on

Monday. You know that I won't give anyone in. About that — I am certain. And committing suicide? I have the possibility to do it now in the same way that our dear friend, whom I think about so often these days [Shosho Simon, a member of the Central HaChalutz in Holland, was caught in January 1943 while attempting to cross the Belgian-Dutch border with certificates and other valuables intended for rescuing friends. According to the police, Shushu committed suicide in the prison in the town of Breda]. I am still at full strength. At night, I overcome the aches, the pressure in - - - so that I look like I'm awake during the investigation. And I want to keep on going...

Regards to all of you, maybe for a long time, and if we don't see each other again, I hope that our common work will be a sacred momento to you for life.

May God bless you,

Joop

The letters of the Dutch Yup Westerweel were written in the Vught concentration camp. He was shot in the forest near the camp on August 11, 1944 as he attempted to escape.

Letter 107

My One and Only Beloved Mamaleh!

I would like to go down on my knees and ask forgiveness from you for the terrible pain that I have caused you. This is the most severe of all my sins before the Lord and I pray to Him every day to forgive me for this. You have sacrificed everything for me and did everything possible. Yesterday I said goodbye to Remus forever. I think that I don't have to say anything else, because you must have certainly sensed what was going on within me during these last days. I promised Remus to do whatever is possible to grant life to our child, whom we love even before its birth, and if it's a boy to call him Arno Alexander. He should be baptized with the name Alexander at the Russian church. Mamaleh, I ask, I plead with you, that you should be strong and live for the sake of my child, don't forsake my child. Love him as you've loved me, and you will have more happiness from him than you've had from me. In the name of the Lord and Jesus Christ, who commanded eternal love and peace, I ask you to forgive me and to pray for my sake as I pray for you all the time. My belief in the Lord and in his eternal love is strong and solid. I leave my child at the mercy of Vera [Vana?] and Mrs. Eugenie, Ina and Sergei. Send my regards to my friends and ask them not to forget me. Please send me one of your icons, perhaps they will permit this. I have with me your passport photo; you know, the last one that you took. It is very comforting and sort of like a shelter for me. And I still hope that we will return and see each other. I think about you, I dream about you, I love you madly. Mamaleh, my dear, I know that you love me and forgive me. I hug you and kiss you a thousand times *kushka-mama* [Russian for pussycat].

Yours always.
Lanoshka

◆ ◆ ◆

Berlin Plötzensee
Koenigsdam 7
August 5, 1943
My Dear Beloved Mamaleh!

This is the end. Today, at dusk, your Lianka will no longer be alive. My solace and hope is little Eirka who, thank God, has no idea about what's going on around her. Mamaleh, you were the best mother in the world to me. You have done for me whatever is possible. Forgive me for my death, forgive me for any offense that I inflicted on you, for any upsetting word; I ask of you, I plead with you, rally your maternal strength to its peak and be strong!!! You must remain healthy and alive, you must live for my little Eirka lying in her cradle, completely orphaned. Protect her, take care of her, live for her sake. As one who owes you a debt, I am going to my death with full confidence that my precious one is in good hands. You must fulfill the last request of your child who is going to die. Raise Eirka to be a bright woman, energetic, make her learn as much as possible. Teach her to believe with a solid faith in the Lord and His eternal love, kindness and justice. She must love and honor the memory of her parents, baptize her in the Greek-Orthodox church. Save for her my curl of hair and my picture, the letters from Remus, my books and personal articles. Divide my clothes between Vera [Vana?] and Gerda, send my wishes and kisses from me to Mrs. Rehemehr. Ask her to take care of herself for the sake of Eirka, this was also the last wish of her son, as she can read in his last letter to me. To Uncle Milia, Ina Senska, Vera [Vana], Aunt Jenny and to all the friends, send my wishes and ask them to take are of Eirka, if she needs it. I believe in the Lord and in eternal life and we will return and see each other. In the next world I will pray for you and for Eirutska and I will watch over you. I am calm and in control of myself and I'm not afraid of death. All of the articles that belong to me according to the will of Henni Berkovitch, I leave for Eira with a request that you take care of them. More than this, I appoint you — and also Mrs. Rehemehr and Dr. Dmitri Yevseinku if something happens to you — to be the guardian for Eira. The last few months, especially since I parted from Eira, have been unbearable for me and on the one hand I'm happy now that these tortures will be coming to a quick end. The Lord has granted me great kindness. He allowed me to experience all that a woman can experience: He gave me a child. At least I was — even for a short time — a mother, and this is the most beautiful thing on the face of earth. And again Mamaleh, be strong, be brave, love your daughter and live for Irka, now I will direct my thoughts and senses to the Lord and prepare for my encounter with Jesus, confident of his love and mercy. I am making the sign of the holy cross. Take Eira to your home after the danger of bombings from the air passes, so that she will have a home and a beautiful childhood like I did.

I hug and kiss my Eirka and her sweet, tiny hands and feet. I kiss and hug and bless you for the last time; I kiss your hands and receive your blessing.

Yours, the tranquil and miserable,

Lanka

Liana Berkovitch, daughter for a Jewish father and a Russian mother, lived in Berlin. In 1942, when she was 20 or 21, she was arrested, probably charged with being a member of the underground. In prison her daughter Yirena (Eirka) was born. The father of the baby, Friedrich Rehemehr ("Remus") was arrested at the same time too and executed. Liana wrote to her mother from prison consistently, until the day she was executed. The letters were kept by Liana's father and transferred to Yad Vashem after his death.

Letter 108

Bendin, August 1, 1943
Dear Motek [Kashashivo]!

We received your postcard from August 6. *Szejrita* [Survivor] didn't write for a long time, because she changed jobs. Yank and the others work in their profession and are content. *Achila* [Eating] is not something special, but they'll get used to this. *Michtav* [Letter] doesn't want to be here; *Sakana* [Danger] also doesn't want to. Tell Martzen and the others to write to Paul, Z.'s brother-in-law. Szejrita will be very happy. Write frequently, if possible, and don't worry if we don't write. Send regards to Alf and to Yeliskolsky and ask them to influence Szejrita to speed up the delivery of the package. Perhaps they will also send it to Megin. He will deliver them alright.

Yank, Vladek, M.W., and everyone send you regards.

Yours,
Kashashivo Yakov

Letter 109

From: Gertrude Eisinger, Birkenau
To: Maria Kellenberger, Modra
Birkenau, July 25, 1943

[…] Aunt *Lechem* [Bread] doesn't visit me […]

◆ ◆ ◆

From: Leah Weinberger, Birkenau
To: Yosef Weinberger, Nova Masta
Birkenau, July 25, 1943

[…] On the 27th of this month, it will be two years since our Tzinka has gone; on August 14 — two years since Shendor went to Wolicka. If you write them, [send] regards from me Mr. *Kaddish* […]

[…] You asked me about Marguitte. As far as I know she is together with Willy and I am happy they're together […]

◆ ◆ ◆

From: Ella Mandel, Birkenau
To: Yuta Mandel, Preshev
Birkenau, July 1943

I mainly want to thank you for the package that I received on July 1st. I was very surprised, because I haven't gotten mail from you yet […]

Magda Goldberg works together with me, and the others with the first *Kaddish* […]

◆ ◆ ◆

From: Alice Bala
To: Jan Undrushkehat Assetzadnika
Birkenau, July 1943

Mrs. *Halal* [Slain] is very diligent here. Back home I didn't like it when she would be in my house, but here I'm with here all the time, and I've already befriended her.

Letter 110

Warsaw, October 30, 1942

A long time has gone by since I wrote you. I think it was on July 15, 1942, on the day that I got sick [= beginning of deportations and destruction]. Forgive me for my negligence, but you will understand my situation and the condition of my health specifically. I was forced to go to the hospital [=a safe place] for an operation and I was very worried about the continuation my life. I was very busy with this and therefore I didn't have the chance to write you. I needed an operation because the diet was poor and the different attacks threatened my life every day. Today my condition is relatively better, I am recuperating, going out a bit on the street, and only sometimes to church [...] My illness has destroyed the entire family financially, and we're going through a pretty rough time. We impatiently await the promised help of our Uncle *Ami* [My People]. Let's hope that it won't take long, until then we will have to consult. Fortunately the weather is still pleasant and quite warm, so we don't need heating yet. I also don't know how we'll survive the winter without clothes.

◆ ◆ ◆

Warsaw, December 10, 1942

Your message that Heniak [= probably a party member, who was in the Land of Israel for over two years] is with you, makes me very happy. Why doesn't he write? I am well and working. My cousin [=the party's center in Warsaw] lives together with L. Alpovitz [meaning that 30 thousand Jews remained in Warsaw*] and she is fine.

Her family is with Yosef Bossel. Many warm thanks for your intention to send me a gift parcel, I myself don't need it, but it would be very good if you could send the same thing you had sent Heniak to little Ella [cash]. The packages will be of great use to the little one and I will be very happy if you send her packages. I await your quick answer and I hereby give you a hearty blessing.

*Based on the ל standing for gmatria 30, and אלפוביץ designating 1000 from אלף.

Letter 111

Dear Natan!

Hanka has already written me because of *Ami* [My People]. Next week I will write you in detail. I cannot write when *Kilajon* [Destruction] comes, because he always comes at unexpected times. Also *Zilumet* [Shadow of Death] has written you often lately, and he will actually write you. You must be surprised why many of our acquaintances have not written lately, they are by *Mavetzky* [Deathsky], that's why they don't have time to write you. I send you many wishes, and also my whole family, we are well, working and content. Also Father, whom you've written to, thanks you for sending regards in my postcard.

Avramek P.

Letter 112

Budapest, November 3, 1943

Dear Aryeh,

I am surprised that I have not received a reply from you yet. Perhaps you did not receive mail from me. You cannot imagine the beauty of Budapest. My mother is excited over it, and it's a pity that you cannot be here with me to marvel over it. Lately I have - - - I feel again as usual. It is fortunate that I am here with my dear sister. We are afraid that Aunt *Mavetia* [Deathia] is liable to visit us. Please, write Uncle *Dror* [Liberty] that Aunt *Alya* [Aliyah - Immigration to the Land of Israel] should take us. It depends on him. I spoke with him already on the phone.

I am here with Tushia, Olek G. and the others. They send you warm regards. How are you, are you healthy? It's a pity that I cannot speak to you personally. Yes, Aryeh, life does change. I personally have gone through so much already. My only hope is that I would still meet my parents.

Respond immediately. I seek your regards,

Helena

Letter 113

Sosonowitz, October 3, 1942

As you see, I am here now and I am well. If you do not know who I am exactly, you should know this: The brother of Regus Orbach from Versols Aveyron who has already notified you about things on September 26. Did you get our letter from Rivesalte. It's a pity that it all happened so fast. I have been here for the past two weeks, and I'm really pleased that I can tell you, that thank God I lack nothing.

- - - gives them from time to time, despite my financial situation which deteriorated greatly. The ability of Geulah [Redemption] has greatly disappointed me. Every year she learns well, and she always fails the exams. Tante Tikwa [Aunt Hope] is fighting with her last strength. The doctors don't give her any hope. The regards from Misha and Moledet [Homeland] always give me happiness. It makes me happy that you have work and that you are healthy. The best of wishes to you, your family, your acquaintances, to Misha (the Zionist worker) and to Usha.

Yours,
Zvi

Letter 114

Dear Natan!

First of all I must apologize to you that there was no sign of life from me for ever so long. But it wasn't my fault that the diseases of *Ami* [My People] make it so hard for me.

I received your postcard and all the parcels with deep thanks. Mr. *Gieruss* [Deportation] is staying with us and bringing with him also Mr. *Mawed* [Death]. And then we hope very much for *Hazalah* [Rescue]. How are you besides this? I expect to hear news from you soon and part from you with warm wishes,

Yours

Riva

Riva Sara Nisdovska of Bendin sent her letter to Natan Schwalb in Geneva.

Letter 115

Warsaw, October 16, 1943

Beloved Aunt *Moledet* [Homeland],

We thank *Kaspi* [My Money] for the news and for the regards from our friends. 38 thousand [people] are here. We wrote you and sent you twice a permit. Last week our friends went to *Haganski* [Defenski]. The last days were very hard for *Ami* [My People], who has meanwhile gotten sick. We paid a lot to Dr. *Mavet* [Death]; the children go to him regularly and we cannot do a thing against this. It is hard for us to take care of Mr. *Mivrak* [Telegram], he will write to you in a while. We will surely move to another place, because here one awaits mortal danger. Our reporter was very sick. Your friend Mokos has arrested us [meaning a South American passport], perhaps it will help us. We don't know whether the letters [passports] have reached the others. Lately we haven't received any food packages. We wrote you a few times and it seems the letters got lost. Despite this we write to *Hatzofeh*. We are with Mrs. Novogratzka Shemuna.

◆ ◆ ◆

December 6, 1943

My Dear,

I am healthy now and pleased you are feeling well. I have gone through and suffered so much, and I cannot write to you myself, because during the fire I was burned. True, I am alive, but I am full of fear.

I am hurrying because I must hide, conceal myself. I thank you for the money because I need it very much. Josik is here, the others have unfortunately [...] I don't want to write because I am afraid. You will soon hear about everything in detail, and I will try to get out of here.

I thank you very much for the packages [food]. If you can, send me tea, coffee. I would very much want to see you.

Meanwhile I end and kiss you strongly.

Josik

We received with thanks the 40,000 rm'.

Letter 116

The Zychlin Ghetto, February 24, 1942
My Dear Friends,

Yosef's wife asks me to write you, especially to the father. He is sick, and so is Alter from Zychlin, with the same disease that Yosef the Righteous had for 12 years [imprisonment]. They are in need of mercy. Also the community of Israel needs of plenty of mercy. We have parted from you many times, and after all it is in the power of God to save us. This morning Yosef Prinz died at lightening speed when he was shot in the face. On Sunday Yitzchak Kovitz's bride, the sister of Avramele Rosenberg, died in the street; she also died from the same disease. How are you feeling? Be well and may you merit redemption.

And now for what concerns us. We know that our days are numbered. There is neither policeman nor officer - - - we are abandoned to our fate. Now, my dears! You know my name. If I stay alive — good, and if not — you will have to pray also for the elevation of my soul. The "Sermon-Book" [probably a manuscript of the writer of this letter] is in the cellar on the southern wall. May you all be blessed and healthy. My family sends regards. I have not broken down, thank God, after all, it is all from the Creator of the World. I should not wonder [about my fate] until the last moment.

I ask from all of you forgiveness,

**Your friend, sending regards to everyone in the family,
one by one.**

I request an answer.

Letter 117

April 15, 1943

Luckily I myself can still write you [...] Last Friday they did by us a 'thorough cleansing'. Our grandfather's factory was working at full force. About 1,500 pairs of shoes (mainly for women and children) were destroyed. In Zloczew it was the same thing. We had a miracle from Heaven. Y. is rescuing us all.

[...] For your birthday, I pray to God that your hopes and our hopes will come true.

◆ ◆ ◆

May 4, 1943

[...] Today you are 26 years old, and it's 4 years since you've stepped on the Holy Land. In my mind, I review what all of us, and everyone as individuals have gone through, and I pray to God to save us so we can see each other again. We had by us in April a big 'storm' that uprooted big, young trees with their roots. In Zloczew, it was the same [...] Heavy clouds cover the sky and we fear an awful storm [...] You probably don't understand our situation yet. Perhaps it is better like this.

◆ ◆ ◆

June 6, 1943

[...] This week an awful storm lashed about destroying the entire city. Only those that found "shelter" from the thunders were saved [...] A storm like this went over Zloczew a few weeks ago [...] By us there is nothing new, if only it wouldn't get worse until the end of the war [...]

Summary

I have read three sayings about writing: "Writing is everything except reality". (Denton Welch); "Of all that was written, I like only that which was written in blood" (Friedrich Nietsche); "Writing is not a profession, but an act of misery" (George Simenon).* The letters in this book were written about reality, in the midst of reality, and only reality emerges from them, and indeed their words were written in blood. Perhaps Nitsche meant that writing that comes from pain is genuine and honest; if so, the letters before us are genuine and authentic — but reading them shocks us, and it would have been better had there been no need for them to be written. "An Act of Misery" — this title is appropriate for these last letters. A cry of misery emanates from them, and we remember and commemorate the writers with awe and compassion.

Zwi Bacharach

Our thanks to all the people who have given over their letters throughout the years, and to the translators who enabled us to publish this volume.

* Great Book of Quotes pages 278–297

Index of Concepts and Topics

Ringelblum Archives 41
Rosh Chodesh 22, 100, 310
Sages 40, 76, 186
Shavuot 29
six million 11, 51, 200
skepticism 58, 60
Socialists 9
S.S. 24, 132, 322
Star of David (Magen David) 22,
    103, 138
suicide 12, 14, 25, 48, 50, 63–66,
    69, 143, 229, 342, 345, 346,
    370
Talmud 27, 41, 65
testimony 8–13, 15, 19–22, 24–27,
    30, 36, 41, 45, 51, 66, 74, 126
Torah 41, 56, 104, 184, 186, 233,
    248, 249, 252, 305
tradition 11, 28, 42, 43, 48, 50, 55,
    65, 69
Ukrainians 24, 132, 322

Underground 25
underground fighters 14, 50
universal-humanistic 45
visas 33
Warsaw Ghetto revolt 67
Western civilization 213
Western culture 56
wills 12, 40, 41, 236
World to Come 65
World War I (the World War) 39,
    73, 77, 210, 213, 293
Yahrzeit 12, 22, 28, 43, 44, 100
Yizkor 11, 73, 74, 76, 77
Yom Kippur 42, 109, 248, 276, 329
Zion 105, 128, 179
zionism 38
Zionists 9, 11, 16, 50, 73, 75, 77,
    78, 80, 121, 128, 175, 177, 178,
    206, 211, 290, 323, 326, 381

INDEX OF PLACES

INDEX OF PERSONS